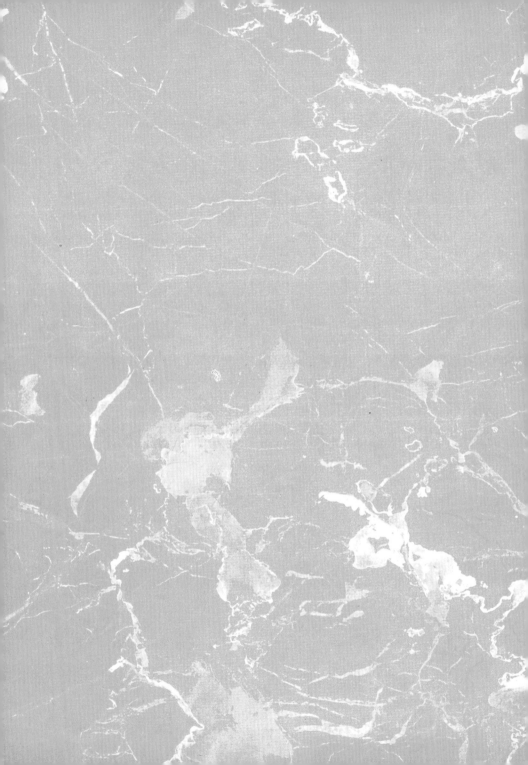

PRESENTED TO

FROM

DATE

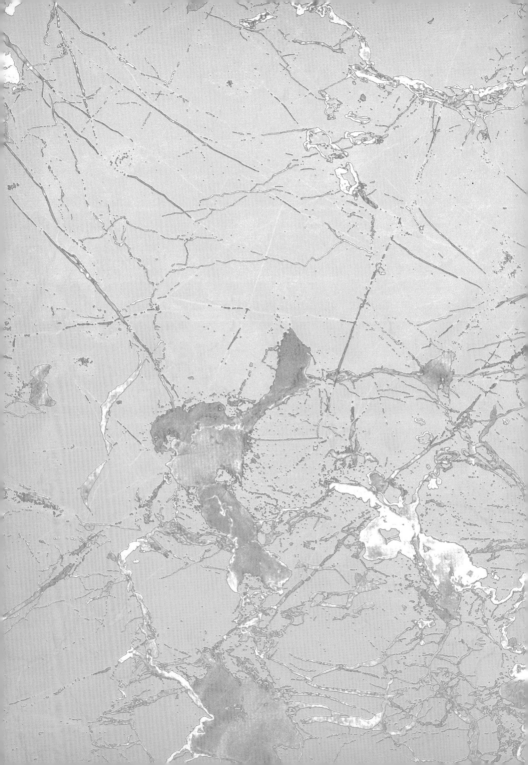

UN
SHAKE
ABLE

365 DEVOTIONS FOR FINDING
UNWAVERING STRENGTH IN GOD'S WORD

CHRISTINE CAINE

ZONDERVAN®
.com

DEDICATED TO MY BELOVED
NIECE, MISSY PRICE HARPER

INTRODUCTION

All of creation will be shaken and removed,
so that only unshakable things will remain.
HEBREWS 12:27 NLT

Everything in our world that can be shaken will be shaken. From a global scale to our personal lives. And yet, the Bible assures us it doesn't matter what happens politically, morally, socially, or economically in the world around us if we have Christ in us—if we have the kingdom of God within us—because with Christ and in Christ, we can have unshakeable faith.

The kind of faith that is impossible to change, shake, or beat down. The kind of faith that is confident in knowing Jesus, our rock and mighty fortress. The One who promised to never leave us nor forsake us. The One who causes us to triumph over any hurdle or situation trying to destabilize us or stop us from fulfilling our God-given purpose.

God wants you to live on mission. On point. Fulfilling all that He has called you to do. So as we journey through this daily devotional together, it is my prayer that your faith grows bigger than any storm you encounter. That your faith grows bigger than any fear shaking your world. That you grow unshakeable faith for every opportunity ahead.

Faith grows when we believe and declare God's Word in our lives. When we stand on His promises . . .

Greater is He who is in us than he who is in the world (1 John 4:4).

If our God be for us, then who can be against us (Romans 8:31)?

With the help of our God, we can advance against a troop and scale any wall (Psalm 18:29).

We can do all things through Christ who strengthens us (Philippians 4:13).

I can't wait for us to dive in and walk through the next year together. I believe that our best days are ahead of us and not behind us, so let's get started!

Therefore, since we are receiving a kingdom that cannot be shaken, let us be thankful, and so worship God acceptably with reverence and awe.
HEBREWS 12:28

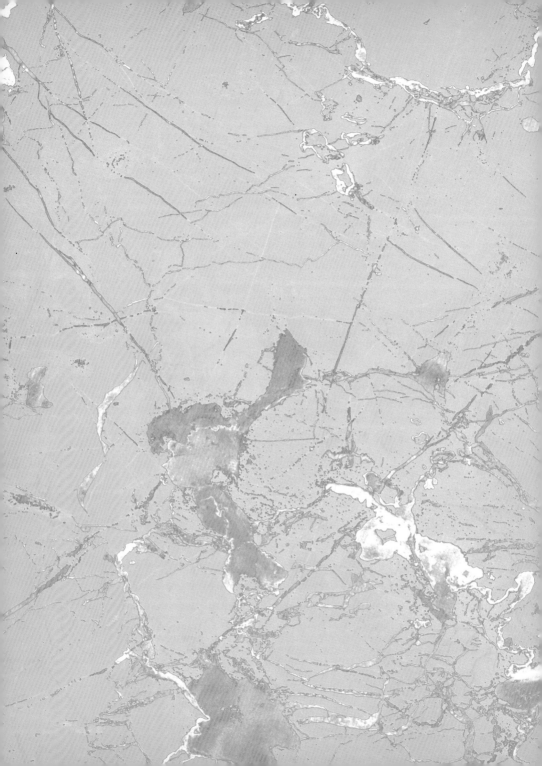

JANUARY

For no one can lay any foundation other than the
one already laid, which is Jesus Christ.

1 CORINTHIANS 3:11

A FRESH START

Let your eyes look straight ahead;
fix your gaze directly before you.

PROVERBS 4:25

I love new beginnings. The first day of a new year always inspires me to take an honest look at every aspect of my life and schedule, and to decide any necessary adjustments. I want to always be sure I'm staying the course—laser focused. I love how Proverbs 4:25 tells us, "Let your eyes look straight ahead; fix your gaze directly before you."

I remember when my husband, Nick, bought me a Vespa—complete with driving lessons. The most important point my instructor made was that where I looked was where I would go.

What great advice for the start of a new year! God wants us to be diligent in keeping our eyes firmly fixed on Jesus—laser focused. He wants us to stay the course, and where we focus is where we'll go.

Let's commit to focusing on Jesus—the One who calms the storms. Then we won't be overwhelmed by our circumstances, problems, challenges, or feelings. We won't fear any waves of opposition. Instead, faith will rise up and make us *unshakeable!*

Lord, help me to stay focused on You,
every moment of every day.

GOD'S STORYLINE FOR YOU

It is for freedom that Christ has set us free. Stand firm, then, and
do not let yourselves be burdened again by a yoke of slavery.

GALATIANS 5:1

The longer I live, the more I see how God has been writing a great story in my life. Its plot illustrates His power to transform a life shaped by shame into a life full of freedom—a life I live as a champion, Spirit-filled and Spirit-led. As a child and a teen, I never could have imagined such a beautiful story for myself. But God is a magnificent author, and I am so thankful I get to live His story for my life every day.

God wants to do the very same thing for you. He created you for a specific purpose. He has a powerful plan—a significant reframing—for your life. And guess what? Slavery has no place in God's storyline. Jesus came to set you free from every bondage—shame, fear, doubt, pain—from whatever has enslaved you. Yes, the Enemy will always try to throw his weights back on you, but when you feel them start to pull you down, declare today's verse over your life. Personalize it and remember to "stand firm" in your God-given freedom.

It is for freedom that Christ has set us free. Stand firm and confidently move forward in God's new story for your life.

Lord, thank You for creating me to live free—
and help me walk in that freedom each day.

LOVING GOD WITH ALL WE ARE

"'Love the Lord your God with all your heart and with all your soul and with all your mind.' This is the first and greatest commandment. And the second is like it: 'Love your neighbor as yourself.'"

MATTHEW 22:37-39

God took all the commands and laws and summarized them into two critical points: love God and love others. That's because His love *in* us heals and transforms us—and His love *through* us heals and transforms the world around us. Imagine how much He has entrusted to us! We can't help but share His perfect love and help others be made whole. What a gift! That's why God wants us to keep growing in loving others well.

Learning to love God first—and loving Him so completely that you love Him with every fiber of your heart, soul, and mind—is a lifelong process. It comes from daily meeting with Him, seeking Him, and allowing Him to change your heart to be more like His. Learning to love others next is how we cooperate with Jesus and His mission to win the lost and disciple others.

As you continue to grow in loving God with all your heart, soul, and mind, show your love for Him by loving those around you. Fulfill the greatest commandments. Love God. Love others. Be the love of Jesus everywhere you go.

Thank You, Jesus, for working in me so I can better love You with all my heart, soul, and mind— and show Your supernatural love to others.

RENEWED PASSION

His power . . . is at work within us.

EPHESIANS 3:20

Your life in God is an adventure of faith—and the fuel to keep you going is your passion. Our passion is that unapologetic willingness and enthusiasm to do what God has called us to do. *Enthusiasm* comes from two Greek words: *en*, which means "in," and *theos*, which means "God." So if you are in God, you have enthusiasm. When you live from a place of passion, you take performing your work and living your life from a place of "have to" to a place of "get to." You don't do anything out of obligation, but out of excited gratitude.

Passion will enable you to do what you never thought you could.

Passion will enable you to keep going when you want to give up.

Passion will help you to inspire everyone to come along on the journey with you.

We are filled with the Holy Spirit of the living God; therefore, we ought to be the most passionate people on earth. So, when you feel your passion begin to wane, stand on God's promise to us: "Even youths grow tired and weary, and young men stumble and fall; but those who hope in the LORD will renew their strength. They will soar on wings like eagles; they will run and not grow weary, they will walk and not be faint" (Isaiah 40:30–31).

Your faithful, unfailing love keeps me going, Lord. It guides, heals, empowers, transforms, protects, and provides for me. Thank You.

OUR REJOICING GOD

[The Lord your God] will take great delight in you; in his love he will no longer rebuke you, but will rejoice over you with singing.

ZEPHANIAH 3:17

How else can we respond to such unconditional love except with gratitude and praise—rejoicing right along with Him? He loves us so much that He sings over us!

When you find it difficult to connect with God, or feel as though you can't hear His direction in your life, start praising Him for all He is and thanking Him for all He has done. Whether you sing it or say it, express your gratitude like the Word says, entering His "gates with thanksgiving and his courts with praise" (Psalm 100:4). Magnify His name with prayers like the following:

"Father, You are wonderful. Thank You for being such a good God, who is so good to me. Thank You for being so faithful to me in every season. Thank You for never leaving me nor forsaking me. Thank You for always working all things for my good—even when I can't see You at work."

Lord, the idea that You sing over me in delight both thrills and humbles me. Thank You for Your love! Show me how to delight in You right back!

LEARNING TO TRUST

Those who know your name trust in you, for you,
Lord, have never forsaken those who seek you.

PSALM 9:10

At some point in our lives, we undoubtedly develop defense mechanisms—those habits we form to protect our hearts and minds from hurt and pain. We decide to never be truly vulnerable again. Or we become the person trying to control every aspect of our lives—and even those around us.

We think these mechanisms create a life that is easier to deal with than trusting an unknown future to a known God. But learning to trust God is actually the antidote to getting rid of all of our defense mechanisms. It's the journey He wants us to take.

Yes, learning to trust will take time. It will be helped by experience with trustworthy people. It will involve accepting challenges, undergoing trials, and coming out the other side. It will mean taking the risk of following God despite our fear.

Trust grows slowly. So, be patient and kind with yourself, knowing that "the Lord is not slow in keeping his promise, as some understand slowness. Instead he is patient with you, not wanting anyone to perish, but everyone to come to repentance" (2 Peter 3:9).

Lord, I know You are trustworthy—even when
I don't feel it. Heal me, and lead me along
the way to complete freedom in You.

LETTING GO OF THE PAST

See, I am doing a new thing! Now it springs up;
do you not perceive it? I am making a way in the
wilderness and streams in the wasteland.

ISAIAH 43:19

At my house, I firmly believe in having a place for everything and everything in its place.

I love to purge my house, office, car, and any other space of needless junk and clutter. If something has not been used recently or is simply taking up too much space, out it goes! (Nick and the girls often leave notes on their possessions, begging me to not give them away or throw them away.)

A harder assignment, though, is to purge our minds from past events. If we spend time replaying every scene when we failed or when someone hurt us, abused us, or disappointed us, then we will struggle to move forward.

If you hang on tightly to past memories, you might miss out on the life God wants you living today! Yes, it takes courage to let go of the weights you have carried around for years—whether those are actual, physical things (such as clothes, cars, jewelry, or houses) or intangible weights (relationships, bad habits, wrong thinking, or emotional baggage). It's time to clean out your mind. Then your hands will be free to hold the good things God has for you. The new things He wants to give you!

Lord God, I want to pursue the adventure You have for my life. Please help me see and release the things I don't need.

DELIGHT IN GOD'S STRENGTH

For Christ's sake, I delight in weaknesses, in insults, in hardships, in persecutions, in difficulties. For when I am weak, then I am strong.

2 CORINTHIANS 12:10

No child wants to grow up to be a pipsqueak. They all want to be big and strong! Even we adults prefer operating out of our strength rather than our weakness. But God keeps allowing us to be in situations where our weakness shows. Why? Because only in our weakness can we know His strength.

Your powerful God is never limited by your limitations. Whenever He calls you to step out of your comfort zone, you can be sure He wants to do something in and through your life. God chooses people for His work not because they are big enough and strong enough and smart enough, but because He knows who will stay focused on the truth that *only God* can do that work. Our God of the impossible chooses people who will follow Him, trust Him, and be His hands, feet, and voice as He does what only He can do.

What a relief to know that God's changing work is done because of God's strength, not yours or mine. So when you see your weaknesses, "delight" like Paul! You can expect God's strength to be revealed in amazing and beautiful ways.

Lord God, please pour Your strength into my weak places and use me for Your eternal purposes. What a privilege and a delight!

SERVING BEHIND THE SCENES

Samuel took the horn of oil and anointed [David] in
the presence of his brothers, and from that day on the
Spirit of the LORD came powerfully upon David.

1 SAMUEL 16:13

When David was anointed by God to be king of Israel, he was merely a boy tending his family's sheep. He was serving in obscurity—separate from his older brothers and where all the action seemed to be. Still, God knew David was the one and He used David mightily in Israel's history.

Maybe you are serving the Lord in total obscurity and anonymity. Maybe you're given jobs no one else wants. If so, welcome them. Like David, there could be something great that God is maturing you to do. If you feel disregarded by your family, your boss, or your coworkers, then you are in David's good company. David was disregarded and dismissed—until it was time for God's plan for David to unfold.

Have confidence in God's plan for you—regardless of what today looks like. Remember that you are not unseen by God. He knows your name, your faithful service, and your heart. God knows your giftedness, your potential, and your faithfulness to Him when no one else does. Know that the God who assigned you to your current place will find you when it is time for your promotion.

*Lord, reading these words makes me excited about the
role You have for me in Your kingdom. I believe that
You are using today to prepare me for tomorrow.*

WHEN GOD IS READY

"Have the whole army give a loud shout; then the wall of the city will collapse and the army will go up, everyone straight in."

JOSHUA 6:5

Throughout my life I've faced many kinds of walls. They blocked me, slowed me down, and challenged me to grow in my faith. The process of standing and obeying God until they fell shaped me. The process always stretched me, but God eventually used those walls for something beautiful. And He'll use the wall you're facing today to do the same for you.

When the Israelites were facing the ominous walls of Jericho, the facts of the situation were bleak: the walls were high and thick and tightly shut. God's perspective was different: He saw Jericho already delivered to His people. The promise was a done deal.

But Joshua and the people had to walk through a God-ordained seven-day process. During those seven days, they were to march around the city (Joshua 6). They were promised that they'd get to witness a miracle, when at their shout, God would bring the wall down. And that's exactly how it happened.

When we take our eyes off God's promises, all we see is a wall. But God is using that barrier to stretch us and shape us according to His purposes. That barrier will come down when He is ready. Our job is to keep marching, worshiping, and following Him, until He gives us the order to shout in celebration—when His promise is fulfilled!

God, thank You for the refining, shaping work You are doing. I believe You'll make my wall fall down.

WONDERFULLY MADE

You created my inmost being; you knit me
together in my mother's womb.

PSALM 139:13

Before I was formed in my mother's womb—whosever womb that was—God knew me.

I was thirty-three years old when I first learned that I was adopted. The underpinnings of my world shifted radically and immediately, but because of my faith in God, they resettled in a more secure place as I comprehended such emotional news.

As I stood in my mother's kitchen, looking at her, my brother, and my sister-in-law, I remembered God's Word. I knew He knitted together my innermost parts and fashioned all my days before there was even one of them. I knew I was fearfully and wonderfully made. I knew that God had always known I was adopted, and He had always loved me. I may not have been who I thought I was, but I was still who He said I was. And I was loved. I was His.

In the wake of that life-changing discovery, God's very real love for me was holding me together. I knew His love was always relentless, unyielding, passionate, unfailing, perfect. And a feeling of peace—of supernatural peace—engulfed me. This loving God was in control of my life.

And He is in control of yours. If you've been rocked by an emotional earthquake, look to Him; His love will hold you together too.

Your gift of love, God, sustains me when my world turns
upside down, and I am grateful. I love You, Lord.

PRESSING ON

Not that I have already obtained all this, or have
already arrived at my goal, but I press on to take hold
of that for which Christ Jesus took hold of me.

PHILIPPIANS 3:12

If we allow little things to interfere with our relationship with Jesus, enough of those small obstructions will, over time, result in blockages that clog our spiritual arteries and harden our hearts. Yet when we *press on*—to use Paul's phrase—we exert a steady force against a hardened heart.

Stay committed to continually pressing *against* those things that would pull you away from Jesus and *toward* those things that help you run unhindered. Don't allow complacency, apathy, weariness, indifference, hurt, offense, insecurity, fear, doubt, bitterness, or unforgiveness to clog your spiritual arteries. Keep your heart strong so you can keep pressing on.

If you're challenged today, exercise one of these characteristics to keep moving forward: diligence, love, compassion, acts of kindness, faith, forgiveness, or perseverance. Don't be too hard on yourself, but take a first step. Paul emphasized that even *he* hadn't obtained his goal and needed to keep pressing on. We've never "arrived" in this Christian life—so in the love and power of our Father, let's keep inching forward against a hardened heart—and toward an amazing eternity with Him.

Lord Jesus, please give me the energy, strength,
perseverance, and stamina I need to keep pressing on in
my relationship with You. I'm in this race until the end!

RESCUED BY JESUS

The LORD is close to the brokenhearted and
saves those who are crushed in spirit.

PSALM 34:18

When God told us to start the work of A21 (an anti–human trafficking organization), I wanted to learn all I could, so I spent time with women who had been rescued from trafficking. I remember Sonia especially. She had arrived at the shelter the previous day and challenged my motives.

"Why are you here?" she demanded. Her eyes narrowed with suspicion. "Why did you come?"

Taking a deep breath, I introduced Sonia to Jesus.

"There is only one Rescuer who has the power to free any of us from prison. This Rescuer is the God I love—and who loves you and me so much that He left everything to come for us, to die for us, to free us.

"And this God makes all things new. He loves you unconditionally, unrelentingly, and forever. He loves you in your brokenness, and He loves making people like you whole again."

Her questions were legitimate. My answer was truthful. God is the only One who can redeem our lives, heal our broken hearts, and take what the Enemy meant for evil and use it for our good.

My answer was the Answer for Sonia. My answer is the Answer for you as well.

*Lord God, thank You for rescuing me, now and for
eternity! Thank You for making all things new in my life.*

CREATED AND CHOSEN

We are God's handiwork.

EPHESIANS 2:10

God created you for good works. He made you on purpose and for a purpose. He wrote out a plan for your life—full of goodness and hope. Full of a great future. He designed you to fulfill all the potential He placed inside of you.

But then life happened.

And every blow was designed to knock you off your feet and short-circuit God's plan for your life. As you move forward, embracing His love and healing power—as you allow Him to deliver you from all fear, shame, disappointment, and everything else that gets entangled in your mind—hide these truths in your heart so you can remind yourself of who you really are:

- *God created you.* You may not know what your parents felt for each other or even the circumstances of your conception, but you are God's workmanship. You are His masterpiece, intricately woven together, and crafted lovingly by His own hands (Psalm 139:13). This truth is the foundation of your identity and mine.
- *God has chosen you.* You are neither an afterthought nor an accident. Your Creator God knows you, loves you, and has chosen you specifically to be His daughter, a child of the King of kings (Ephesians 1:5).

God, what sense of worth comes with knowing that You created me! What sense of purpose comes with knowing that You have chosen me as Yours! I am Your handiwork!

"TAKE HEART!"

"In this world you will have trouble. But take
heart! I have overcome the world."

JOHN 16:33

Through everything that we encounter in life, we can be grateful that our God is wise, loving, and completely trustworthy. He has told us that we will have trouble—because we live in this world—but when we feel overcome, we can believe that *He has* overcome for us. We can trust Him that it's all taken care of—regardless of what it looks like. We can lean into the strength He gives us so we can hang on and press through.

Just hours before He would be arrested, flogged, and crucified, Jesus experienced a level of trouble we never will, yet He was able to say, "Take heart!" He was essentially saying, "Cheer up!"

Why? Because Jesus, whose Spirit is within you, is greater than anything the world can throw at you—even when it feels crushing (1 John 4:4). In Him, we can press on, knowing that there will be a happy ending, guaranteed. In Him, we can refocus our sight and thoughts to be above the circumstances we're facing. We can rest that the real battle of overcoming has already been won. That's when we can walk in *unshakeable* faith.

Lord God, thank You that You have overcome everything
I could ever face. Thank You for strength to cling to
the truth: You are faithful, wise, and loving—and You
are growing my faith into unshakeable faith!

BIGGER GOD, SMALLER STRUGGLES

---

*We fix our eyes not on what is seen, but on what is unseen,
since what is seen is temporary, but what is unseen is eternal.*

2 CORINTHIANS 4:18

To the naked eye, distant stars are just a speck of light, but with the help of a telescope, we realize those stars are actually huge. In the same way, during our hard times, God can seem distant. When that happens, do whatever it takes to remember how big God actually is—and let faith adjust your lens.

What crisis in your life—what I call a faith-shaker—is currently looming? A medical diagnosis or new boss? Car repairs or depleted finances? Is a treasured friend moving away or a trusted leader leaving your church? Maybe it's issues with your family. Whatever you're facing, God invites you to "fix [your] eyes not on what is seen, but on what is unseen" (2 Corinthians 4:18). There is an eternal, unseen purpose beyond this crisis.

Boost the power of your lens so you can see more of God. Seek Him in prayer and in the Word, and meditate in amazement on His attributes. The bigger God is in your mind, the smaller your struggles will look. During hard times and dark times, remember that God is doing good that you are yet to see. It is coming to a wondrous resolution, in His time.

*God, please help me see more clearly Your wisdom, love,
and trustworthiness—and know that You are close.*

FEELING NO SHAME

Adam and his wife were both naked, and they felt no shame.

GENESIS 2:25

The Bible tells us that in the beginning Adam and Eve "felt no shame." They were created perfectly and set in a perfect environment. But when they sinned, and sin entered the world for the first time, so did shame—and they felt shame for the first time.

God placed this key point in Genesis because there's a freeing truth for us to grasp. God wanted us to know that shame was never His plan for us—that the perfect state for humankind is a shame-free life. After Adam and Eve sinned, God knew that shame would be one of our Enemy's most harmful weapons, so He gave us the ultimate defense: Jesus. "Anyone who believes in him will never be put to shame" (Romans 10:11). He makes us clean, He teaches us truth, and He restores us to Himself, just like humankind was originally created to be.

So the next time you feel the dark pull of secret shame or embarrassment, or that feeling of just not being enough, remember you weren't created to live that way. Open your heart to Jesus, and He will bring light to the dark places. After all, He knows everything, and He loves you fully.

I'm so grateful that Your unconditional acceptance of me banishes shame, and I can walk in Your perfect peace.

YOUR LIFE-PRINT

Body and soul, I am marvelously made! I
worship in adoration—what a creation!

PSALM 139:13 The Message

It is no coincidence God gave each of us a distinct set of markings unique to every person: our fingerprints. I believe this is one of the ways God reminds us that each of us is an original, a unique person with a unique purpose. Psalm 139 says:

> You know me inside and out, you know every bone in my body; you know exactly how I was made, bit by bit, how I was sculpted from nothing into something. Like an open book, you watched me grow from conception to birth; all the stages of my life were spread out before you, the days of my life all prepared before I'd even lived one day. (vv. 14–16 The Message)

I love that! Just as God gave us fingerprints, He prepared for each of us a "life-print" that is completely our own. Sadly, many women never truly discover there's a divine "life-print" for them because they're too busy trying to fit into someone else's. If you feel the urge to become a carbon copy of the wonderful women you see around you, let me remind you: she's got her life-print, and you've got yours. Yours was made for you! So seek God for your purpose, and accept it—because you were "marvelously made."

God, thank You for giving me my own life-
print. When I compare myself to others, remind
me of what You put here to do.

THE GRACE OF FORGIVENESS

John saw Jesus coming toward him and said, "Look, the
Lamb of God, who takes away the sin of the world!"

JOHN 1:29

It's important to understand: Why exactly did Jesus, this wonderful Son of God, have to die (John 3:16)? The answer lies in the very nature of God—and the very nature of humankind.

God is without sin—and we human beings are not, so we cannot stand before our holy God in our sin. But there is a bridge that enables us to connect with God—Jesus.

Jesus was the spotless Lamb of God. He was spotless because He never sinned. He perfectly kept the law of Moses, He perfectly loved God with all He was, and He perfectly loved people (2 Corinthians 5:21). Jesus' victory over sin and death was necessary because it secured our forgiveness and allowed us to be in contact with our holy God.

When we invite Him into our hearts to be the Lord of our lives, He moves in. He forgives. He redeems. He restores—regardless of what you have done or what has been done to you. That's why I often say to let what He has done for you become bigger than what anyone has done to you. That's the grace of receiving forgiveness and extending it to others.

*Lord, You see my faults more clearly than I
do, yet You love me with a gracious, forgiving,
cleansing, and redeeming love. Thank You.*

CALL IT WHAT IT IS

Without the shedding of blood there is no forgiveness.

HEBREWS 9:22

If I ripped the label off a bottle of poison and replaced it with a label that said "chocolate syrup," you would think I was crazy, if not utterly evil. I may have done real harm by mislabeling the liquid. Accuracy in labeling is important in more ways than one.

These days, for instance, many people do not like us to use the term *sin*, but I think it is important that we correctly label a poison so that we know exactly what antidote to administer. Romans 3:23 tells us, "All have sinned and fall short of the glory of God." Sin is to miss the mark, and sin is why God sent Jesus into the world to redeem us.

So when you're tempted to dismiss something as a mistake or a slipup, make sure you're using an accurate label. Ask your heart, "What's the real problem, and what's the necessary cure?" Only when we call out sin for what it really is will people know to go to Jesus, the Lamb of God, and be washed clean by His forgiveness and sacrifice. Ask Him to open your mind today to call sin what it is—and to draw you to Him for the cure He freely gives us.

Thank You for opening my eyes to the truth about my sin and for forgiving me for it. Help me boldly use the right labels so others can know the blessings of forgiveness and eternal life.

FORGIVEN—AND FORGIVING

"When you stand praying, if you hold anything
against anyone, forgive them, so that your Father
in heaven may forgive you your sins."

MARK 11:25

Our loving God is concerned with our spiritual health and our overall well-being. He'd never want us to hold on to something that was hurting us. That's why God commands us to both receive His forgiveness and forgive others.

Forgiveness goes in two directions: we are forgiven for our sins, and we forgive those who have sinned against us, who have hurt, offended, or abused us.

Asking God to forgive your sins frees you to enjoy your relationship with Him. You are better able to hear His guiding voice, and you can be confident that nothing is blocking your prayers (Matthew 6:12; 1 Peter 3:12). Yet sin comes all too easily to us. We sin in thought, word, and deed. Asking God's forgiveness is essential to our relationship with Him.

The other side of the coin, forgiving others, can be difficult. Maybe the hurt still stings, or you are still dealing with the consequences of those actions. Forgiveness doesn't mean reestablishing the relationship: that's not always safe. Forgiveness doesn't mean forgetting: pain offers lessons you need to remember. But forgiving others is a gift of freedom you give yourself.

Lord, You know my struggles. But, like all Your commands,
Your instruction to forgive is for my good. Thank You for
the strength to forgive for my good and Your glory.

SECOND CHANCES

If we confess our sins, he is faithful and just and will forgive
us our sins and purify us from all unrighteousness.

1 JOHN 1:9

Just like in a race, when you trip and fall in your effort to live a Christlike life, you are not disqualified. You are out of the race only if you don't get back up and carry on. But the Enemy wants you to believe that because you've fallen, you are no longer fit to run. That's just not true!

God's grace is greater than most of us realize. He never gives up on us. He is the God of second chances, third chances, fourth chances—an endless number. On this side of eternity, there is always another chance with God.

Sin may have consequences, but no matter what you have done, you can still finish your race. And you can live free of guilt and shame when you get back up and take your sins to Jesus, and leave them with Him.

Lord God, I have plenty of reasons to need Your
forgiveness. Thank You that when I bring my sins to You,
You forgive me and free me to continue my race.

A NEW "HERE"

The LORD makes firm the steps of the one who delights in him.

PSALM 37:23

We all want to get from "here" to "there"—wherever "there" is for us. For some of us, it's a promotion we've worked toward, completing our degree, getting married, or moving through a struggle. And when we do, it's a celebration!

I love it when I realize I'm standing in a "here" place that used to be a "there" place. As I reflect on all the steps I took—being obedient, faithful, staying my course through all the hard times—I realize how my heart and endurance are what got me "here." Not a gift or talent. I am always so grateful for all God has done to get me "here."

Psalm 37:23 promises us that the steps of a righteous woman are ordered and established by the Lord. What a promise!

Every step you take today to move you from "here" to "there" is ordered of the Lord. Rest in this assurance, resist the temptation to obsess about where you will end up someday, and trust God by being faithful where you are now. Before you know it, you'll be celebrating a new "here"!

Lord, thank You for bringing me from where I
was to where I am. Teach me to be faithful and
trust that You are ordering my steps.

GRACE FOR RUNNING THE RACE

Nathan replied, "The Lord has taken away your sin."

2 SAMUEL 12:13

David was one of the most famous kings of Israel in Bible times. He was about fifty years old and had been successfully ruling the nation of Israel for almost twenty years when He had an affair with another man's wife—Bathsheba.

David had everything going for him, but he made a terrible choice.

The same can happen to us. We can be running our race well, and then we begin to relax. We let down our spiritual guard, and before we know it, we stumble and fall. In circumstances similar to David's, after he realized the magnitude of what he'd done, many people might have thought, *It's all over for me now. I knew better, but I've destroyed my relationship with God. He will never forgive me for this!*

Not David. He knew the truth. Yes, he had taken a spectacular fall, but he got back up, repented, accepted God's forgiveness, and finished his race. David suffered consequences for his actions, but he got up and back on course—forgiven, with a new lease on life.

No matter what you've done—or what's been done to you—get back up. God is for you and not against you. He will always be just as merciful and gracious to you as He was to David.

Thank You, Lord, for Your grace and forgiveness. May I never hesitate to confess my sins to You, confident I will hear in my heart that You have forgiven me.

FROM STRENGTH TO STRENGTH

They go from strength to strength, till each
appears before God in Zion.

PSALM 84:7

I love the adventure of faith God has called us to live. I love that following Jesus is never dull as He takes us on a journey from faith to faith, strength to strength, and glory to glory. In short, I love change. But I realize not everyone shares my enthusiasm!

I have two daughters. My eldest, Catherine, loves to try new experiences, visit different places, and taste new foods. She is a great traveling companion.

But my youngest, Sophia, loves routine and keeping things the same. She loves being home playing with our dog, Ezra Blake.

Sisters. Same mother. Same father. Total opposites.

So, whether you are like Catherine and love change, or like Sophia and prefer things staying the same, change is inevitable whether we want it or not.

God wants us to navigate change so we always flourish through it. He wants us to adapt easily, make the best of things, stay positive, and be faith-filled. Sometimes, that's easier to say than do, but I believe God helps us move one step closer every day. Let's commit together to always grow and always change.

Jesus, I know that change is inevitable. When I face
it, please give me guidance and insight as I grow.

SERVING WITH HUMILITY

Therefore, as God's chosen people, holy and
dearly loved, clothe yourselves with compassion,
kindness, humility, gentleness and patience.

COLOSSIANS 3:12

The fastest way to the top sometimes is to start at the bottom—and to serve in humility with all your heart. Philippians 2:3 encourages us, "Do nothing out of selfish ambition or vain conceit. Rather, in humility value others above yourselves."

Through the years, I've watched people work and serve out of both selfish ambition and humility—and only one succeeds in the long run.

People who walk in humility, who value others above themselves, follow after destiny. They discover their purpose and place. They are willing to work whenever they are needed, wherever they are needed, and on whatever project is at hand. They are willing to lay down their lives for the team and the bigger picture. As a result, they *are* influential. Promotion comes to them.

As you jump into your day, clothe yourself with humility and serve with all your heart. As you do, I believe you'll get to the top faster than you ever imagined!

God, I praise You that in Your economy, the last is
first. You are so gracious and wise. Please show me
how to act in humility when I serve and work.

JUST SAY YES

The one who calls you is faithful, and he will do it.

1 THESSALONIANS 5:24

I love the life of faith God has called you and me to live. Yes, it's a risky life—a life of believing Him, trusting Him, and stepping out in faith. It's a constant exchange of:

- the known for the unknown,
- the predictable for the unpredictable,
- the comfortable for the uncomfortable,
- the certain for the uncertain, and
- the explainable for the unexplainable.

But it comes with a promise: "The one who calls you is faithful, and he will do it" (1 Thessalonians 5:24). Our life of faith doesn't have an age limit or a time limit. We don't have to know how the details will unfold, or when the timing will fall into place. All we have to do is trust that the One who calls us is faithful, and know that as we risk stepping out in faith, He *will* do it.

So, whatever God has called you to do, whatever next step He's shown you to take, risk it. Just say, "Yes!" and keep moving forward.

*God, the unknown can scare me, but I am so
thankful that You are faithful to bring me through.
Show me how to take risks for You.*

ACKNOWLEDGING THE TRUTH

Jesus said, "If you hold to my teaching, you are really my disciples.
Then you will know the truth, and the truth will set you free."

JOHN 8:31-32

For the truth to set us free, we have to receive it and allow God to penetrate our hearts with it—working that truth into every area of our lives. Learning to face the truth about some areas is a great step in moving forward in our spiritual growth.

Whatever you've found challenging to overcome, first let go of blaming others for your situation, your actions, or your choices. No, we cannot change the past or delete our life experiences. But we are gifted with the power to take responsibility for how we process those experiences, and for any actions resulting from those experiences. God has blessed us with the power to move forward.

Invite God into the depths of your heart. Invite Him into the challenges of your past. We invite God into our mess so He can deal with it and help us deal with it. When we invite Him into our calamities, He can get us out. Jesus' teachings set us free. Acknowledging the truth about our life is freeing too.

Lord, please give me the courage to look at the truth—and thank You for never leaving me, no matter what I may see.

RECEIVING GOD'S LOVE

I will praise you, Lord my God, with all my heart; I will glorify
your name forever. For great is your love toward me.

PSALM 86:12–13

Accepting as truth that God loves you unconditionally is profoundly difficult when you have lived your life as a performance-driven, accomplishment-oriented, earn-people's-acceptance woman. Plus, if you bear deep scars of being rejected in the past and if you have been filled with shame either by that experience or by choices you yourself made, you might find it hard to believe God loves you. You may also be battling true guilt (you are indeed guilty of something you shouldn't have done) or false guilt (feeling guilty for no legitimate reason) and are therefore keeping your distance from God.

To learn to receive the unconditional love God has for you, simply seek Him. Be in community with His people: they will give you a taste of His love. Choose to believe and commit to memory Scripture that says in no uncertain terms that God loves you. Share your doubts and questions with Him in prayer. Ask Him to reveal to you what is keeping you from accepting His love, and let Him gently lead you back to Himself.

Thank You, Lord, that You want me to know Your
love for me and truly live in that reality. Please
free me from whatever is holding me back.

YOU ARE VALUABLE

He has saved us and called us to a holy life—not because of
anything we have done but because of his own purpose and grace.

2 TIMOTHY 1:9

God created you on purpose and for a purpose. He's called you, positioned you, and equipped you. There is a realm of influence—a group of people—that only you can inspire, encourage, and lead. There's a plan only you can complete. That's how valuable you are!

As you keep moving forward, giving it all you have, know that God is aware of all you do—and He will reward you: "I will cry to God Most High, Who accomplishes all things on my behalf [for He completes my purpose in His plan]" (Psalm 57:2 AMP).

What a reason for celebration! Whether you've been walking in your purpose for a long time, or have just begun the journey of discovery, God will help you fulfill what He's called you to do. He's the One who promotes you—and rewards you.

*Dear God, please keep me strong in my purpose.
And thank You for bringing it to pass!*

THE WONDER IN YOUR HEART

"Truly I tell you, unless you change and become like little
children, you will never enter the kingdom of heaven."

MATTHEW 18:3

Albert Einstein once said, "I have no special talents. I am just passionately curious."

Being curious is "wanting to know." Children are naturally like this. They ask lots of questions—often to the point of exasperating us! I can remember when mine were little and always asking, "Why?" It seemed no answer I gave was sufficient, because their next breath was again, "Why?"

But even Jesus told us to be like little children, childlike in our faith, in awe of the greatness of our God: "Truly I tell you, unless you change and become like little children, you will never enter the kingdom of heaven" (Matthew 18:3).

Being curious, like a child, is how we keep the wonder God placed in our hearts to continually seek Him, learn, and grow. It's how we keep our hearts hungry for who He is and eager to know what He's called us to do.

Being curious about others increases our capacity for empathy and caring, because to care about someone, we have to wonder about them first. One of the best ways to learn is to be interested in people and ask them questions.

Being curious is essential to problem solving and learning. When we open the door to increasing our knowledge and understanding, we grow in innovation and creativity.

So let's stay curious!

Holy Spirit, please pique my curiosity today about You,
Your world, and the ones You place in my path.

FEBRUARY

May the God of hope fill you with all joy and peace
as you trust in him, so that you may overflow with
hope by the power of the Holy Spirit.

ROMANS 15:13

INTENDED FOR GOOD

You intended to harm me, but God intended it for good to accomplish what is now being done, the saving of many lives.

GENESIS 50:20

I love this verse. I often say it's my life verse because, just as it did for Joseph, it accurately depicts what God has done with my life. He's used it—every detail of it—for the saving of many lives. That's because God is in the business of turning anything bad into everything good—including the details of your life.

In the Old Testament, Joseph was sold into slavery by his brothers, falsely imprisoned by his enemies, and forgotten by two men he befriended there. Looking back, though, Joseph could see God's hand in the events of his life and how He used those events to preserve the nation of Israel.

What Joseph recognized as true then is no less true today: anything the world intends for evil, God can use for good. God is able to take the mess of our past and turn it into a message for saving others. He is able to take our trials and turn them into a testimony to encourage others.

So trust God with everything that's happened in your life. Rejoice even now that He's going to use all of it for the saving of many lives.

I rejoice in the hope that what the Enemy meant for evil, to harm me, You will use for good, for the saving of many lives. I celebrate Your work in my life!

WE WANT TO GET WELL

When Jesus saw [the invalid] lying there and learned
that he had been in this condition for a long time,
he asked him, "Do you want to get well?"

JOHN 5:6

Do you want to get well? It seems like such an odd question posed to someone who obviously would want to be well. And yet, Jesus found it necessary to ask.

Jesus was engaging the man's faith, inviting him into the healing process. Receiving our health and wholeness isn't just receiving Jesus doing something to us; it's us actively taking hold of what He's offering.

Jesus wisely asked the man who had been unable to stand or walk for thirty-eight years if he wanted to be well. He really was asking him if he was ready to participate, to cooperate, to engage his faith in the process.

Everything Jesus offers us is something we have to choose to receive—to reach out and take. Whether that's forgiving others who have hurt us, or letting go of anger or bitterness, there is always a part for us to play in receiving our healing and wholeness.

So choose today to engage in the process. Choose to receive your healing—by forgiving, letting go, and freeing others from being indebted to you.

Lord, I want to be well, to be free and whole. I release
others and receive all that Jesus has for me.

RELEASING CONTROL TO GOD

I am like an olive tree flourishing in the house of God;
I trust in God's unfailing love for ever and ever.

PSALM 52:8

You might think you have to protect yourself from broken trust, betrayal, or pain in relationships by grabbing too tightly to control in an attempt to avoid further hurt. It's a natural reaction. You may too readily want to share what you've learned in hopes of helping someone avoid what you have suffered. Neither course of action is healthy or helpful.

God offers another, more balanced way.

A healthy approach to relationships is to love others enough to let them make their own choices instead of succumbing to your need to control and insisting on your choices. And, yes, this means trusting people despite the fact that your trust muscle has been strained, if not torn. It also means trusting "in God's unfailing love," trusting that He will be with you whatever impact other people's decisions have on you (Psalm 52:8).

As you learn to trust God to keep you through everything, you learn to relax and let go of control. Doing so will bring you the peace you were trying to grasp in your own strength.

So take a step of *unshakeable* faith. Trust God. Trust others to God. And let go.

Lord, please free me from my need to control, and grow my trust in You, Maker and Keeper of all things and people.

YOUR PILGRIMAGE ON EARTH

Consequently, you are no longer foreigners and
strangers, but fellow citizens with God's people
and also members of his household.

EPHESIANS 2:19

Do you realize that if you are a follower of Jesus, this world is not your home? You are already a citizen of heaven but living temporarily on this earth as you journey toward eternity with Him. The purpose of our time on earth is to learn to walk with Him, abide in Him, and live through Him—and then share that light with others.

Growing up in a strict and very orthodox home, I remember being told each Sunday, "Christine, you'd better behave in church because God is watching you!" I soon learned that fun did not happen at church, and I compartmentalized my life. That meant I was Christian Christine for a few hours every Sunday, and during the rest of the week, I lived the way I wanted.

Only when I surrendered my heart to Jesus did I realize that He is with me in every situation, each day, and not just for a few hours on Sunday. This new perspective changed the way I live. It reminded me that every day, I am on a pilgrimage with the very Person whose image I want to reflect.

The point of your daily pilgrimage is to become more like your Savior, Jesus, not just for a few hours a week, but in your deepest self. It's to realize He's preparing you for what He's prepared for you—which is your purpose here on earth and your place in eternity (John 14:3).

Lord, thank You for walking with me in this
pilgrimage, each and every day, toward my
purpose here and then with You in eternity.

CONSUMPTION HABITS

"The things that come out of a person's
mouth come from the heart."

MATTHEW 15:18

I'm a caffè latte sort of chick, and I love a good, strong coffee. Shortly after becoming pregnant with my eldest, I was told caffeine wasn't good for the baby. Enough said! I not only stopped drinking coffee; I removed any temptation by giving my coffeemaker and all the coffee in the house away! In the same way, when it comes to our God-given dreams, we, too, have to adjust our consumption habits if they are to fully mature.

Our eyes and ears are the gateways to our heart—just as our mouth is to our stomach—and our dreams flow from our heart. As a new Christian, I had no idea I had to control what entered my heart. I maintained the same old diet of negativity, gossip, and doubt and then wondered why I was not growing in the purposes of God. In time, I became aware I had to change certain things in order to grow—like filling my mind with preaching, teaching, good books and music, and things that glorified Him, instead of things that stunted my growth.

So what are you consuming? Let's choose to put good things in; then we can expect good results and full maturity!

Lord, I choose to feed my heart with good things!
As I choose what goes in, remind me of the purpose
and dreams You are maturing within me.

DESPITE THE ODDS

I know that you can do all things; no
purpose of yours can be thwarted.

JOB 42:2

Once, when I faced a situation where the odds stacked against me were especially high, God reminded me that being in such a predicament never bothers Him in the least: "Yes, the odds are stacked against you. Overwhelmingly, in fact. Yes, the giant you're facing can make you think there's no way forward. But no odds and no giant can stop Me, and when you do My will, they can't stop you either."

God is always with us, always making a way for us to do His will. Yet that's easy to forget in the face of overwhelming odds. But it's still true.

Maybe you're asked to speak at church but think, *I can't! I'm too shy.* You want to volunteer at a homeless shelter, but your schedule tells you that you're too busy. You want to give money or groceries to a family who has lost their home, but your checkbook says there's not even enough in your account to pay your own bills. You want to make a career change and follow what you know is your calling, yet a voice inside mutters: *Stay where you are. The risk is too high!*

Whatever the odds stacked against you, it certainly will never stop what He wants accomplished through you!

Lord God, I like Your odds. You are infinite in
power, knowledge, wisdom, love, kindness,
faithfulness, patience, and everything good!

WOUNDEDNESS REDEEMED

[The Lord] heals the brokenhearted and binds up their wounds.

PSALM 147:3

Years ago, on a family ski trip, I totally wiped out. I remember being in the air and hearing the awful popping sounds in my knee. I snapped my ACL, tore my MCL, tore my meniscus, and fractured my knees.

When I had surgery on my right knee, the surgeon told me that after the required physical therapy, my right leg would actually be stronger than my left—if I was willing to endure the pain of recovery. He explained that the hard work of returning to normal the knee that had been injured would strengthen the muscles and connective tissue. And he was right.

I believe this same principle holds for our hearts when they are broken. No matter what you're going through, *believe that your wounds can indeed make you stronger.*

I believe in every trial there is a gain God wants us to receive. But that perspective requires us to trust Him at levels we might not have before. It requires us to open our hearts to new ways of looking at our circumstances. It requires us to press through the pain knowing an even stronger faith is on the other side.

Thank You, Lord, for healing my broken heart and making me stronger and wiser—about You, about relationships, and about myself. Thank You for bringing good out of every negative I ever encounter.

REMEMBER HIS BENEFITS

Praise the LORD, my soul, and forget not all his benefits—who
forgives all your sins . . . and crowns you with love and compassion.

PSALM 103:2-4

A benefit is an allowance to which one is entitled. It's an advantage. God is telling us in Psalm 103 that there are benefits to being a Christian. This entire psalm is loaded with benefits—promises from God—that He does not want us to forget.

- He forgives *all* of our sins. To forgive is to remit, let off, pardon. He has set us free from all guilt and condemnation (Romans 8:1).
- He heals *all* our diseases—both physical and spiritual. I know not everyone is healed this side of heaven, but they are healed one way or another. My own father passed away from cancer. I know that kind of pain and suffering. But I will always pray for healing. I will always believe for life, because His Word says He heals *all* our diseases.
- He redeems our lives from the pit. That means He delivers us and frees us from every stronghold: addiction, abuse, fear, even our stupid mistakes.
- He crowns us with love. Imagine that. Right after He redeems us, He crowns us with love and compassion.

God's benefits are for you today. Read this list over and over because He doesn't want you to ever forget them. He wants to give you every advantage.

*Thank You, God, for daily loading me with benefits.
For giving me every advantage to succeed.*

A GOD-GIVEN BLESSING

God made him who had no sin to be sin for us, so that
in him we might become the righteousness of God.

2 CORINTHIANS 5:21

I experienced so much pain as a child that I thought there was something wrong with me. I also thought that if I could *be* good enough and *do* enough good things, then perhaps I could compensate for the things that were obviously wrong with me. When I brought that thinking into my relationship with God, I tried to perform for His acceptance. But that wasn't necessary.

Through Jesus, God had already made me what I was trying to become: righteous.

Isn't it comforting to know that our righteousness is found in Christ alone and that there is nothing we need to do to earn it? Being saved is a gift, not a reward we receive based on our performance. In a word, salvation is *grace*: it is an unearned, undeserved, unmerited, God-given blessing.

It took a long time for that truth to sink deep into my heart and soul, but when it did, it brought such freedom into my life. I could relax. Rest. And just receive His unconditional love. If Jesus is your Savior, He has made you righteous.

Thank You, God, for making me righteous. There is nothing
I can do to earn any more of Your love than I already
have. I am pure, good, and worthy because of You.

FOCUSED ON THE CROSS

For the joy set before him [Jesus] endured the cross, scorning
its shame, and sat down at the right hand of the throne of God.

HEBREWS 12:2

For the joy set before Him . . . that's us! When Jesus was on the cross, the joy that kept Him going—the passion that fueled His endurance of pain—was knowing the freedom His death, burial, and resurrection would produce in our lives.

Nothing demonstrates God's love more powerfully than the cross. Jesus wasn't forced to die. He wasn't overpowered, outnumbered, or tricked into it. He chose the cross because He loves you and me. Jesus' passionate love for us took Him to the cross—with its pain, humiliation, and complete separation from God—and then on to the resurrected life that means victory over sin and death for you and me. What passion!

Throughout our lives, we have opportunities to show God we love Him. Again, we do these things not to earn His love but in response to His unconditional, unstoppable love. Because our hearts burn with the same kind of passion that lives in Him. So, activate that passion in your life today. Worship Him passionately. Seek Him first passionately. Share His love with your family passionately. Reach out to others passionately. Let's turn our lives, our families, our communities, and the world around for Jesus!

What amazing grace! What indescribable love!
Jesus, thank You for dying on the cross for my sins—
and teach me to live a life of passionate thanks.

OFF THE TREADMILL

The LORD has dealt with me according to my righteousness;
according to the cleanness of my hands he has rewarded me.

PSALM 18:20

I will never forget the freedom I felt when I finally stepped off the performance treadmill and reveled in God's acceptance of me just as I was.

When I stopped trying to make myself right with God through my own good works, I discovered His grace. I didn't have to earn His acceptance. I didn't have to live a perfect life. I didn't have to be in control of everything.

I found He was readily available to help me up when I fell down, and He kept me going when I wanted to quit. Nothing saps the life out of us faster than trying to make ourselves right with God. Only our faith in Jesus Christ and His redemptive work on the cross brings us into right standing with God.

God's grace changed me, so over time I stopped thinking about all the things that were wrong with me and I started thinking more about all the things that were right with Jesus. I have since discovered that we become what we behold, and as I beheld Jesus, I started to become more like Him because God's Spirit was at work in me.

You, too, can hop off the performance treadmill. Jesus' righteousness is your righteousness.

I am righteous! Thank You, Father, for such truth
and freedom in my life. Thank You that I do not
have to perform for Your acceptance.

THE BRIDGE THAT MATTERS MOST

For there is one God and one mediator between
God and mankind, the man Christ Jesus.

1 TIMOTHY 2:5

I was blessed to grow up in one of the most beautiful cities in the world, and I have walked across, run under, and driven over the Sydney Harbour Bridge dozens of times. I sometimes simply stare at her in awe, captivated by the engineering and beauty. When I look at photos of Sydney without the bridge, it seems somehow incomplete.

When the bridge opened, so did new opportunities for travel, commerce, employment, leisure, and more. People who once had little or no access to the city suddenly had a way in. That is what bridges do: they join things that were separated, providing a means of connecting and community.

That's one reason I love the fact that Jesus Christ is often called the *bridge* between humanity and God. Jesus made a way where there was no way. In the ultimate act of grace, Jesus died on the cross as the sinless Lamb of God and perfect sacrifice, and He made it possible for us to be reconciled to our holy God.

Jesus has sent us into the world so everyone can learn about Him, the Bridge to our great and gracious God. He is a glorious route to a new, and eternal, life.

Please use me, Lord, to be a messenger of Your grace. Help me to be a bridge-builder too, as I direct people toward You.

HE SEARCHES EVEN FOR ONE

"When [the shepherd] finds [the lost sheep], he
joyfully puts it on his shoulders and goes home."

LUKE 15:5–6

If you have one hundred sheep and one wanders off, Jesus tells us, that's the one you go after to rescue. Isn't the one as valuable as each of the ninety-nine?

In natural disasters and in time of war, medical personnel often perform something they call *triage.* It means that they examine the injured and determine which ones they have the best chance of saving. They concentrate their efforts on those they think they can save—and, with regret, allow the others to die, or perhaps to rally and recover on their own.

Jesus doesn't do triage. He leaves the healthy ninety-nine safe in their pen while he goes out into the night, looking for the one who's lost, sick, depressed, disappointed, wounded, enslaved. And when He has found it, He lays it across His shoulders and in celebration calls together His neighbors, saying, "Rejoice with me; I have found my lost sheep" (Luke 15:6).

How could an almighty God do any less? He promises to come after the one, because each one is precious to Him. Each one.

If you feel lost today, emotionally, spiritually, or physically, Jesus will find you and lead you home. He loves you and will never leave you to wander alone.

Lord, thank You for never giving up on me.
Thank You for always leading me home.

OUR SEEKING GOD

"In the same way there will be more rejoicing in heaven
over one sinner who repents than over ninety-nine
righteous persons who do not need to repent."

LUKE 15:7

In Luke 15, Jesus told three stories about how easy it is to be lost—and how remarkable it is to be saved. Jesus first told the story of a lost and rescued sheep. Then, as if to be sure we don't miss the message, He told about a lost coin that was found and a lost son who returned home. All to remind us He is in the business of finding, saving, and celebrating.

These stories can help us remember important truths that reflect God's infinite grace. He says to us:

No matter how deep the pit, I will always seek you and rescue you because I love you with an everlasting love. Even when you mess up, even when you're careless or mistaken or afraid or broken or weak, even when you deliberately sin, I still love you. Even when you are incapable of doing anything for anyone or even helping yourself, I still love you. I come for all those who have made mistakes, those who are overlooked, devalued, and despised. I come for the lost, whether the lost is a silly sheep, a silver coin, a squandering son . . . or you.

Lord, I am all too aware that my heart is prone
to wandering. By Your grace, tether my heart
to Yours. Thank You for finding me!

WILLING AND AVAILABLE

The number of the men who had eaten was five thousand.

MARK 6:44

God works with the available, not with the qualified, or those who look "good on paper." This is one more truth illuminated over and over in the Bible, and ever so subtly in the story from Mark 6 about the boy and his five loaves and two fishes.

In the reporting of this miracle, Mark counted the number of men only—because women and children were not considered important in that day. But God always uses people others overlook—in this case, a little boy. While we might expect God's miracles to come through people we consider important—the accomplished, the wealthy, or the talented—He chooses people we might not see. In fact, God will use anyone who is willing to be used, regardless of whether any onlookers think that person is qualified. God is not looking for *ability* as much as He is *availability*.

Consider that truth when you are overwhelmed by the magnitude of a need. Don't do nothing just because you can't do everything. God is not asking any one of us to do everything, but simply to do something—and then He will do the rest. Look for opportunities to put your little into the hands of a big God, and watch Him use it to do the impossible.

Lord, may I never miss an opportunity to make my little available to You. Thank You for using it for Your great plans.

WORKS OF GRACE

He who began a good work in you will carry it on
to completion until the day of Christ Jesus.

PHILIPPIANS 1:6

What good work has God begun in you? What purpose has He called you to fulfill? Rest assured, *every* good work He's started, He will complete. He will see you all the way to the finish line. And it all starts with the first work of saving you . . .

If you are seeking Christ, He is beginning and carrying on a continual cycle of good works in you. It starts like this: The more we become like Christ, the more readily and genuinely we love people. The more we love people, the more we want to serve them. We best serve them when we rely on God's power, His resources, and His ways—so we rely on Him and become even *more* like Him. It's a miraculous cycle of renewal.

In your Christian life, you are in the process of increasingly "[living] a life worthy of the Lord… growing in the knowledge of God" (Colossians 1:10). And at the same time that Jesus does this transformational work *in* us, He is transforming the world *through* us.

God has a perfect plan for your life. A purpose for you to fulfill. And He will complete what He has started in you—what He has planted in your heart.

Jesus, I trust You to complete what You have begun in me. I will complete all that You created me to do.

GIFTED AND TALENTED

Each person should live as a believer in whatever situation the
Lord has assigned to them, just as God has called them.

1 CORINTHIANS 7:17

When my girls, Catherine and Sophia, were little, they each had many different toys, but I can guarantee the only one each one ever wanted was the one the other was holding. I wanted to teach them to be satisfied with what they had and to stop comparing and coveting what the other one had. And I always want to remind myself of that too!

As Christians, we know in our heads that God has a great plan for each of us, and He has given each of us the talents we need to live according to His plan. But, like children, we desire someone else's talent regardless of the talents God has given us. Let's refocus on what we've been given, so we'll never miss out on the joy and satisfaction of doing what God has called us to do.

There's no use pining away to be one thing when God has specially gifted and ordained you to be another. God wants you to live with a deep contentment, and you can experience this when you embrace *His* plan. His plans for you are good!

God, You have gifted me in a certain way for a certain
reason. Please help me know that purpose, use my
talents for Your glory, and be graced by contentment.

TRANSFORMED AND RENEWED

We all, who with unveiled faces contemplate the Lord's glory, are being transformed into his image with ever-increasing glory, which comes from the Lord, who is the Spirit.

2 CORINTHIANS 3:18

As God transforms us from the inside out, He gives us the amazing gift of renewing our minds. In that process, some things we always thought were true are suddenly revealed to be completely different than we thought they were. Where we might have had a harsh viewpoint, suddenly we develop a more loving perspective. Here are some amazing transformations He's shown me:

- The goal of Christian faith *is not* to earn God's favor. *The goal is to become more like Christ—and receive all He has for me.*
- I become more like Jesus *not* by doing good works. *I am transformed by Christ at work in me, and He works through me to touch the world.*
- Christian community is not where I go to be assigned more works to do. *Christian community is where transformation happens. It's where discipleship happens and I grow into a more mature believer.*

How freeing to know that a life in Christ is powered not by us but by Him. It's full of hope, not chores, tasks, and assignments.

So keep reading His Word and listening to His Word. And let it transform your suppositions into freeing truth.

God, thank You for always welcoming me into a deeper relationship with You and into fellowship with others. Thank You for transforming my mind!

WALKING BY FAITH

Without faith it is impossible to please God, because
anyone who comes to him must believe that he exists
and that he rewards those who earnestly seek him.

HEBREWS 11:6

Is there a gap between what you are doing and what you want to be doing? Then that's a gap for the God of the impossible to step in. Do you feel nervousness about doing what you feel called to do? That nervousness is space where the Holy Spirit wants to step in. Welcoming God to interrupt, step in, and fill those spaces is *walking by faith.*

When we walk by faith, we choose not to trust in our human planning or solely rely on our God-given abilities. We don't factor God out of the equation of our lives. We don't try to fill up the gaps ourselves by controlling every aspect of our lives so much that there is no room for God to interrupt and disturb our plans for His good purposes. Think about it: if your goals are achievable *without* God, are they even *from* God?

Our faith is what pleases God. Not our capability or ability to plan, wrangle, and do it on our own. Yes, diligence is important, but so is allowing God to interrupt our plans and move us past the gaps in fulfilling our calling. So seek Him, and watch Him reward your faith.

Lord, build in me a faith that pleases You. I welcome
You to step in and change things to go Your way!

CRUMBLING WALLS

The LORD gave and the LORD has taken away;
may the name of the LORD be praised.

JOB 1:21

We all have walls to overcome—those seemingly impenetrable forces standing between us and our freedom. They can be walls representing sin, such as unforgiveness, or a circumstance in our lives we have to emotionally and physically overcome—like being a single mom, or suffering a great financial loss, or losing a job.

I know many courageous people who have faced high and thick walls blocking their way in life, and who watched those walls come down. Despite their pain, often dire circumstances, legitimate concerns, and pressing needs—they chose to pursue God and trust Him when He told them what to do. And that made all the difference.

It is never easy, but courageous people choose to put their faith in what they know about God—about His trustworthy nature—instead of what they don't know about their future. They bravely choose to run to God, not away from Him, even when everything inside of them wants to pull back and protect themselves.

Be courageous. Pursue and trust God. Believe in His Word. Believe His promises to you. Believe in His power to destroy any walls in front of you.

Lord, You know the pain, circumstances, concerns, and needs that make up my walls. Thank You that today, those walls come down!

IMPOSSIBLE IS WHERE GOD STARTS

"What is impossible with man is possible with God."

LUKE 18:27

Impossible is where God starts. Miracles are what He does. I don't care what you're facing today, God can turn it around.

Mental illness, unforgiveness, infertility, an eating disorder, anxiety, depression, addiction, poverty, abortion, a divorce you never expected, an affair you regret. Nothing is too big for our God.

Go to His Word. Find the verses that speak to your situation. Wrap your heart and mind around Luke 18:27 and believe it for your circumstance.

Regardless of what others have told you, I'm telling you the truth. God is able to do abundantly more than you can fathom, contemplate, hope for, or consider. And He wants to. But it is according to the faith, confidence, determination, big thinking, and expectation in you.

It's not enough that God is big in stature if He's not big in you. So make God and His truth bigger than anything staring you down.

There's no problem He cannot solve.

There's no question He cannot answer.

There's no enemy He cannot defeat.

There's no difficulty He cannot overcome.

There's nothing our God cannot do. Impossible is where He starts. Miracles are what He does.

Lord God, help me trust You, obey You, and put more faith in You, who can tear down any wall.

NO DARKNESS AT ALL

God is light; in him there is no darkness at all.

1 JOHN 1:5

Jesus said, *"I am the light of the world"* (John 8:12).

He also said, *"You are the light of the world"* (Matthew 5:14–15).

He wasn't contradicting Himself, but rather showing us the progression of how when His light floods our souls and swallows up all the darkness, then we, too, become the light of the world. His light illuminates our darkness, heals our hearts, and then shines through us to others.

Jesus wants to shine brightly through you.

Wherever you live, you have a realm of influence. You hold a great deal of power and persuasion. At your job, in your family, among your friends. You may be the glue that holds everyone in your world together. And the Enemy knows that if he can shake your confidence and make you second-guess your value, it can have ripple effects on everyone around you.

So, let's agree to shine brightly together today. Let's continually allow God's light to shine through us, in us, and on us to change our world.

Thank You, God, that because You are the light of the world, I can also be the light of the world. I choose to shine brightly today and be a beacon of hope to everyone around me.

CHARACTER BUILDERS

Let us run with perseverance the race marked out for us.

HEBREWS 12:1

If you've played sports or music, you might give a shudder and a smile at the term "character builder." Memories of endless rounds of warm-ups and drills are commonly referred to as character builders. And those exercises come with their fair share of tumbles and mess-ups.

All of us—at one time or another, again and again—stumble and fall. But the good news is, we can pick ourselves up and continue running our race. And we can be better for it.

Remember: God is bigger than any of your past mistakes. Jesus has redeemed your life so that you are forgiven for your sins in the past, you are graced with a fresh start today, and you have solid hope for the future.

Don't believe the lie that somewhere along the way you have been disqualified for stumbling or for being weak. Instead, get back up and keep building that character. You are not out of time. God will give you enough time to do all that He has called you to do. As long as you have breath in your lungs and your heart is still beating, there is always hope and always a future. Your falls and your failures cannot keep Jesus' perfect plan for you from unfolding.

Lord, thank You for helping me to get up when I stumble, stay on track when I fail, and always trust You who guides, strengthens, and redeems.

WELCOME TO THE NEIGHBORHOOD

The Word became flesh . . . and moved into the neighborhood.

JOHN 1:14 THE MESSAGE

Imagine what might happen if Jesus literally moved into your neighborhood. No doubt there would be some changes as He made Himself at home—and miracles per capita would skyrocket! When you give God full access to your soul and He moves in, He changes things around for the better. He heals your soul with His presence and allows you to flourish. *When God moves in, you move on in life* because you're able to.

Without Him, you cannot move on from past hurts. You will inevitably become weary and run out of steam. But God's power is made perfect in your weakness (2 Corinthians 12:9). The healing you receive is not at all about *your doing more for God.* It's about giving God greater access to more of your heart and soul so *He can do more in you.*

What a concept! This was revolutionary for me. It was my true introduction to grace beyond the grace that saved me. He didn't just save me to leave me how I was, but to set me free with His grace day after day. It's a process of walking in greater freedom every single day of our lives.

Let God move into your neighborhood—so you can move on in every area of your life.

I praise You, Lord, for Your grace that frees
me to live an abundant life in You.

A DIVINE EXCHANGE

"I will give you a new heart and put a new spirit in you; I will remove from you your heart of stone and give you a heart of flesh."

EZEKIEL 36:26

Defense mechanisms can be great, if they're serving their purpose. You duck and cover when something comes flying at you. But spiritually, defense mechanisms can be a problem.

As I allowed the Lord to heal my heart from my painful childhood, I saw my faith and courage increase. Instead of constantly trying to protect myself, I gave myself over to the Lord bit by bit. I let Him change my heart of stone into a pliable, tender heart of flesh. It was a supernatural, divine exchange—one that He wants you to experience as well. Let God replace your broken heart with "a heart of flesh." After all, healthy hearts mean healthy and fruitful lives.

This divine exchange may begin quite subtly. But over time, you'll see transformations like these:

- Hurt people hurt people, *but helped people help people.*
- Broken people break people, *but rebuilt people build people.*
- Damaged people damage people, *but loved people love people.*
- Wounded people wound people, *but healed people bind up wounds.*
- Bound people bind people, *but freed people lead others to freedom.*

Lord, thank You for giving me a heart of flesh to replace my heart of stone. Thank You for using me to lead others to freedom.

VICTORIOUS OVER THE PAST

We are more than conquerors through him who loved us.

ROMANS 8:37

The apostle Paul knew trouble, hardship, persecution, famine, and danger, yet he declared that in all such circumstances God's love made him a conqueror. Paul learned that he was defined not by the things that happened to him, but by his amazing, all-powerful, all-loving God. He made what God did for him bigger than anything anyone did to him—and that process made him a conqueror.

God has called you to be a conqueror too. He wants you to let go of the past—of the tough times, the disillusionment, the emotional pain. He wants you to let Him use what you went through and redeem it. He wants to make you stronger and to give others hope. He wants to increase your capacity for all of Him—compassion, wisdom, love, trust, maturity.

Let Jesus help you see that you are not defined by your past. You have a life beyond it—both here on earth and forever in His kingdom.

Let this hope of a better future give you the strength and courage you need to work through the pain and hurt you still deal with. Jesus is not content to let you simply survive your past; He has equipped you already to conquer it and live victoriously in the present.

Jesus, thank You for redeeming my life and my experiences by making them helpful for others. Please use me to help others conquer their past and live victoriously in the present.

FREE TO RUN

Sin shall no longer be your master, because you
are not under the law, but under grace.

ROMANS 6:14

We're running a race that takes stamina, faith, and joy. It's the race of this Christian life. And it requires we run with the lightest load possible. If it were a literal race, we wouldn't lug along, say, a bowling ball. And yet, holding on to sin does the same thing to us in our spiritual race. Jesus paid the price for sin and rose victorious, so we can run our race victoriously too.

Jesus made forgiveness from any sin possible—but whether we receive that gift is up to us. He already did the heavy lifting, by dying on the cross, so sins that keep us from fulfilling our God-given purpose could be removed easily. When we confess and then actively turn away from sinful behaviors and thought patterns, we are releasing our grip on that which hurts us.

Be honest with yourself as you deal with your sin and cast it aside. God always will forgive you, but—in His strength—you still need to confess and then drop the things that are holding you back from all the life He has prepared for you. As you shed what's weighing you down, you will know what it's like to run freely.

I praise You, Lord, for grace that forgives me, that
empowers me to turn away from sin and run this
race of life glorifying You in all I say and do.

LOOKING THE PART

If I give all I possess to the poor and give over my body to
hardship that I may boast, but do not have love, I gain nothing.

1 CORINTHIANS 13:3

I'd never skied before, but my friend—a professional skier—loaned me her top-of-the-line ski gear. She said, "At least you'll look the part!" Well, it was apparent on my first day that looking great had no bearing on my performance on the slopes. I didn't have any of the knowledge, skill, experience, or strength that a real skier needs. Looking the part didn't count for much at all.

Similarly, we Christians can look the part by having the best gear (our Bibles, devotionals, commentaries), by avoiding certain behaviors, or by going to church and even singing on the worship team. But if our choice of gear and behaviors does not stem from a genuine love for Jesus, we have nothing.

Jesus wants authentic followers. Far beyond collecting the trappings of faith, those followers welcome and willingly yield to His transforming grace—allowing Him to change them from the inside out. But this transformation into Christlikeness does not happen overnight. Let's be committed to strengthening our spirits and growing our love for Jesus so we really shine His light to those around us. Then we will look like Christ-followers outside, because we truly *are* Christ-followers inside!

Lord, please transform me from the inside out so I can live
out a genuine faith in You. I want people to know I'm Yours.

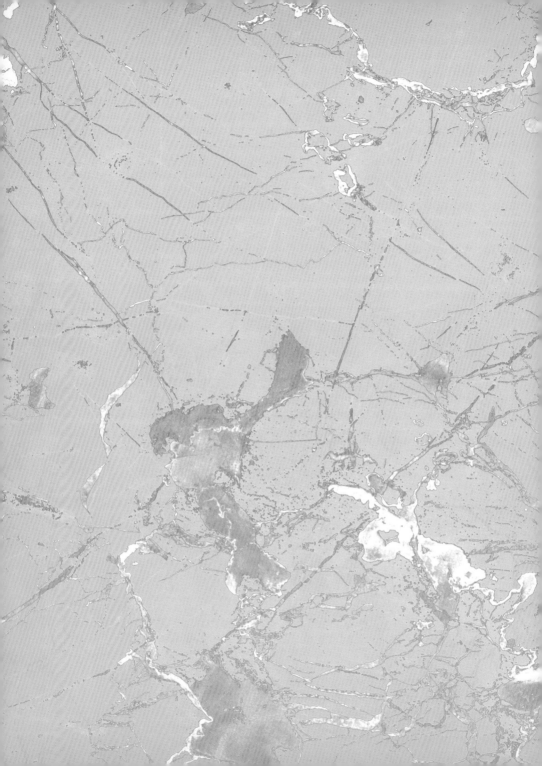

MARCH

We have this hope as an anchor
for the soul, firm and secure.

HEBREWS 6:19

LOVE ONE ANOTHER

"As I have loved you, so you must love one
another. By this everyone will know that you are
my disciples, if you love one another."

JOHN 13:34–35

You want prosperity, education, comfort, and safety for yourself and those you love. These are wonderful things. But Jesus would not have you stop there. When you want for other people the good—education, comfort, and safety— that you want for yourself, you are following His command and loving others as you love yourself.

One sign of Jesus' work in you is that you start extending His love and compassion to the broken, the marginalized, and the hurting. As Jesus' character is formed within you, you will find yourself acting more according to His priorities. Because you'll have His heart, you won't be able to ignore or remain disconnected from the needs of the people in your community and around the world—people He loves.

Injustice and suffering go untended because we are so often distracted, preoccupied with our own concerns. Would people looking at you know you are Jesus' disciple? As Jesus works in your heart, ask for inspiration and wisdom for new ways to love His children. That's one thing He will freely give (James 1:5). There is more than enough love to share.

*Lord, I don't want to be preoccupied with myself
when Your people are in need. Please show
me who to love and how to love them.*

THE LORD LOOKS AT THE HEART

Search me, God, and know my heart.

PSALM 139:23

Image seems so important to people—but not to God. First impressions seem to buoy people up or sweep them under, no matter how fair or unfair those impressions are. Oftentimes, God's call contradicts appearances or overwhelms first impressions—and that's good!

Imagine how David might have felt when the prophet Samuel thought that Jesse's oldest son and David's older brother, Eliab, was surely going to be the next king. But God told Samuel to anoint David. Jesse never thought that his youngest son, David, was even in the running to serve God as king. Do you think it was demoralizing for David to realize that neither the prophet nor his father considered him good enough to serve in the way God was calling him to serve? As a king?

If David felt this way, he certainly didn't let it keep him from stepping into his calling. If you face opposition based on other people's impressions and opinions, remember that ultimately, what other people think does not matter. The only opinion that matters—the only vote that counts—is God's, and first and foremost He considers your heart. If He calls you, no opinion, appearance, or impression can stop Him from working His wonderful plans and purposes through you.

Lord, thank You that what You think of me is far more
important than what others think. I believe Your
purposes will be fulfilled in my life no matter what.

WILLING TO SERVE

There are different kinds of service, but the same Lord.

1 CORINTHIANS 12:5

I'll always remember a letter I received from a social work professional implying that I needed training at her university before I would be qualified to work with young people. At the time I was directing a youth program that—by God's grace—seemed to be thriving. If I were to continue long-term in youth services, though, she said I needed formal training.

It is wise to consider such input—the source, the motive—and get counsel from trusted people of God. The woman had a point: technically, I was unqualified to do the very thing I was doing, so I considered resigning. Yet something inside me—I'm convinced it was God's voice—said, *No, don't quit.*

To the world, I looked unqualified, but God has blessed my work for more than twenty-five years since that letter came. It seems God cared more about my willingness to serve than my qualifications.

Many ministries in God's kingdom do require a baseline of training, such as music, medicine, law, accounting, and art. But once you recognize the role God has called you to, seek training if you need it, and serve with an unrelenting heart. But remember, He can work wonders with willingness. And ultimately, He's the One who enables you to serve. He's the one who qualifies you.

Lord, make me open to Your call, and show me when to sharpen my skills so I can serve You with excellence.

CLEARER VISION

My eyes are ever on the LORD.

PSALM 25:15

As our bodies age, one of the first symptoms can be a diminished ability to see. Impaired vision can cause headaches, lead to accidents, and even keep us from driving. But with corrective lenses, many of us can turn back the hands of time and start seeing things clearly again.

Impaired *spiritual* vision also comes from the wear and tear of time. As we are bombarded with the inevitable disappointments and discouragements of life, we might begin to lose sight of God's greater purpose for our lives. But there is a way to reverse vision loss.

My theory is *love and compassion*. When God calls you to a specific place to love others on His behalf—your home, neighborhood, church, workplace, kids' sports team—you just may find a purpose uniquely designed for you. Choosing to fulfill these purposes keeps us spiritually alive, focused, and maturing. It restores our sight.

So practice love and compassion rather than dwelling on difficulties, fears, and discouragements—which are like scales or cataracts forming over your spiritual eyes. Jesus gave sight to the blind, and He will give spiritual vision to you.

Lord, thank You that I can look to You, and keep my heart free of attitudes that form scales over my spiritual eyes. I want the clear vision You offer.

FISHERS OF PEOPLE

"Come, follow me," Jesus said, "and I will
send you out to fish for people."

MATTHEW 4:19

Not every one of us is called to stand on a platform and preach or to be part of the church's evangelism team or worship team. But every single one of us believers has the ability to tell people about Jesus' love and grace.

That's what Jesus meant when He said He'd send us to fish for people. Whatever our personalities, gifts, and talents, Jesus will use us to draw people in to His saving grace.

Some Bible versions say that Jesus will *make* us fishers of people or of men, and the word *make* means "to shape, to frame, to form, to construct." In other words, Jesus will take you as you are and transform you. This transformation is different from a gift or a calling. It's you becoming more like Jesus as you continue to follow Him. That kind of soul beauty draws people in to Him.

How can you fish for people? Ask God to reveal to you the special tools He gave you so you can touch others with His love. Ask Him to give you His heart for others. Follow Him; then stay open to every opportunity. He will turn you into a fisherman yet.

Lord, transform me to be like You, so I can draw others
in to saving hope. Make me ready to share the gospel
when someone asks what makes me different.

THE TRUTH

"The reason I was born and came into the
world is to testify to the truth."

JOHN 18:37

We live in a world where authenticity makes a big impact. Truth sticks out in the midst of all the media, politicians, advertisers who manipulate for their own ends. The idea of truth in general is often compromised. That's why living authentically for God is so powerful—and why you can change the world by testifying to His truth.

We do this by living it. Perhaps that's why Jesus did not say that He came into the world to *tell* the truth. Rather, He came to testify or *bear witness* to the truth. He lived an authentic life where His words, actions, thoughts, and deeds all bore witness to the same message of truth: the message about people's sin, God's love, Jesus' death and resurrection, available forgiveness, adoption as God's children, and the Holy Spirit within us and transforming us.

As a Christian, never underestimate the impact you can have simply by walking your talk, not only at home and at church, but in the neighborhood and larger community as well. The world has enough people professing one thing and living another. You are blessed to be different. As you live a life of integrity and consistency, God will use you to draw people to Him.

Holy Spirit, please show me how to be consistent in my walk
and talk. I want to be a beacon of Your truth in this world.

REMEMBERING PROMISES

The Lord is trustworthy in all he promises and faithful in all he does.

PSALM 145:3

Sometimes we have to be intentional about remembering what we want to remember. Birthdays, meetings, errands, appointments, oil changes. We write things down or put them in the calendars in our phones so we remember *what* we are supposed to be doing *when*.

For the same reason, it's important to be intentional about remembering the promises of God that we read in His Word. Otherwise, naturally, we will forget them. We need to remember, for instance, that greater is He that is in us than he that is in the world (1 John 4:4); that God brings beauty out of ashes (Isaiah 61:3); that He will never leave us nor forsake us (Deuteronomy 31:6); and that nothing can separate us from His love (Romans 8:38–39).

When we remember promises like these, we will find courage to step out in faith. When we forget what God has said, we more easily react to our circumstances in fear. Faith activates us; fear immobilizes and even cripples us. Today, as you make your to-do lists or calendar, remember God's promises too—so you are able to walk in faith and not fear.

Lord, help me remember Your gracious promises to me.
Seal them in my heart, so I can walk without fear.

WHAT DO YOU HAVE?

___

"How many loaves do you have?" he asked. "Go and see."
When they found out, they said, "Five—and two fish."

MARK 6:38

I have always loved the account of the fish and the loaves. It delights my heart that God always uses the least likely to achieve the unimaginable. He'll do that for us too—when we *recognize* and offer what we have to Him.

Seeing the crowd's hunger, Jesus first asked His disciples what food they had. He asked for a count—for recognition and identification of those resources, no matter how small. Like most of us would have, the disciples saw the enormity of the crowd and their small bundle of food, and they undoubtedly concluded that nothing could be done. But Jesus made them examine what they *did* have because, whether or not we see it initially, the elements for a miracle are always within our reach.

Miracles always begin with a recognition of what we do have—an inventory, and an offering—not a list of all the things we don't have. Jesus can multiply what we recognize.

God had the elements for this miracle in a child's brown bag. What small things can you offer? Take a moment of reflection today to identify and offer your gifts. And never underestimate what God can and will do with whatever you offer Him, however small it seems.

Almighty God, in Your hands, nothing I offer You is too small. Thank You for that truth—and for this hope!

A LOOK IN THE MIRROR

Jonah ran away from the Lord and headed for Tarshish. He went
down to Joppa, where he found a ship bound for that port.

JONAH 1:3

How many times has God asked us to do something that we didn't want to do?

Perhaps the Lord asked you to be the first to apologize when you disagreed with your spouse—and the argument wasn't even your fault. Or He asked that you take a meal to your grumpy neighbor even though He knew you already had made other plans for the evening. Or perhaps God asked you to give away the new jacket you absolutely loved and had worn only once.

It's easy to act when the task is in our wheelhouse, or when we like the person who asks us to help. But we need some help to stretch past our limits when the cost of obedience feels too high, or when we simply don't like the people to whom He has sent us.

Did you realize you have so much in common with Jonah? He had to learn to build faithfulness, even when he didn't like where he was sent or who he was sent to. His first instinct was to run away, to resist what God had called him to do.

If you're running the other way, turn around now. Shake off that reluctance and embrace what God has called you to do.

Lord God, thank You for using Your living and active Word
to make me a stronger and better follower. Show me
how to stay committed to Your calling in all situations.

DISCERN YOUR PURPOSE

"I have raised you up for this very purpose, that I might show you
my power and that my name might be proclaimed in all the earth."

EXODUS 9:16

If you have been struggling with uncertainty about what unique gifts you bring to the table of life, here are a few questions you can ask yourself to successfully determine God's dreams for your life:

1. What is it that I've been good at since an early age?
2. What do others look at me doing that would be hard for them, but seems effortless to me?
3. What is it that I consistently find myself sharing about or helping others with?
4. Why do I think God created me?
5. What am I most passionate about?
6. What things enrage me and what problems in the world do I have a passion, over and above all others, to solve?
7. What subjects could I talk about for hours and days without a loss of momentum?
8. What scriptural truths and subjects have been those that most bear witness to me and speak life to me?

Over the course of the day, reflect on your answers. I believe as you do this, you will begin to see how your specific destiny is a God-ordained puzzle piece that fits perfectly into His purposes. You'll begin to discover His dreams for you!

Lord, thank You for the unique gifts You've given me. Please give me insight and guidance on how to use them best.

MY GRIEF, GOD'S GRACE

[The Lord] has not despised or scorned the suffering
of the afflicted one; he has not hidden his face
from him but has listened to his cry for help.

PSALM 22:24

Pregnant with our second child, I went to a routine doctor's appointment, looking forward to hearing my baby's heartbeat. As the doctor began to listen, he seemed to take a long time to find it. Then I saw on his face that something was seriously wrong and heard the crushing words "Christine, I'm so sorry. I can't find a heartbeat."

It was a loss that sent me reeling. Could I still believe that God is good? Would I ever be able to fully trust Him again? Could I find strength in the truths of His Word despite this devastating loss?

In the days after we lost our precious baby, I spent as much time as possible in church. And amazingly, at a point when I was worshiping, God healed my heart. He took away my grief and filled me with renewed hope about my future. I believe He acted in this gracious way because I had chosen to worship Him despite my heartache. I learned through that act of grace that we can trust Him with our grief, no matter what happens.

Holy Spirit, You know my heartache. I welcome
You as my Comforter—and please help me hold
on to You and trust You once again.

STRONGER THAN YOU THINK

Finally, be strong in the Lord and in his mighty power.

EPHESIANS 6:10

You are stronger than you think! That's because God's strength is unlimited and always available to you. He never meant for us to accomplish everything on our own. I can't tell you how many times I've declared Philippians 4:13 over my life because I want to succeed *in His strength*—instead of my own: *"I can do all things through Christ who strengthens me"* (NKJV).

Whatever you've faced this week, take it to Him in prayer and trust Him with it. Then let these truths strengthen your heart and encourage your faith:

- There is no disease God cannot heal.
- There is no heart God cannot mend.
- There is no relationship God cannot restore.
- There is no person God cannot save.
- There is no pain God cannot redeem.
- There is no sin God cannot forgive.
- There is no bondage God cannot break.
- There is no need God cannot meet.
- There is no enemy God cannot defeat.
- There is no mountain God cannot move.

There is *nothing* our God cannot do. And *in Him*, you are stronger than you think!

God, Your promises are overwhelming. Thank
You for Your strength and power in my life!

LIVING AN INTENTIONAL LIFE

So be careful how you live. Don't live like fools, but like those who
are wise. Make the most of every opportunity in these evil days.

EPHESIANS 5:15–16, NLT

Today's verse tells us that God wants us to lead intentional lives—believing and understanding that He has a unique plan and purpose for us: "So be careful how you live. Don't live like fools, but like those who are wise. Make the most of every opportunity in these evil days" (Ephesians 5:15–16 NLT).

And He wants us to live this intentional life *daily*. He wants us to live knowing we are a product of eternity, positioned in time and given giftings from God to serve our generation—inside the normality of our daily routines. That is what makes everything in our lives have meaning:

- Our parenting
- Work
- School
- Relationships

Inside our day-to-day life is where our influence resides—when we share a meal, encourage a friend, cheer someone on to greatness. When we train our children, lead our teams, or inspire a lost co-worker. And approaching those moments with intentionality is how we fulfill our purpose and reach our destiny—and help others reach theirs.

As you step into your today, stay focused on living an intentional life.

*God, thank You for caring about the details of my
life. As I walk, make me careful to get the most
out of every interaction and opportunity.*

HIDE AND SEEK

The LORD God called to the man, "Where are you?"

GENESIS 3:9

When Adam and Eve disobeyed God in the garden of Eden and ate the fruit from the Tree of the Knowledge of Good and Evil, they felt ashamed. And they hid.

But God, in His great mercy, went looking for them. When Adam and Eve heard God "walking in the garden in the cool of the day, they hid" (v. 8).

Nothing has changed in thousands of years. Just like Adam and Eve, isn't that our first instinct when we feel shame? To hide?

But just like in the garden, God comes looking for us. He calls to us. He seeks us out.

Why? Because just like with Adam and Eve, He loves us and wants to fellowship with us. He wants to break the power of shame in our lives.

Is shame part of your story? Do you feel less than? Not enough? Inadequate? Even when you can't perceive it, God is searching for you. He's calling you to come out of hiding and into His grace, into His unconditional acceptance. He loves you. He always has, and He always will.

Lord, please show me the ways You are searching for my heart. Help me come out of hiding and experience Your healing, transforming love.

YOU ARE NO MISTAKE

[Adam] answered, "I heard you in the garden, and
I was afraid because I was naked; so I hid."

GENESIS 3:10

Just because you've made a mistake doesn't mean you are a mistake. What freeing words. Guilt and shame researcher Brené Brown described shame as "the intensely painful feeling or experience of believing we are flawed and therefore unworthy of acceptance and belonging."[1] God never wanted that for us. We can learn more from Brown's definition of *shame* versus *guilt*:

Guilt says: "You've done something bad" or "You've made a bad choice."

Shame says: "You are bad."

There is a big difference between "You *made* a mistake" and "You *are* a mistake."[2]

I put it this way: Guilt is about my *do*. Shame is about my *who*.

In today's verse, Adam admitted to shame, not guilt. What if Adam and Eve had confessed what they did (guilt), instead of trying to hide who they were (shame)? They would have still faced consequences, but with honesty, acceptance, and forward motion instead of blame and finger-pointing.

Today, you can come to God without shame for any mistakes you've made. He loves you and wants to purify you—because you are no mistake (1 John 1:9).

Lord, when I need to, please help me come
out of that hiding place, knowing that You
forgive my mistakes and make me whole.

ALL-SUFFICIENT GRACE

"My grace is sufficient for you, for my power
is made perfect in weakness."

2 CORINTHIANS 12:9

In today's world, we have so many places we can turn to when trials, tribulations, and weaknesses come—but as Christians, we should run to Jesus. When hard times come—and they will!—we must choose to run to God *first* and listen for His guidance. Instead of avoiding, panicking, having a breakdown, running to friends, denying the reality, or numbing the pain, we can run straight into the arms of our gracious and loving God.

Friend, God never sleeps nor slumbers, so there's no point in both of you staying up all night. So cast your cares and anxieties over on Him (1 Peter 5:7). Peace that surpasses all understanding will keep you sane.

There are many small, positive things we can do to treat our symptoms during hard times. But if we rely on vitamins, exercise, counseling, "self-care," lifestyle changes, or other such healthy interventions, we'll find that they're never fully sufficient. We'll never get to the deepest root need: Jesus' restoration of our soul. His grace and His power are the only things that are *fully* sufficient in our trials. After all, He has already won the ultimate victory for us at Calvary! We can face our challenges from a position of victory, because the victory has already been won.

*Lord, thank You for Your all-sufficient grace
not only during trials, but always.*

COMPASSION MEANS ACTION

"On the next day, when [the good Samaritan] departed,
he took out two denarii, gave them to the innkeeper,
and said to him, 'Take care of him; and whatever more
you spend, when I come again, I will repay you.'"

LUKE 10:35

You might be filled with compassion for the hurting in this world. Your heart might break over the fact that you can't serve everyone in need. But that's not what God's called you to do. He's only asked you to respond to the ones in your path.

When I read the story of the good Samaritan, the Lord convicted me of this truth. And then He had more to say to me: *The key difference between the Samaritan and the religious people was that the Samaritan actually stopped. This traveler went to the broken man in need and stooped down to lift him up.*

Compassion is only an emotion until you first stop and then you stoop to help. Compassion means action. You go to them.

I wanted to weep because, in my mind, I saw Jesus. He stepped down from heaven to earth, stopped to help bandage our hurts and heal our wounds, and then stooped to bear the cross for us. His compassion translated to world-changing action. God showed me that when compassion turns to loving action, it glorifies Him and helps the people in our path.

Jesus, please help me honor Your ultimate
act of sacrificial service by being willing to
serve the ones You place before me.

LIFE-GIVING WORDS

The word of God is alive and active.

HEBREWS 4:12

Words have power, and they can change you for the better. Who and what you listen to can influence what you will do in life, determine the risks you will take, and shape who you become.

If you constantly hear that you are a failure or that you are not good enough, not talented enough, not pretty enough, or not smart enough, then you eventually will begin to believe those lies. Listening to the wrong voices will cripple and immobilize you. But God has empowered us to hear Him— and His is the voice of the Good Shepherd (John 10:27).

If you are listening to affirming, life-giving, hope-filled messages from the Word of God, you will be better able to hear His voice when He calls you. You will be stronger and take greater risks because you will have the faith to believe that Jesus is who He says He is and that He will do what He has promised.

God's Word is living and active: it breathes life back into dead bones, weary souls, and broken hearts (John 7:38). God's Word sustains and empowers; it guides and encourages. Its truth brings freedom, hope, and joy. His Word is for you—and it will accomplish His loving plans for you (Isaiah 55:11).

I live in a noisy world, Lord, and I've heard unhelpful, untrue messages about myself. Help me counter the noise and the lies with the calm, life-giving truth of Your Word.

THE MAIN THING

"My food," said Jesus, "is to do the will of him
who sent me and to finish his work."

JOHN 4:34

Distractions. We all face them on a daily basis. Whether they're relatively harmless or destructive, God wants us to resist them and keep the main thing the main thing—fulfilling our purpose.

None of us wants to live a life where we can say we have done many things but not the one thing God assigned us. We want to cultivate a habit of focus, and the motivation that comes from a clear vision. We want the grit to complete our task, and the guts to say no when we need to. Extraordinary accomplishments in the kingdom of God are rarely happenstance. They result from our daily choices and everyday actions. But we must decide to be single-minded and focused on the task He's given us. I cringe to think of the great works for God that were never finished because people grew distracted from their purpose.

Determine in your heart today to stay focused so you can finish well what God has called you to do. He promises to instruct you on the way you should go and to guide you as you follow Him (Psalm 32:8).

Lord God, please show me which tasks You
have for me, and thank You for strength as I
persevere and complete those tasks.

YOUR GREAT PROJECT

"I am carrying on a great project and cannot go down. Why should the work stop while I leave it and go down to you?"

NEHEMIAH 6:3

If you are committed to the work God has given you, you'll find it easier to say no to any lesser thing. You'll be able to focus on your mission and say no to distractions—just as Nehemiah did.

Nehemiah and his men had begun the formidable task of rebuilding the walls of Jerusalem that had been destroyed by the Babylonians. He faced opposition and ridicule, but he was determined to finish this assignment God had given him. When his enemies invited him to meet with them, they hoped they could make Nehemiah stop his work.

But Nehemiah was committed to what God had called him to do. He would not be sidetracked or tricked into coming down. Nehemiah wouldn't engage in petty debates or get involved in any activity that would take him away from his God-given task to rebuild the walls.

What pressures and tactics are coming at you today? What's keeping you from working on your "great project"? Ask God for discernment and guidance, and with His wisdom, determine which things you *won't* stop for. Then you can say: "I have set the LORD continually before me; because He is at my right hand, I will not be shaken" (Psalm 16:8 NASB).

Lord, it is a privilege to be given work that makes a difference for Your kingdom. Show me how to keep my focus!

THE TRUE MESSAGE

Faith comes from hearing the message, and the message is heard through the word about Christ.

ROMANS 10:17

We are blasted by media images telling us we are "not enough," "too much," or "not normal." I can't tell you how many creams I've bought over the years to reduce wrinkles—because apparently I'm *never* supposed to have them, even if I live to be 150 years old! But none of those intimidating images reflect who we truly are in Christ.

If we want to build our faith in God and who He says we are, then we need to turn down the volume of those voices and turn up the volume of God's Word.

In today's verse, the apostle Paul taught that hearing the truth of God's Word is the source of faith, and hearing it over and over is how we sustain and encourage our faith (1 Timothy 4:6). So throw aside any distractions or messages that could disrupt your plans to study or hear God's Word.

We are so blessed in this day and age. We have access to the Word in all shapes and forms. It's at our fingertips! Let's keep the Word before us. Let's read it. Hear it. Discuss it. And just keep it going in our hearts and minds. Then God's truth can drown out any untrue message.

God, Your Word is such a gift. Thank You for the privilege to study it and allow its truth to fill my soul and build my faith in You.

GETTING PAST THE GIANTS

With your help I can advance against a troop;
with my God I can scale a wall.

PSALM 18:29

Goliath wasn't the only giant in the Bible. An entire society of big, burly adversaries were occupying the promised land when Moses and his twelve leaders arrived to take possession of it. When they saw those giants, ten of the leaders gave up: "We can't attack those people; they are stronger than we are" (Numbers 13:31).

They saw only the difficulties and apparent impossibility. They saw giants and were afraid: "All the people we saw there are of great size.... We seemed like grasshoppers in our own eyes, and we looked the same to them" (Numbers 13:32–33).

Then, as now, possessing what's ours in God sometimes requires getting past the giants in life. It requires making God bigger on the inside of us than the obstacles we're facing—than anything coming against us. If we do that, we can get past any giants. Nothing is too difficult for God, and that's a promise (Matthew 19:26)!

So, whatever you're facing today, go to the Word. Find God's promises for you and make that truth bigger than your giant. Then, you can advance against an entire troop and scale any wall.

Almighty God, when I encounter giants, I make
You bigger than anything I'm facing!

HEALING LIGHT

"I have come into the world as a light, so that no one
who believes in me should stay in darkness."

JOHN 12:46

Like me, you probably spent years covering up your emotional wounds. Mine were mostly rooted in shame, and I worked hard to hide them. When I began the journey to be free, exposing them was the last thing I wanted to do. Allowing ourselves to be vulnerable is the *last* thing any of us want to do. We would rather stay put in the dark than risk opening ourselves to things that might cause us to feel even greater shame—or any kind of pain. It's a cycle that God longs to free us from.

I have learned through years of walking out my freedom that what you don't reveal can't be healed. When I bring something out of the darkness and into God's light, it no longer has power over me.

So, let's agree to never be ashamed to admit that we need healing. God didn't make us to stay in the dark. No, Jesus came "as a light," so we can be cleansed by His healing power. Choose to step into His light, and let His light dispel all the darkness and empower your freedom.

*Lord God and my Great Physician, please grant me
courage to reveal—to bring into Your light—what needs
to be healed. I don't want to stay hidden any longer!*

BUILDING ON A SURE FOUNDATION

"Everyone who hears these words of mine and puts them into practice is like a wise man who built his house on the rock."

MATTHEW 7:24

You and I live in uncertain times—so it's a good thing our faith is built on the solid rock of Jesus Christ. All around us are unprecedented political, social, moral, educational, environmental, and spiritual ideas, theories, movements, and change. The spiritual tectonic plates of the earth have shifted, and they are never going back to the way they were. We are living in a new era. So, to stay steadfast in our faith and immovable in our commitment to Jesus, we need to be empowered by the Holy Spirit and follow His leading.

That doesn't mean we disengage from the world (John 17:18). Quite the contrary. To live victoriously, we must not only understand our world but also know how to live in it.

What it does mean is that we need to draw closer to God than ever before. Let's refocus on Him and establish ourselves in His Word. Let's look to Him for comfort, wisdom, insight, and discernment to navigate these uncertain times. Let's remember that when we simply do not know what to do, He always does. We can always go to Him for counsel, direction, and guidance. His truth is timeless and eternal, and His leading is sure.

Lord, show me how to build my life on Your truth and follow in Your ways. You alone offer a strong foundation.

WHEN YOUR WORLD IS ROCKED

Jesus Christ is the same yesterday and today and forever.

HEBREWS 13:8

My world was totally rocked when—at the age of thirty-three—I learned that my brother George and I had been adopted. My mother and father had kept it a secret to protect us because they loved us. But still, it rocked our worlds.

I remember thinking, *What other "facts" about me aren't true? Can I ever trust anyone again?*

Had I kept on that train of thought, I would have derailed completely. But I had spent many years hiding God's Word in my heart. So, in that moment, those truths offered immediate comfort and a light for this new path. Because I knew the Word, I stood strong on God's truth, His promises, and His character.

After a few seconds of being stunned, I almost surprised myself with the words I spoke: "Well, before I was formed in my mother's womb—whoever womb that was—God knew me. He knitted together my innermost parts. I am fearfully and wonderfully made." It was the Word of God (Psalm 139:14), not words of hurt or shock.

When your world is turned upside down, let God's Word rise up out of your heart and come out your mouth. Speak the truth and declare your trust in Him.

Lord, in this ever-changing world, I praise You for being the same yesterday and today and forever. Thank You for the security and strength and peace that is in You.

YOUR DEFINING MOMENT

Who knows but that you have come to your
royal position for such a time as this?

ESTHER 4:14

At some point in your Christian life, you'll be faced with a crossroads decision. We face them when we consider changing jobs, moving out of state, or going back to school. We face them when we have to choose between looking out for our own interests or the interests of others.

Esther was a queen in the Bible who faced such a decision. An evil adviser had persuaded her husband, King Xerxes, to sentence her people, the Jews, to death. Her uncle Mordecai pointed out that she was uniquely positioned to save the people—to petition the king. But it was dangerous. Esther chose to put God and the people first.

I call that a defining moment—and eventually, we all have them. Maybe yours hasn't happened yet, but at some point you will have the opportunity to make an eternal difference in the lives of others. It may be something as simple as driving someone to the doctor or skipping a movie to be with a hurting friend, but it will be a defining moment. A moment when you choose to do the right thing and it affects someone's life.

Keep close to God and attune your heart to His plans around you, so you don't miss any defining moments.

*God, please show me the defining moments You send
my way. Thank You for opportunities to make an eternal
difference in someone's life today and every day.*

A REKINDLING

Do the things you did at first.

REVELATION 2:5

If your relationship with Jesus has felt as though it's become distant, know that your feelings of connection with Him aren't lost forever. In fact, what has worked reigniting relationships with others can work in your relationship with Jesus. You can rekindle your passion for Him by doing with Him and for Him the things you did when you first discovered His love.

Yes, it will take some intentional investment of your heart, soul, and mind. Yet working on a relationship isn't burdensome when you love the Person and when the "work" is spending time with Him, sharing your hurts and dreams, listening for His voice, and walking through life—both the mountaintop experiences and the deep valleys—with Him at your side. Even in your darkest hour, Jesus will still love you and care for you, and He will never leave you (Matthew 28:20).

Your love for Jesus need never diminish, grow stagnant, or cool down. Just do the things you did at first. Nurture it, watch it grow, and you'll find it fueling you as you act in love toward Him and His people.

Jesus, please show me my part in nurturing and strengthening my friendship with You. I want to live with You as my most treasured relationship.

THE TIME IS NOW

---

*"Now this is eternal life: that they know you, the only
true God, and Jesus Christ, whom you have sent."*

JOHN 17:3

The human heart loves a good story. The Bible is full of great stories, but let's remember that they are not *just* stories. The people are not *just* characters. When we see these Bible heroes as people in a fairy tale, we think of them as somehow different from us, and we too easily conclude that they didn't struggle with family issues, stress over decisions, or feel emotions. But if we believe that the Bible is true and its "characters" are people just like us, then we will read it very differently.

We will realize that the same issues are at stake—that the people we meet in Scripture needed to overcome the same fears, doubts, and challenges that we do. Legends like Abraham, Moses, Esther, David, and Paul overcame to choose courageous acts of obedience—and generations were saved.

What courageous acts of obedience are you willing to conquer? Never underestimate what your obedience can accomplish, especially when people's eternal future is at stake. Whatever is before you—and whoever will cross your path—God will empower you, just as He did His people in the Bible, to share your faith, to stand up for what's right, to lead and lead well.

*Lord, thank You for calling me to be in this time
and this place. Show me how to act for You,
and lead me toward those who need You.*

THE WISDOM OF SILENCE

Though he slay me, yet will I hope in him.

JOB 13:15

Oh, if we could only replicate those times we've said just the right thing at just the right time, straight out of God's wisdom. Those times are beautiful and encouraging for everyone. Yet it's wise to admit when it's *not* one of those times. We can use the gift of compassionate silence when we really, truly don't know what to say. God gives us the freedom to not know it all, all the time.

Job, a man in the Bible who lost everything, had three friends. When they heard about his unimaginably tragic losses, they "met together by agreement to go and sympathize with him and comfort him" (Job 2:11). Grieving with and for their friend, these men sat with Job for seven days and seven nights. They said nothing. Their very presence with their hurting friend spoke volumes about their compassion and concern.

When you don't know what to say, try *showing* God's love. It will be much more helpful and healing than any empty words could be. "Be strong and take heart and wait for the LORD" (Psalm 27:14).

When friends are hurting, Lord, show me how
to simply be with them. Give me wisdom, and
let me be quiet evidence of Your love.

LOVING OUR NEIGHBORS BY SHARING GOD'S TRUTH

"Go and make disciples of all nations, baptizing them in the name of the Father and of the Son and of the Holy Spirit, and teaching them to obey everything I have commanded you."

MATTHEW 28:19–20

If someone new moved into your neighborhood and you wanted to be a good neighbor, you'd probably show him or her the ropes. You'd recommend the closest grocery store, the best plumber, or a great babysitter. How much more should we tell our spiritual neighbors where to find the ultimate Good in life?

Today's passage, also called the Great Commission, is directly related to the Greatest Commandments—love God and love your neighbor. If you love your neighbors as yourself, you will want them to know the good things you've experienced, like salvation from your sins and how to live in God's loving presence. And He will empower you with His Holy Spirit (Acts 1:8).

Ask God to help you show love to your neighbors by discipling them—pointing them to the life-saving power of Jesus. Let your heart get excited to share, to lead others to Jesus, and to teach them to follow Him. If you are discipling people, you are loving them with your actions and passing on the greatest gift you've ever been given.

Thank You, God, that when You call Your people to do something, You enable us to do it. Please give me the courage and the words I need to share Your life-transforming truth.

DIVINE CORRECTION

Guide me in your truth and teach me, for you are God
my Savior, and my hope is in you all day long.

PSALM 25:5

God is in the business of healing broken hearts, binding up wounded souls, and renewing minds with His truth. Have you ever been reading the Bible and noticed that your thoughts—about yourself, about life, about God, about holiness, about right and wrong—were about as far away from God's thoughts as you were from the moon? That's the moment when your mind was being renewed.

It was life-changing for me when I realized that I should not believe all my feelings and thoughts, especially when they contradict the Word of God. From start to finish, Scripture contains absolute truth. It is infallible in its presentation of God's character, Jesus' life on this earth, instructions for living, historical accounts, miracles, and the future (2 Timothy 3:16–17).

When, for instance, your feelings tell you that you are utterly unloved, the truth of God's Word teaches otherwise: "I have always been mindful of your unfailing love" (Psalm 26:3). God's love for you is unfailing, constant, and permanent: He loves you now and He always will. When you renew your mind to that truth, then your thinking is on track.

Knowing God's truth can profoundly affect our broken hearts, our wounded souls, and our cluttered minds. Dive into it today, and be guided in truth and renewed with hope.

Thank You, Lord, that You never stop healing
me and renewing my mind with Your truth.

APRIL

For God alone my soul waits in silence;
from him comes my salvation.
He alone is my rock and my salvation,
my fortress; I shall not be greatly shaken.

PSALM 62:1-2 ESV

REALIGNING YOUR THOUGHTS

You were taught, with regard to your former way of life, to put off your old self, which is being corrupted by its deceitful desires; to be made new in the attitude of your minds.

EPHESIANS 4:22–23

We train our bodies to stay fit. We train ourselves to stop bad habits or start good ones. We often forget, though, that we can train our minds. We do this by thinking about what we're thinking about. Yes, we actually can choose what we think about.

Philippians 4:8 tells us to choose "whatever is true, whatever is noble, whatever is right, whatever is pure, whatever is lovely, whatever is admirable—if anything is excellent or praiseworthy—think about such things."

The Devil is ever so crafty, and well aware that most people don't even think about what they are thinking about. He knows they will believe any lie he tells and grab on to any thought he puts in their minds.

Commit to retraining your mind and aligning your thoughts with God's. When you think about what you're thinking about, *test* it;, learn to discern God's voice among all the others in your life. Consciously choose to believe God's Word. Simply put, learn God's thoughts and make them yours. This is the process of renewing your mind, and the result is thinking and living with more freedom.

I am grateful, Lord, that You defeated the deceiver and that You will always help me align my thoughts with Yours.

SPRING CLEANING— AND SUMMER, FALL, AND WINTER TOO

Let us throw off everything that hinders and
the sin that so easily entangles.

HEBREWS 12:1

If you do spring cleaning, you know the fresh, new feeling that comes after a deep scouring of the house. Once that all-over cleaning is done, you can sit back, relax, and enjoy it. And with regular maintenance, that cleaning will do you for the season—until it's spring again.

So it is with our hearts and minds. Cleaning out our internal world requires an ongoing, focused commitment on a deeper level. I wish the "throwing off everything that hinders" were a one-time shot that was never required again, but it's not. In fact, learning to stay focused on Christ in you is a lifelong effort requiring time and diligence. You aren't, however, required to throw off in your own strength whatever hinders you *in order* to run the race. That isn't a prerequisite. Instead, you are invited to throw it all off *as* you run your race. That's part of God's on-the-job training in Christlikeness that happens during the race.

If you want to be unstoppable, keep challenging yourself to clean out the internal world of your heart and mind regularly, so you can focus more clearly on Christ in you, with you, and at work within you. And He will help you with that spring—and summer, fall, winter—cleaning!

Holy Spirit, I yield to Your transforming work to make me
more like Jesus. Thank You for showing me what to throw off.

THE ABSOLUTE GOSPEL

"I am the way and the truth and the life. No one comes to the Father except through me."

JOHN 14:6

In a world where we are exhausted with choices and options, we can rest easy that when it comes to eternity, there's only one option: Jesus. We don't have to figure it all out ourselves. The gospel is based on *absolute truth*. Jesus said that *He* is the way, the truth, and the life—the only way to God. Now our task is to take that absolute truth to our world.

Many people believe there are numerous ways to God. In fact, our culture often confuses tolerance with endorsement and dismisses the idea of absolute truth. That's why proclaiming Jesus' absolute message in this world can be both a challenge and an opportunity.

Always, people around the globe are searching for truth, meaning, significance, security, and unconditional love. Jesus is the Source of all that and more. When people can see that faith in Jesus makes a difference in our lives, they are open to hearing about Him.

As Christians we proclaim the gospel of Jesus Christ in many ways—both speaking and acting. To be effective, let your heart rest in certainty of what you believe, and be ready to present the unvarnished truth: there is only one way to God, and that is through Jesus, who welcomes all to come to Him.

Jesus, help me always be ready to share Your absolute gospel truth. You are the way, the truth, and the life!

THE LOVE OF THE FATHER

I am convinced that neither death nor life, neither angels nor demons, neither the present nor the future, nor any powers, neither height nor depth, nor anything else in all creation, will be able to separate us from the love of God that is in Christ Jesus our Lord.

ROMANS 8:38–39

I loved my dad. I was only nineteen when he died, and it was devastating to our family. But as wonderful as he was to all of us, my relationship with him pales in comparison to the relationship we can have with our heavenly Father.

Whatever your earthly father was like—good or bad or nonexistent—God wants you to have the best now. He is a heavenly Father who truly loves you and will never leave you nor forsake you (Hebrews 13:5).

This kind of unconditional love and nurture is almost incomprehensible to us, and so often we feel that we must do something to earn His love. But God's love can't be earned, and it can't be stopped. And yet I know firsthand that turning away from the impulse of trying to earn it is a daily journey.

We have to renew our hearts and minds to truly believe His love is a gift. It is pure grace. So, together, every day, let's open up our hands and hearts to accept it.

Father God, Your love for me is truly incomprehensible! Help me learn to accept it and live my life confident in Your love for me.

STOP PERFORMING

We all stumble in many ways.

JAMES 3:2

I'll never forget a conversation with one of my team leaders years ago that shook me to my core. She revealed that I had been so focused on reaching my goals that I didn't see destruction in my wake.

My poor team member painted a picture of her experience under my leadership—and it wasn't pretty. My unrealistic deadlines. Pushing for impossible performance standards. Being more concerned with results than with people. She had put in long hours, tremendous effort, but it was never enough for me. I did not take this news well. In fact, I was defensive and devastated. But thanks to her courageous honesty and some painful digging, God revealed to me that my performance-driven nature was a by-product of my own unmet needs, my own brokenness. I was carrying shame's baggage into ministry.

For my sake and everyone else's, it was time to drop that baggage. Only then would my heart be softened so I could embrace others in our *mutual* lack of perfection and control, and embrace God's control and love for each one of us.

As you run your race, don't be too hard on yourself and others. God is at work in you, softening you, teaching you to receive love and to love as He does.

Lord Jesus, please deliver me from perfectionism and a performance mentality. You are perfect, and that is enough.

A PIECE OF CAKE

He is before all things, and in him all things hold together.

COLOSSIANS 4:17 ESV

Think about the ingredients you need to make a chocolate cake. It's quite a list. Yet when that slab of chocolaty deliciousness is sitting in front of you, the last thing you think of is the individual ingredients. Yet each ingredient is key to its success. Once baked, it's impossible to separate the ingredients again—not that you'd want to!

Similarly, every area of our life is interconnected and mixed together: spiritual, relational, emotional, and physical. The whole, which is who we are, is the sum of each of these parts.

Simultaneously, I am a Christian, a mother, a wife, a daughter, a sister, a friend, a speaker, an author, and all the other facets that make me, me. I used to wrongly think that my priorities in life had to be in a certain order. I was constantly frustrated because I never seemed to have enough time for anything, especially God, and He was at the top of my list!

God never intended for life to be a juggling act, nor for us to feel that if we nurture one aspect of our lives, it will be at the expense of another. Together, they make us who we are—and He made us whole.

Lord, thank You for all the things that make me,
me. Help me view everything as interconnected,
so I can be all You made me to be.

SELF-DEFENSE

We demolish arguments and every pretension that sets
itself up against the knowledge of God, and we take
captive every thought to make it obedient to Christ.

2 CORINTHIANS 10:5

Whenever any old lies you've believed about yourself come back to visit—saying that you're ugly, stupid, worthless, flawed, incapable, inadequate—you have the power in Christ to take those thoughts captive. You can think new thoughts based on God's truth. You can talk back to the lies.

So speak truth to yourself. Encourage yourself. Build yourself up. When the past screams, "You are hopeless! You are useless! You aren't good enough! You'll never measure up!" tell yourself truths like these:

- I am fearfully and wonderfully made (Psalm 139:14).
- I am the righteousness of God in Christ Jesus (2 Corinthians 5:21).
- Greater is He who is in me than he who is in the world (1 John 4:4).
- I am greatly loved by God (Romans 1:7; Ephesians 2:4; Colossians 3:12).
- I can do all things through Christ Jesus (Philippians 4:13).
- I am God's workmanship, created in Christ for good works (Ephesians 2:10).

And the list of biblical truths about you could go on and on. Find these truths and treasure them—they speak of God's love for you!

I thank You, Lord, for the truths in Your Word. I declare them and make them a permanent part of me so I can use them to defeat untruth whenever it rears its head.

STAND UP WITH TRUTH

I keep my eyes always on the LORD. With him
at my right hand, I will not be shaken.

PSALM 16:8

Even when she was in kindergarten, my daughter Catherine was confident about who she is. One day she had an argument with a boy in her class over who was going to take the teddy bear home that night. At one point, the boy grabbed the bear from Catherine and said, "Catherine Bobbie, you are dumb, and you are ugly!"

Catherine didn't hesitate to stand up to that boy. "No, I'm not," she answered. "My daddy says I'm intelligent and beautiful."

Catherine trusted with all her heart what her daddy told her every single day. She accepted as truth the words Nick spoke to her, and she was confident enough to speak them aloud herself. Then she took back the teddy bear and walked away. That's my girl!

You can accept what your Father in heaven says about you in His Word of truth. Believe you really are who God says you are in His Word, and like Catherine, you'll stand strong—because you know what your all-powerful and loving Daddy says about you.

Lord, when I struggle to completely believe the truth of
Your acceptance of me and Your love for me, give me
childlike faith to believe. Thank You for being my Father!

NEVER IMPOSSIBLE

The gates of Jericho were securely barred because of
the Israelites. No one went out and no one came in.

JOSHUA 6:1

God promises you freedom. Even when it seems impossible. But just as He did for the children of Israel, He will make a way. When the promised land seemed within reach, they hit a wall. Literally.

The entire city of Jericho was surrounded by a wall made of heavy mud bricks. But God had promised His people this land: it was the endpoint of their march to freedom after slavery in Egypt.

So just when the people thought, *At last! After forty years in the wilderness, we are actually entering the promised land,* God said, "I want you to take that new territory right over there. Yes, right there behind that massive, impenetrable, unscalable wall."

Isn't that like our lives? God promises us freedom, and it seems impossible sometimes. But He always has a plan to tear down the walls blocking our way.

He gave the children of Israel a strategy to build their faith and trust Him with the wall—just as He does for us. Their wall came down, and so will yours. Keep trusting Him. Keep seeking Him. Keep believing that if He brought you this far, He's taking you all the way into the promised land.

Lord, You know the wall I face and the condition of
my heart. But I know this truth: for You, nothing is
impossible. I'm glad we face this wall together.

WORK IN PROGRESS

[Be] strengthened with all power according to his
glorious might so that you may have great endurance
and patience, and giving joyful thanks to the Father.

COLOSSIANS 1:11–12

I am so grateful for the healing grace and power God has poured into my life, yet I am well aware that I am still a work in progress. Growth this side of heaven goes on and on. And there is no shame in that.

My wounded heart that once sought comfort and validation in busyness, accomplishment, achievement, and perfectionism now finds peace in God and His perfection.

My hands that once held so tightly to the reins of control have loosened their death grip. I have learned to control less and to yield more to God's guidance. My heart that was so full of fear, doubt, insecurity, low self-esteem, anger, bitterness, unforgiveness, and rejection has been softened. Many of its protective walls have been torn down, leaving more room inside for love, joy, peace, and patience. I've discovered that I was not created to bear shame because Jesus bore it for me.

I've been letting God rebuild my true identity as His beloved daughter, precious and redeemed. This is His will for me, and for you. Today, open yourself up to Him, and let Him continue the beautiful work in progress that is you.

Praise You, God! You don't let me stay crippled
by my past, but You grow me in the present
for Your good plans for my future!

MEETING THE GOD OF THE BIBLE

"For God so loved the world that he gave his one and only Son, that whoever believes in him shall not perish but have eternal life."

JOHN 3:16

When I was young, my initial view of God was shaped in the church I was forced to attend with my family. In all those years I cannot remember ever hearing that God loved me. I am sure many of the church leaders believed this to be true, but either no one told me or I simply did not hear or understand it.

My perspective of God was also influenced by relatives and friends who had never read the Bible for themselves. These were sincere and good people, but they were sincerely wrong about God. But somewhere along the journey I met the God of the Bible, who is big in grace, big in mercy, big in love, and big in forgiveness—and I was transformed.

If you've had rough experiences with church on this earth, take heart. Just as God did for me, He can reframe your understanding of church. He can show you authentic Christianity—the kind that comes from a vibrant, living relationship with Jesus. Let the true God of the Bible help you "to be made new in the attitude of your minds; and to put on the new self, created to be like God in true righteousness and holiness" (Ephesians 4:23–24).

Thank You, God, for showing me who You really are and the gift of Your church to me.

YOU ARE VALUABLE

God demonstrates his own love for us in this: While
we were still sinners, Christ died for us.

ROMANS 5:8

I once saw an illustration in a church service that profoundly affected me. The speaker held up a brand-new, crisp $100 bill and asked the congregation if anyone wanted it. Of course everyone did. The speaker then scrunched up the bill and jumped on it. He held it up again and asked who wanted it. Again, everyone did.

Then he told us that the $100 bill had been stolen, used to buy drugs, and used to pay for sex with a prostitute. Then he asked if anyone still wanted it. Undaunted, everyone did because they understood that the value of money is not determined by what it experiences or how it looks. Its value is determined by the government that printed the bill.

You're just like that $100 bill. Regardless of your history, regardless of all you've been through, God will always want you. He sees you just the way He made you—beautifully, wonderfully, and full of great value.

Thank You, Lord, that You see me as valuable. Thank
You for shedding Your blood on the cross for me. I know
that because You love me, the truth sets me free.

LOVING WITH GOD'S LOVE

Praise be to . . . the God of all comfort, who comforts us
in all our troubles, so that we can comfort those in any
trouble with the comfort we ourselves receive from God.

2 CORINTHIANS 1:3-4

I remember one time when God prompted me to walk across the street and meet one of my neighbors. I had been in the midst of a busy season in my life and hadn't yet met her. What a divine appointment!

Her husband had just left her, and she desperately needed love and encouragement. Isn't that just like God? To send someone to us at just the right time to comfort us and to love us.

When we cry out to God, He is endlessly creative in comforting us. Yet one reason God brings healing into our lives is so we can comfort others as He does His healing work in their lives.

God can use you to comfort others. As you share God's love with hurting people, you are loving Him. You show your devotion to Him when you seize opportunities to be the hands and feet of Jesus, seeking to ease the pain of hurting people.

So ask God to open your eyes to the hurting around you. Pray for sensitivity to minister to them. You'll find your love burning brighter and stronger when you do.

Lord God, thank You for loving me. Show me how to
tell others, with my words and actions, how much
I love You—and how much You love them.

RAISED UP AND INCLUDED

"You did not give me any water for my feet, but she wet
my feet with her tears and wiped them with her hair.
You did not give me a kiss, but this woman, from the
time I entered, has not stopped kissing my feet."

LUKE 7:44–45

I'm always struck by the number of women Jesus encountered in the Gospels. Some supported His ministry out of their own means (Luke 8:3). Others benefited from His ministry of healing and deliverance. And it was women to whom He first appeared after He was resurrected (Luke 24:1–10).

Jesus valued women—then and now. Despite the culture of the time, He set an example and gave women opportunities to prosper and to take an active part in His ministry. In His day, women were regarded as inferior to men, always accompanied by a father or husband, doubly veiled in public, and forbidden to speak to male strangers. Despite such social norms, Jesus refused to exclude women from His life and ministry. He always treated them with the same kind of honor He extended to men. And He extends that love and respect to you today. Regardless of how others have treated you, Jesus always honors you, esteems you, and values you—whether you're a man or a woman.

Let His example heal your heart, encourage you, and show you how to treat others.

Holy Spirit, please help the truth of Jesus'
unconditional love for me penetrate my heart,
so I can rest in knowing how valuable I am.

THE COMPASS OF YOUR HEART

[W]alk humbly with your God.

MICAH 6:8

The greatest thing you can do for your future today is not to work out a big strategic plan that covers years of your life, but rather to make sure the compass of your heart is right. If you do, you'll reach the destiny God has for you.

For example, I recently took three flights: one from Atlanta to New York (two hours), then from New York to Los Angeles (five hours), then from Los Angeles to Bangkok (eighteen hours). If the pilot had set his instruments just one degree off between Atlanta and New York, we still would have made it with a minor course correction. But one degree off between New York and Los Angeles takes you to an entirely different state! Between Los Angeles and Bangkok, one degree off lands you in the middle of the ocean.

The best way to reach your destination is to make sure your heart is set on Him today. Make those incremental, intentional decisions with your time, talents, and resources that keep you on course. Guard that one degree in your life. Pay attention to how you use today—so you stay the course to where you are destined to go.

Lord, show me how I need to adjust my course toward You today, and keep my focus on living for You in the now.

EMPOWERED BY GOD'S LOVE

Let us love one another, for love comes from God.

1 JOHN 4:7

Whenever God's love and grace captivate your heart, you learn—among other life-giving truths—that His plans for you are for good and not for evil, that He is for you and not against you, and that He is ever so trustworthy. That's life-changing. And it gives you a real source of fuel when loving others seems too hard to do.

Let's face it: in our own power, we wouldn't do such a great job of loving one another. But the good news is that the power doesn't come from us or our good behavior, or how "nice" we are to each other. We don't need to put on a performance in an attempt to earn God's love and approval. Instead, we choose to love because He loved us; it's a "want to," not a "have to." As Scripture says, "Dear children, let us not love with words or speech but with actions and in truth" (1 John 3:18). Your good works of loving others are empowered by His love for you, and those words and actions are your grateful response to that love.

Knowing you are already deeply loved, valued, and accepted by God frees you to give of your heart to others for their good and God's glory.

Thank You for the love and acceptance You offer me, Lord. Show me how to genuinely share Your love with others, showing them what Your love has meant for me.

EQUIPPED TO SHARE

"Return home and tell how much God has done
for you." So the man went away and told all over
town how much Jesus had done for him.

LUKE 8:39

Since Jesus' day, He has entrusted us with the good news. We are uniquely gifted to boldly and freely share the gospel of Jesus. And we all know, once you have met Jesus—once you have experienced His love or forgiveness—you can't keep His good news to yourself. As you go about your day, remember these truths and share them to encourage others:

- Jesus banishes fear from our hearts (1 John 4:18).
- His love is stronger than death (Romans 6:9).
- Jesus meets our needs (Philippians 4:19).
- He restores hope (Romans 5:5).
- Jesus heals diseases (Matthew 8:17).
- He blesses us with peace in the biggest of life's storms (John 14:27).
- Jesus forgives sin and redeems failures (Romans 8:28).

Jesus has entrusted you and me with the knowledge of these amazing truths, and He has called us to share them with our world. Let's go and tell!

It's a privilege to be entrusted and called, Jesus. Show me
the people who need to hear Your good news today!

RESHAPED BY GOD

As [a man] thinks in his heart, so is he.

PROVERBS 23:7 NKJV

Many people believe that who we are is the result of our upbringing, socioeconomic background, education, gender, or ethnicity. Of course those factors help shape us, but our sense of who we are also comes from what we *think* about our background, circumstances, and experiences. So we have to ask ourselves, "Is our thinking accurate and helpful? Is it based on things that aren't true?"

If you are feeling discouraged and stuck in a place of hurt, ask the Lord to help you first to evaluate the thoughts behind those feelings and then to make changes that will move you toward truth, freedom, and wholeness.

You end unhealthy thinking by replacing it with God's healing truth (2 Corinthians 10:5). God reaches out to you through His Word, inviting you to believe the truth found there, and applying it to your life. You are loved. You are seen. And your Father will help you renew your mind and nurture it in a way only He can.

As you read God's Word today, compare what it says to what you think. If they don't agree, then exchange any of your wrong thinking for His truth. Let His Word reshape you—and your thoughts.

Lord God, thank You for freeing me as I renew
my mind with Your Word. Thank You for Your
truth in exchange for every lie I've believed.

UNCHANGING IDENTITY

In Christ Jesus you are all children of God through faith.

GALATIANS 3:26

Good times and hard times come and go, but your identity always stays the same: loved, wanted, known, and created by Christ. He identifies you as forgiven, cherished, planned, and given purpose.

Whenever your sense of identity is shaken, focus on who you are in Christ. When life is calm, prepare for its storms by establishing your roots deeper into God's Word. Then when life's challenges do come, you will find yourself able to stand strong in God's truth rather than being overcome by circumstances. When I think about my own story, especially about learning in my early thirties that I was adopted, I honestly believe that I avoided years of grief, anger, resentment, confusion, and even therapy because I knew the Word: when I saw my birth certificate for the first time, and it said I was unnamed, I knew God's Word says He called me before I was born and from my mother's womb He spoke my name (Isaiah 49:1).

When your sense of identity is challenged, you'll find sure defense by fully grasping who you are in Christ—who you are in His Word. You are His child created in His image—loaded with all of who He is (Genesis 1:27).

Thank You, God, that I am Your child. I am wanted, cherished, known, valued, worthy, and loaded with purpose. I am so thankful for my life in You.

IT'S GOOD TO REMEMBER

[God] has caused his wonders to be remembered;
the LORD is gracious and compassionate.

PSALM 111:4

Often when I'm tempted to give up, I pull out old journals to remind myself of God's faithfulness. When I do, I see all the good things God has done; I see that He has never left me alone or forsaken me. I remind myself that He who was faithful before will be faithful today and tomorrow (Hebrews 13:8). I also focus on all He has blessed me with, from family to ministry to my healing and restoration. Every time I look back on how my life has unfolded, I see God's grace, redemption, and protection. Why not try this yourself?

Let your past fuel your future. Let your past encourage you that if God brought you this far, He'll take you the rest of the way. Your story is unique, and God has woven it. So look back over your own life to see God's gracious hand. See how far He has brought you and remember specific moments when He showed His faithfulness. Let those powerful memories carry you through difficult seasons and give you strength to face challenges that come your way (John 16:33).

You aren't alone when troubles come. Remembering God's faithfulness, you can stand on the truth of His presence with you.

You are faithful. You are present with me. You bless me lavishly. Thank You for truths like these that give me a solid foundation for life.

THE LIGHT THAT MEANS HEALING

The unfolding of your words gives light; it
gives understanding to the simple.

PSALM 119:130

God's Word gives light, and that light exposes all the darkness in our lives—those places that need healing and restoration. Those places of pain, shame, hurt, or unforgiveness. When His light shines on our wounds, it frees us, gives us understanding, and takes us to the next level of growth and maturity. God longs to heal us physically, emotionally, psychologically, and spiritually—in every way—because He wants the best for us.

If you've been nursing wounds or pain for a long time, they may have crippled and immobilized you—whether you realize it or not. Maybe you're holding back, shrinking back from being who you really are. Maybe you diminish yourself, not ever fully exposing yourself and being truly vulnerable and authentic.

Jesus wants to free you so you can live your life fully alive, fulfilling all He's called you to be and do.

Invite Jesus to shine in your heart today. Let Him engage in the process with you of making you whole. Let Him shine His Word and love into those places you've long protected. Risk trusting a faithful and tender Savior.

*Thank You, Lord, for Your light of truth, understanding,
healing, guidance, and hope! Thank You for shining
Your light on what needs to be healed.*

NO MORE STICKS AND STONES

From everlasting to everlasting the Lord's
love is with those who fear him.

PSALM 103:17

Remember that old saying, "Sticks and stones can break my bones, but names can never hurt me"? That thought may help you keep a resilient will, but it's not true about the heart. You can be hurt plenty by labels like *stupid, ignorant, alcoholic, addict, criminal, weak,* or *pitiful.* If you allow those labels to loom larger in your heart and mind than the promises of God, they can fool you into missing God's truth about who you are.

When your head insists that God created you in his image and loves you, but your heart and emotions keep punching away at that knowledge with thoughts like, *What's wrong with me? I never seem to do anything right!,* the blows can give you an overwhelming sense of worthlessness and rejection.

But, the truth of God's Word gives you the power to fight back. When we stop believing the lies in our thoughts, we stop giving them power. None of these labels can stand up in your mind to God's loving truth about who you are.

Hand over any of those old sticks and stones to your loving Father. Trust the truth of God's love for you and His promised faithfulness to you. Truths that last forever.

Holy Spirit, please blow through my mind and heart,
replacing lies and labels with Your everlasting love and truths.

THE HANDOFF

One generation commends your works to
another; they tell of your mighty acts.

PSALM 145:4

I love watching the Olympics—especially the runners. I have run for years, and their stamina and endurance have always inspired me. One of my favorite events is the relay race, because it speaks volumes to me about our Christian race.

When the runners round the track and ready themselves to make the handoff of the baton, it's their moment. And when the handoff goes well, the next person takes off like a shot.

That's what our race is like—a race where we hand off truths from one generation to the next—and this is *your* moment. Who are you handing the baton off to each day?

Your children? Your coworkers? Your friends? Whoever is in your sphere of influence, always be ready to pass on the baton of truth. It's the joyful culmination of all that training and running you've been doing!

Look for opportunities to hand off one baton of truth after another every day. Your supply of batons is unlimited! It's exhilarating to run in good company toward the goal—eternal life with Jesus (Hebrews 12:1–2).

Lord, this is my moment. Empowered by You,
I freely, effectively, and in love share Your
gospel truth with those I encounter.

YOUR BEAUTIFUL STORY

I will meditate on your wonderful works. . . .
I will proclaim your great deeds.

PSALM 145:5-6

I remember the first time a friend invited me to Hills Christian Life Center—which grew into Hillsong Church in Sydney. From the moment I walked in the door, I felt that I had found the home I didn't even know I was looking for. There, immersed in fellowship and worship, mentored in God's Word, loved, valued, and accepted, I became so alive and on fire with purpose.

There's something about our beginnings in our relationship with Christ that is so powerful, so moving, so very real. If you're like me, it was something I couldn't wait to share.

Maybe the first time you heard the gospel, God enabled you to recognize the truth, and you committed your life to Jesus. Or maybe God placed people in your life at several points, some sowing seeds of truth and others watering them, until your decision to follow Jesus finally blossomed.

Whatever your story of God's gracious revelation of His truth, it's too good not to be shared. Sharing our stories of faith is all about revealing God's glory on this earth. As your story continues, as you continue to run the race, keep sharing. And remember that God will provide the strength and energy you need. (Isaiah 40:31).

Almighty God, please use my story to share Your truth with the ones You place in my life. Thank You for writing it for me!

GOD'S PERFECT TIMING

Wait for the Lord;
be strong and take heart
and wait for the Lord.

PSALM 27:14

When I was pregnant, people would ask, "What is your due date?" I answered based on the date the doctor had given me, knowing it might not be the exact date—because how could anyone but God really know when a baby will be born? When my daughter did not arrive on her expected date, people's question changed to "How far past your due date are you?" Then I realized that my baby was not overdue; she was coming right on time.

Just like a baby being right on time, so is God. He's never early and never late. We may think He is, but that's because we confuse due dates with due seasons. And we set ourselves up for disappointment.

In the New Testament, when God promised us, "Let us not become weary in doing good, for at the proper time we will reap a harvest if we do not give up" (Galatians 6:9), He did not state a specific date. Yet, we mysteriously hold Him accountable to a deadline we prescribe. It's time we start trusting in God's perfect timing and shift our hearts and minds to adapt to His methods of timing.

God is always on time. He's never late—and He's always faithful.

Lord, thank You for working out the perfect timing for Your good plan for me. Please help me stay on Your schedule.

THE GRACE OPTION

In the Law Moses commanded us to stone such women
[caught in adultery]. Now what do you say?

JOHN 8:5

We live in a time when the media specializes in broadcasting people's moral failures and passing judgment. The Pharisees were the same way in the Bible story about the woman caught in adultery (John 8). The woman was dragged out of bed and paraded through the streets, eventually being brought to stand before Jesus. She had violated the law—and the lawful punishment was not only deep shame but a death sentence.

The Pharisees were not seeking justice. They were trying to trap Jesus with the letter of the law, and this woman was their bait. Would He support stoning her, or would He violate the law? They didn't foresee that Jesus offers a third option: forgiveness.

Jesus challenged the people, saying that if anyone was without sin, they were to cast the first stone. They all slowly walked away, leaving the woman alone with Jesus. That's when He extended the powerful act of love and grace. He told her He didn't condemn her and to go and leave her life of sin (John 8:11).

Forgiveness is an option that's more powerful than any amount of worldly shame—an option that sets us free.

Lord, like the Pharisees, I can fail to recognize
that forgiveness is an option. I thank You that You
never pass on an opportunity to forgive me.

GOD IS TRUSTWORTHY

Sovereign LORD, you are God! Your covenant is trustworthy,
and you have promised these good things to your servant.

2 SAMUEL 7:28

Uncertain times can fill us with fear, but we can trust that our Father God is still trustworthy to carry us through.

If you're like so many of us, you are receiving a constant newsfeed of updates, alerts, and posts that can make us feel anxious. News reports and projections imply that everything—the economy, the environment, terrorism, crime—is bad and growing worse. It's overwhelming. So much, in fact, that a large part of our population requires prescription medication to combat these very emotions. The day-to-day wear of anxieties drives us to find relief—yet the more permanent cure for our hearts and souls is remembering God's trustworthiness.

The world will always be constantly changing—but God never changes. He is the same yesterday, today, and forever (Hebrews 13:8).

Choose to remember the unchanging truth that God is in ultimate control of the world. When you accept what you cannot change and take responsibility for the things you can change, you will experience greater peace.

When everyday anxieties start to run you down, remember who is in charge. Your sovereign God is trustworthy, wise, and good—and He is looking out for you (Psalm 121:5).

I praise You, God, for You are sovereign, trustworthy,
wise, and good. I want to build my life on that fact.

DEFAULT TO TRUST

"Who of you by worrying can add a single hour to your life?"

LUKE 12:25

Every single thing in your life is important to God. So when you pray, unload every worry, fear, joy, or thought in your head. He wants to hear about all of it (1 Peter 5:7).

And then leave it there. God tells us to cast our cares and anxiety over on Him because He cares for us. We weren't designed to carry all of our cares—but He is.

So when something today sparks worried thoughts, you could talk to your friends or just keep it to yourself. But I suggest that you first, before anything, talk to God about it. Worrying with your friends won't add an hour or a minute to your life or theirs; praying to your trustworthy God will bring you peace.

You can trust Him with your concerns—always. Believing the truth, for instance, that God is good and that He does good, will help you trust Him—even when your circumstances are not good, and you are overwhelmed with worry. Your God is powerful, faithful, and loving—and He treasures you (Deuteronomy 7:6). Whatever your concerns, make praying to your Father your default reaction to worried thoughts, and you'll see your trust in Him grow. When you do, He blesses the hours of your life with peace.

Lord, I believe in Your goodness, love, and trustworthiness. So I ask You to change my default from worry to trust. You are powerful to achieve it!

BREAKING FREE

God is love.

1 JOHN 4:16

You already have access to the key that sets you free from any ball and chain you've been dragging around. You've probably felt the heaviness of shame, regrets, or the fear of being unworthy, but you don't have to be weighed down by them anymore.

What will set you free?

The truth of God's love (John 8:32).

God's great love broke some of my chains—and it can break your chains too. He brings this freedom to us through the truth He gives in His Word. His truth can break through any lies you believe—lies about yourself and your value—and reveal the truth of who you are and why He created you. In this truth, you can be comfortable with who you are in Him.

Breaking free from the shackles of shame does not happen instantly or according to a ten-step process. It's a beautiful, everyday journey. It involves ongoing discoveries of the depth of God's love for you and His limitlessness of power to transform you, re-create you, and continually renew you. Ask for help from the Holy Spirit. Seek, pray, and discover more about God's love and power. Let Him free you with His unfailing love.

Lord, help me hear Your voice of love rather than the lying voice of shame, so I can live with confidence and hope in You.

A MATTER OF TRUST

"Father, if you are willing, take this cup from
me; yet not my will, but yours be done."

LUKE 22:42

When I worked in youth ministry, I sadly watched some young people walk away from God. Yes, they wanted to follow Jesus, but on their schedule. Rather than follow after God based on His principles, they wanted to do things their way. But that never works.

Over the years, I have seen that we cannot always do what we want to do, when and how we want to do it, and still follow Jesus. His plan is greater than ours—and always what's best for our lives—and our challenge is to give up our plan when it conflicts with His.

Our good God has a great plan for our lives, and we can trust Him with the *what*, the *when*, and the *how*. So let's shift our thinking so that we go when He calls, and let Him take care of the outworking of our future. Like Jesus Himself, let's subordinate our will to the Father's.

We can rest confidently in the truth that what God has for us is better than anything we can imagine. God's will is always our ultimate good. Always.

Help me, Lord, to trust You with the when, the how,
and the what that You have for my life. Thank You that
You work all those elements together for my good.

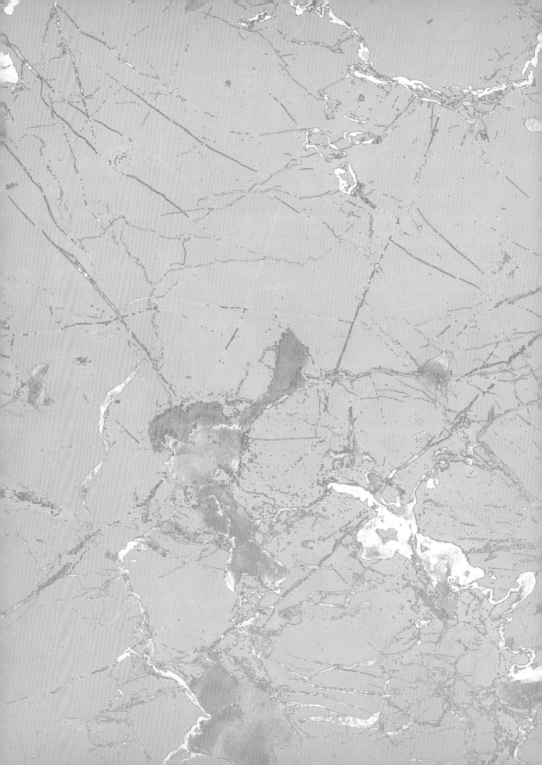

MAY

———————

The Lᴏʀᴅ is my light and my salvation,
whom shall I fear?
The Lᴏʀᴅ is the stronghold of my life,
of whom shall I be afraid?

PSALM 27:1

WHAT FAITH CAN DO

"If you have faith as small as a mustard seed, you can say to
this mountain, 'Move from here to there,' and it will move."

MATTHEW 17:20

God said, "Go," and Moses and the Israelites—and Abraham before them—
went. And how did they go? The Bible tells us, "by faith" (Hebrews 11:27). By
faith, they arrived at their promised land, and by faith you will too.

For the Israelites, setting out on their journey made no sense. Leaving
everything they had, leaving the safe and familiar for the unknown, wasn't
rational. But the life of faith requires venturing out into the unknown and
expecting the unexpected, the unpredictable, the awe-inspiring, and even the
outrageous.

Faith is your turning point when you're in doubt, when you're in want,
when life is difficult, and when the path ahead is unclear. We can't touch or
see or smell or hold faith, but it is real—and it is powerful. Faith can shut the
mouths of lions, quench the flames of fire, escape the edge of the sword, raise
the dead, end torture, and release the imprisoned!

And your faith can take you right to where God wants you. After all, God
is able to make a way where there is no way. Have faith in His perfect plans for
you! That's how you keep developing *unshakeable* faith!

Thank You, God, that Your "Go!" means adventure
and expectation of Your good plans coming
to pass. May I go with confidence in both Your
trustworthiness and Your presence with me.

STEPPING OUT IN FAITH

When I am afraid, I put my trust in you.

PSALM 56:3

I love a good plan, don't you? Sometimes it's comforting to have your day mapped out, proportioned, confirmed, and predictable. You know exactly what to expect and how to spend your energy. Yet days rarely run according to our plan—especially when doing God's work.

Consider the Galilean fishermen who heard Jesus say, "Follow me," dropped their nets, and walked away from their boats (Mark 1). They exchanged a very predictable life for a very uncertain future. The only certainty was that Jesus would be leading them—and that made all the difference.

Likewise, when Jesus says, "Follow Me into the place or position or job or ministry I have for you," we cannot wait until we have the entire blueprint before we get up and start moving. Like the fishermen, we must leave our schedules and plans behind and embrace the uncertainty. Trusting Jesus, we step into the future, not knowing how it will end. His presence with us will make all the difference.

Flexible and ready for adventure, you can give up ultimate control over the direction of your life and choose to walk by faith, not by sight. Though you might naturally feel nervous or afraid, you can trust that the One you follow is going somewhere wonderful.

Teach me, Lord, to take steps of faith
into Your plan for the future.

OPPORTUNITIES TO TRUST

Now faith is confidence in what we hope for and
assurance about what we do not see.

HEBREWS 11:1

Confidence. Hope. Assurance. According to today's verse, that's what faith gives us. Those very things mean the difference between believing in our hearts and taking bold steps of faith in the world.

Think for a moment about the great men and women of the Bible, about the early church, many of whom were martyred, and about believers today who suffer for Jesus around the world. The accounts of their lives are glorious and inspiring—because these men and women not only *had* faith in their trustworthy God, but also *took* steps of faith, steps into the unknown.

Now think about times when you've taken a step into the uncertain. Maybe you didn't actually have a choice: the company relocated; your child entered kindergarten; the bank didn't approve the loan. Still, you suddenly found yourself stepping into the unknown and needing to trust God. Looking back at that experience, what did God do to grow your faith?

Whether you're about to take a step into the unknown now or you're preparing to sometime soon, remember all the ways God has proved Himself trustworthy when you encountered the new and unfamiliar. Rest in what He has matured in you—*unshakeable* faith!

Opportunities to trust You are opportunities for me to
grow unshakeable faith in You. So, Lord, I thank You for
the unfamiliar, uncertain, and difficult times. When I
see You work, I see once again Your trustworthiness.

THE DARKROOM

Whenever the spirit from God came on Saul, David would
take up his lyre and play. Then relief would come to Saul;
he would feel better, and the evil spirit would leave him.

1 SAMUEL 16:23

Remember when cameras used film that needed to be developed? The process required a darkroom, a special red light, and trays of chemical solutions. You couldn't take shortcuts or expose the room to light, and the development process determined the quality of the prints.

In the same way, David spent a long time in God's darkroom before he became king of Israel. He was a teenager when—unbeknownst to Saul—he was anointed as the future king of Israel. But King Saul was still on the throne with apparently no plans to step down. Neither Samuel nor David had any idea when David would take the throne. Fifteen years passed before David was crowned at thirty. In the meantime, David served Saul and was faithful where he was.

Maybe you think you're in God's darkroom today. Trust that He is developing and preparing you. He's preparing you for the roles He has for you in your future. God always uses other people, time, and circumstances to transfer the image of Christ onto our souls. When we emerge from God's darkroom, nothing can destroy the image of His Son developed in our lives.

Lord God, thank You for preparing me to do Your work in
this world. Please keep making me like Jesus in the process.

ROOTED IN GOD'S LOVE

The LORD is compassionate and gracious,
slow to anger, abounding in love.

PSALM 103:8

I want to remind you of something important: Whatever you've given or not given, no matter what you have said or have not said, what you have thought or have not thought, what you have done or have not done, what you have accomplished or have not accomplished, *God loves you*. And He always will.

Love is not only what God does, it is who God is. He cannot stop Himself from loving us because He *is* love (1 John 4:8). His love far surpasses any earthly love we may have experienced. It is based entirely on His character, not our performance. There is nothing you can do to make God love you less; there is nothing you can do to make Him love you more. God loves you with an unfailing, indescribable, and unending love.

Of course, the Enemy would like you to believe otherwise. But you don't have to be plagued by his onslaught of thoughts and feelings of inadequacy, guilt, shame, condemnation, insecurity, fear, doubt, and unworthiness. Decide today to not listen to those lies, but to stand on the truth of God's Word. And His Word states again and again that *God loves you*. He always will—no matter what.

Lord God, please seal into my heart the magnitude of Your love for me. As I face each day, may it be the running background to all my thoughts and actions.

TAKE TIME TO PRAY

Rejoice always, pray continually, give thanks in all circumstances; for this is God's will for you in Christ Jesus.

1 THESSALONIANS 5:16–18

Countless women have asked me how I balance all I do. I certainly don't have it all figured out, but I can tell you that prayer is indispensable.

You might feel you don't have time for prayer, because "Oh my gosh, I have a zillion things to do today: drop the kids off at school, go to work, cook dinner" . . . and on the list grows. Believe me, I completely understand. I'd convinced myself that I didn't have time to pray, until I discovered this one thing: prayer has no formal location or time-slot requirement!

Simply put, prayer is a way of life. It's an attitude of God-consciousness and God-surrender that we carry all the time. Prayer is how we communicate with our Father, and it's an opportunity for us to bring our gratitude, needs, and concerns before Him. So, I pray when I go for walks on the beach. I pray when I'm lying in the hammock. I pray as I walk around the house, getting ready for another trip. I pray on airplanes, in terminals, wherever I am! It's an ongoing conversation, an attitude of my heart, a lifeline I can't live without!

Lord, whenever an issue comes up in my day, no matter how big or how small, remind me to stop for a moment and talk to You about it. I do have time to pray!

TRADING FEAR FOR FAITH

God has not given us a spirit of fear, but of
power and of love and of a sound mind.

2 TIMOTHY 1:7 NKJV

Our Enemy doesn't need to use physical danger to make us fearful and immobilize us. He is just as effective when he whispers, "What if you fail? What if you embarrass yourself? What if . . . ?"

When that whisper comes, listen instead for God's voice of reassurance, reminding you of His power, love, presence, and trustworthiness. The moment you taste fear, realize that you've just recognized an opportunity for God to grow your faith in Him. Learn to see areas of fear as places where trust is about to grow, and your fear will give way to courage.

Your spirit of power, love, and a sound mind will know in those times to reach for Jesus. Review biblical truths about God's faithfulness. Reflect on how He has walked with you through hard times. Remember that the God who loves you has good plans for you that nothing and no one can thwart.

Fear is a feeling, and it will pass. Christ with you and Christ at work in you and through you—that is eternal reality. He is on your side, protecting you always (Psalm 46:1).

Lord God, when I hear "What if . . ." and taste
fear, lead me back to You. Thank You for the ways
You are growing my unshakeable faith.

RETHINKING FAILURE

Though the righteous fall seven times, they rise again.

PROVERBS 24:16

You can probably think of a failure or two in your life. Perhaps, if you're like most people, those failures seem to replay on a loop in your head when you least expect them to. Despite what the world, the voice inside your head, or the Enemy himself may tell you, failure is not an entirely bad thing. Really!

You *will* falter, fumble, and fail in life, but failing at something does not make *you* a failure. Failure is not final—unless you choose to not get back up. The key to growing from failure is refusing to quit.

The same goes for your life of unshakeable faith. It's not so much about what you accomplish for God, but that you are becoming more like Jesus. When you bring your failure before God, He reminds you to live with humility and in reliance on Him.

Champions fall, and champions fail. They stumble, but then they reach for help. They flee, but they return. They strike out in anger, but they accept rebuke and correction. Champions are never perfect. Only Jesus is perfect. But champions press on. They persevere. They will not be stopped. They know that God builds their character through adversity. "In all these things we are more than conquerors through him who loved us" (Romans 8:37).

Lord, I'll gladly take the scrapes and bruises if they mean I'm closer to victory in You. Thank You, trustworthy God, for using my failures for my good and Your glory.

PARTNERS

Praise [God] for his acts of power; praise
him for his surpassing greatness.

PSALM 150:2

When God invites you to stop and help someone He has placed on your path, He never asks you to go alone. You are His partner, and He goes alongside you (Hebrews 13:5).

What does this truth mean for your ability to meet someone's needs? It means that while you may think you don't have enough time, money, resources, or know-how for the task, God will use and bless what you have. He will back you up with acts of power.

You can go wherever God calls you with confidence, with assurance, and in anticipation of the good that will happen. And this confidence has nothing to do with you, your skills, or your passion. It comes because you serve a great God. The apostle John put it this way: "The one who is in you is greater than the one who is in the world" (1 John 4:4).

Remember that truth whenever Satan whispers that your contribution will be so small that you may as well do nothing. You don't have to be afraid of insignificance, of not making a difference, of trying and failing. Even if you don't immediately see the fruit of your actions, you can know that your service will not be insignificant because you go with God!

*What a privilege to be a partner in Your life-giving
ministry, God—and what a blessing to have You
go with me wherever You call me to serve!*

"I LOVE YOU, LORD!"

We love because he first loved us.

1 JOHN 4:19

Circumstances can change, and our feelings can change with them, but reminding ourselves of God's truths can help keep alive our love for Him.

Did you know that God loved you before you loved Him? One simple way to keep your love for Him burning is to tell Him you love Him … every single day . . . several times a day.

Be fueled by these facts:

- God created your inmost being; He knit you together in your mother's womb (Psalm 139:13).
- He knows the number of hairs on your head (Luke 12:7).
- He delights in you and loves your company (Psalm 149:4).
- He designed you with a purpose and has good plans for your future (Jeremiah 29:11).
- There is nothing you can do to make Him love you more or less (Ephesians 2:8–9).
- And, yes, you are able to love God "because he first loved us" (1 John 4:19).

So build your love for God by speaking words of love to Him every day. Sing of your love. Show your love by spending time with Him in worship, prayer, and reading His Word.

Lord God, You are gracious and kind, patient and
forgiving, steadfast and generous, sovereign and
wise, merciful and good. I love You, Lord!

GOD'S SUSTAINING WORD

"It is written: 'Man shall not live on bread alone, but on every word that comes from the mouth of God.'"

MATTHEW 4:4

Do you long to hear God's voice declaring His love for you? There are so many ways you can drink in the great depths of His love for you. One of those is to read God's love letter to you—the Bible—daily. Don't miss a single opportunity to hear from Him, and you will be nourished in a whole new way.

Not a day goes by, I'm guessing, when you don't talk to or connect in some way with your spouse or best friend. It keeps that relationship healthy. Well, we would be crazy to think that our relationship with God needs any less attention. And the thing is, it's so easy to talk to Him and connect with Him in some way every single day. Not only does it feed your soul, but God loves when you cherish His words (John 14:23–24).

That's why I can't say this strongly enough: read your Bible and other books that deepen your faith, such as this one. My prayer for you is that, as you spend time reading God's Word, you may more fully "know this love that surpasses knowledge—that you may be filled to the measure of all the fullness of God" (Ephesians 3:19).

Lord, give me a hunger for Your Word and the discipline to make reading it a daily priority.

GREATER EXPECTATIONS

Great are the works of the Lord; they are pondered by
all who delight in them. Glorious and majestic are his
deeds, and his righteousness endures forever.

PSALM 111:2–3

Not everything goes the way we pray or believe sometimes. At times our expectations end in disappointment instead of victory:

- When a friend relapses after you've stood with her through rehab again
- When you play the political game at the office and still don't get the promotion
- When someone dies of cancer after a fierce fight of faith

It's in those moments—when faith-shakers rock our world—that we have to trust.

When disappointment eats away at us, we have to persevere and believe God anyway. We have to allow that experience to build our trust instead. We have to believe God is up to something bigger, working all things together for our good (Romans 8:28).

So the next time you face an unmet expectation, let it spark in you even *greater* expectations of what God is up to. Your loving God is "able to do immeasurably more than all we ask or imagine" (Ephesians 3:20).

Thank You, Lord, for the comfort You offer me—
and for the greater expectations You provide
when my expectations go unmet.

A PLACE GOD CAN WORK

Make every effort to live in peace with everyone and to
be holy; without holiness no one will see the Lord. See to
it that no one falls short of the grace of God and that no
bitter root grows up to cause trouble and defile many.

HEBREWS 12:14–15

If you live and work with other human beings, you'll be pretty familiar with the fact that egos will flare, grumbling will happen, ambition will rear its head, and misunderstandings will occur. We're all human and we all have flesh to refuse if we want to walk in the Spirit (Romans 8:6). Such relational strife is very real even for Christians—but I have great news for you. Strife can be a beautiful opportunity to love the way Jesus loves.

People-loving is the work of Christ—and this work brings challenges and growth. God's Word offers guidelines for dealing with strife. The basic instruction is simple: love one another (1 John 4:7).

Loving one another, however, is more than just warm fuzzies. Loving one another means doing the specific work of 1 Corinthians 13, the work of being patient, kind, longsuffering, without envy, and more. Read that chapter to see how to act when conflict arises. Let your words, actions, and decisions reflect Jesus. Whenever strife begins, thank God for this opportunity to put His love into action.

*Lord, when I encounter relational trouble, use me to bring
forgiveness, grace, and love. Let me do it in Your power.*

REST FOR THE WEARY

"Come to me, all you who are weary and
burdened, and I will give you rest."

MATTHEW 11:28

Sleep deprivation can sap our confidence, bring on discouragement, and muddy our thinking—including our thinking about God. Thankfully, we can ask ourselves questions to get to the root of our tiredness.

To take better care of yourself, examine the reasons you're so worn out. Are you getting the sleep you need? Are you exercising? Are you working too much? Are you taking a Sabbath? (Even the Son of God rested [Matthew 14:13]!)

Maybe you're weary because you never say no. Are there handoffs you're reluctant to make? Let people help you according to God's design. You don't have to do it all.

Or perhaps you are trying to control what isn't yours to control. If you may have a blind spot in this area and need wise counsel, seek it out; counselors are ready and willing to help.

Maybe you are weary from waiting. Goals, objectives, and strategies can help you get to where you believe God wants you to go, but you cannot make something happen in your own strength or twist God's arm about the timing. Your due dates may often differ from your trustworthy God's appointed times. But stay faithful, trust your wise God, and get some rest!

Lord, when I get weary, please show me how to get not
only the physical rest but also the mental, emotional,
and spiritual rest I need. Refresh me, I pray.

BUT GOD IS GREATER!

The one who is in you is greater than the one who is in the world.

1 JOHN 4:4

The world is facing problems that the "power of positive thinking" can't touch—serious evil like the corruption of government, the ominous influence of organized traffickers, the pernicious threat of terrorism, the breakup of marriages and families, and widespread chemical abuse. All of this evil appears to have taken hold of our world, never to let go. But God's power is "greater than the one who is in the world," and God lives in you.

The opposition you encounter in everyday life—and especially when you consciously serve God in all that you do—is an invitation to focus your mind and heart on our omnipotent, trustworthy God and pray to Him. Other Christians, your family in faith, can join in, too, to multiply those prayers. There is power in prayer—God's power—which is stronger than any and all opposition.

Consider a time when you faced opposition . . . and your trustworthy God came through for you. The opposition may have been great, but God was greater—and that still holds true today. Even if the almighty God encounters opposition to His goals, it doesn't keep Him from reaching those goals. He is in you, and He will empower you to pray against and overcome the one who is in the world.

God, I find such comfort in the truth that You are greater than any opposition that can arise. You are unbeatable, Lord!

GO WITH HIM

Surely the righteous will praise your name, and
the upright will live in your presence.

PSALM 140:13

As I faced my fear of flying years ago, I had important questions to answer: Was I going to choose fear, or would I choose faith in the One who has overcome the world? Was I going to worry about hurtling through the sky in a metal tube, or trust the One who hung the stars and moon in place?

I had to overcome my fear to fulfill my calling—and so will you. What fear is keeping you from your purpose—from your destiny? Jesus has charged all of us to "go and make disciples of all nations." And He included with it a fear-busting truth: "And surely I am with you always, to the very end of the age" (Matthew 28:19–20).

We're not directed to go *as long as* or *if* or *after* Jesus removes all danger and takes away all our fear. We go *in spite of* and *even if* and *anyway*. He says simply: *Go. Go with Me.*

Jesus has been saying this to me all my life. And every time, He gives me the courage to look fear in the face and dare to go where He is calling me to go—knowing He is with me.

Jesus, thank You for going with me into the
unknown, past my fears, and toward Your glory.
Remind me that You are with me always.

GO FIND SOME DARKNESS

---

*The night is nearly over; the day is almost here. So let us put
aside the deeds of darkness and put on the armor of light.*

ROMANS 13:12

Once, in a Walmart, we bought my daughter Sophia a flashlight of her very own. Sophia flipped it on, trying it out, but none of us could see even a glow. The lights in the store were too bright. "Oh, Mummy," Sophia pleaded, "can we please go find some darkness?"

From the mouth of babes comes the wisdom of Christ. Darkness is everywhere. We live in a world full of fear and in need of light—and we are the light of the world. Jesus said we're to show the hope of our Father in heaven to the world, because our light and hope quench the darkness (Matthew 5: 14–16).

As His hands and feet, we are the force that goes, finds, and conquers the dark. We hold the truth that wipes out fear. "Keep your eyes on Me," Jesus says. His presence in the darkness, in the face of the most primal, serious danger, vanquishes fear. Once fear no longer controls you, and Christ is walking by your side, you are undaunted—and eager to go find some darkness because you are the light of the world!

*Lord God, thank You for making us Your light in the
world. Show me where the darkness is, so I can shine
Your light to those who are so desperately waiting.*

THE CHOICE AND CHALLENGE OF FORGIVING

"Do not judge, and you will not be judged. Do not condemn, and you will not be condemned. Forgive, and you will be forgiven."

LUKE 6:37

It's easier to forgive others when their offense is simple or short-lived. It's easier to forgive someone when they ask for forgiveness—especially if we love them or recognize they are immature and didn't realize how they were hurting us. But to forgive someone who will never ask, who doesn't care, who has wounded us in a deeply damaging way—that's always much harder.

Genuine forgiveness of someone who has hurt you deeply can be a long, slow, difficult process. I traveled many valleys and revisited a lot of pain in order to grant unsolicited forgiveness to my abusers, to be free from my past and free for the future God had for me.

You may be on that same kind of journey. If so, let me remind you that Jesus is *on* your side and *by* your side each step of the way. His Spirit will guide you and reveal to you what you need to know and are able to address. If the effort is overwhelming, I encourage you to get support from a Christian counselor who can facilitate God's healing process. Stay close to your Father God, and He will lead you through.

I know I need to forgive, Lord. You want me
to know freedom. Help me, I pray. Show me
how to forgive those who have hurt me.

OPENED EYES

"Love each other as I have loved you."

MATTHEW 15:12

Years ago, I used to change TV channels when the intensity of bombings and genocide in news reports became unbearable. But not anymore. As my world-view broadened and my empathy for humankind grew, I realized that those people in the middle of their crises can't turn off their pain as easily as we turn off our TVs—and watching what was happening in their world was my prompting to pray for them wholeheartedly. I realized that as the world grows darker, I need to always remember who these trapped and suffering people are: people like you and me made in God's image.

God knows their names, their pain, their fears, even their dreams—and God wants us to make a difference in their lives. Let's remember what Jesus said: "Whatever you did for one of the least of these brothers and sisters of mine, you did for me" (Matthew 25:40). That means, do *something*, not nothing. When you see a circumstance you just can't bear to watch or think about any longer, pray. Ask for guidance. Even ask what you can do specifically. Then do it—and watch the Lord lead you, equip you, and guide you into the role He has for you: the role of loving others as He has all over the world.

Thank You for opening my eyes to the great needs in Your world. Please show me where You want me to serve.

RESCUED

[God our Savior] wants all people to be saved
and to come to a knowledge of the truth.

1 TIMOTHY 2:4

Actions have consequences, but let's face it: many of us secretly feel that if people make their own bed, then they ought to sleep in it. But not Jesus. He came for the mess-ups—including you and me.

Why do we sometimes feel that the seriously lost should be on their own—that they got themselves into this mess and should get themselves out? That's certainly not God's attitude. Imagine if a mountain rescue squad spotted a missing hiker and said, "Sorry. We can't rescue those who get lost because they intentionally skied out of bounds."

No. That's not how Jesus would ever see it.

When someone is trapped in a burning building, you don't try to work out what caused the fire and then decide whether to extend your sympathy. You rush to save that person. Especially if you understand how much it hurts to be burned.

No matter how the treasure of a soul comes to be lost, Jesus wants us to rescue and save what is precious. He said that even God calls the angels together to rejoice over the precious soul that's been found (Luke 15:7, 10). Even the humblest and least deserving of us are of such value to heaven!

*Jesus, give me Your heart for the lost, and make me
compassionate and bold as I reach out to them today.*

THE SECRET OF CONTENTMENT

I have learned to be content whatever the circumstances. I know what it is to be in need, and I know what it is to have plenty. I have learned the secret of being content in any and every situation.

PHILIPPIANS 4:11–12

Learning the secret of contentment helps us endure life's challenges and keeps us in the race for the long haul. Paul learned to be content in the midst of trials, "in any and every situation."

But contentment didn't come naturally to Paul any more than it comes naturally to us. Paul had to learn contentment—and some of the classrooms where he was tutored were brutal. From being imprisoned, shipwrecked, bitten by a snake, to being stoned and left for dead, Paul endured and learned to be content.

True contentment comes when we choose to depend on Christ and to trust that He is doing a good work inside of us despite all of the external challenges to our faith. It's trusting Jesus that He gives us what we need when we need it to endure and overcome.

True contentment is in the presence of Jesus, not in the absence of difficulties. "Be content with what you have, because God has said, 'Never will I leave you; never will I forsake you'" (Hebrews 13:5).

I find contentment in Your presence, Lord Jesus, and I know You are trustworthy. Your presence is more than enough for me.

TRAINING AND TRUST

God's gifts and his call are irrevocable.

ROMANS 11:29

When David was still a teen, he was anointed to be the future king of Israel. Yet, he did not possess the skill, wisdom, or knowledge to lead a nation. How could he? The character and spirit of this anointed king-to-be had to be trained and matured. So God required David to follow and obey Him every step of a long, mystifying, and difficult journey that lasted for years.

God did not tell David His timetable, nor did He hand David a map and itinerary. This future king did not have a clue as to what was going to unfold between his days of tending sheep and his reign as king of Israel. But God was at work in every one of those fifteen years, preparing David for his assignment.

God trains us in the exact same way. Throughout our lives, in all the difficult and dark seasons, in the seasons we don't understand or even in the ones where we don't see any value, He's training us for our assignment—to fulfill our purpose. So, yield to His plan. If you will—He'll get you to your destiny.

Thank You for the privilege of being Your partner
in Your kingdom work. Please help me to follow
Your call and let You take care of the rest.

A PARADIGM SHIFT

I can do all things through Christ who strengthens me.

PHILIPPIANS 4:13 NKJV

Faith-shakers come in all forms—from marriage challenges to parenting concerns to financial stress—but every one of them is an opportunity to develop unshakeable faith. As we overcome and persevere through every faith-shaker, our confidence grows. And our confidence in the face of faith-shakers comes from the resurrected Christ living inside of us. *In Him*, we can deal with anything because:

> No promise is too hard for God to keep.
> No prayer is too difficult for God to answer.
> No problem is too complex for God to solve.
> No person is too hardened for God to save.
> No mountain is too big for God to move.
> No need is too great for God to meet.
> There is nothing our God cannot do!

As Jesus Himself proclaimed, "With God all things are possible" (Matthew 19:26)! so we really can have *unshakeable* confidence and *unshakeable* faith.

Lord God, thank You for helping me transform faith-shaker circumstances into faith-growers. I renew my confidence that all things are possible through You!

CHRIST IN YOU

I have been crucified with Christ and I no
longer live, but Christ lives in me.

GALATIANS 2:20

We each have our own gifts, our own desires, our own passions in life. When we discover and begin to outwork our passion, we begin to see God miraculously work through us in the world around us.

Our passion is our enthusiasm because of Christ living in us. The Gospels have some amazing descriptions of God being "in us": it's like being "clothed with power from on high" (Luke 24:49), like being "baptized" (Mark 1:8), like water being poured on dry and thirsty ground (Isaiah 44:3). The Spirit—besides doing other things—comforts us, teaches us, empowers us, counsels us, leads us, and intercedes for us.

As the Spirit of Christ dwells within you and does these things, you will find yourself passionate about the very things Jesus Himself is passionate about. So invite the Spirit in. Your ongoing openness to God's Spirit will mean a life of unstoppable passion fueled by God Himself.

Thank You, Lord Jesus, for the gift of Your Spirit.
Thank You for helping me stay passionate.

THE WINNING SIDE

This is how God showed his love among us: He sent his one
and only Son into the world that we might live through him.

1 JOHN 4:9

God uses every single trial, every detour, every obstacle in our journey for our benefit, for our good. That's because what the Enemy means for evil, God uses for our good (Genesis 50:20). Sometimes the good is a change in circumstances. Sometimes the good is a stronger faith. But nothing is ever wasted.

Satan used Judas to betray the Lord, but God intended for Jesus to stand trial and be condemned to death. Satan used the scheming of Jesus' enemies to have Him crucified, but Jesus' crucifixion was key to God's plan for securing eternal life for all who believe in Jesus. Satan loses! God wins! Regardless of what it looks like in the process.

As you persevere despite opposition, trust God. Trust that in the midst of everything, He is building you up, strengthening you, and teaching you to trust Him more.

I praise You, God, for using for good what the Enemy intends
for evil. Show me how to persevere toward ultimate victory.

SET THE CAPTIVES FREE

The Lord has anointed me to proclaim good news to the poor. He
has sent me to bind up the brokenhearted, to proclaim freedom
for the captives and release from darkness for the prisoners.

ISAIAH 61:1

We are called to live a life of freedom—and help free others along the way. For those of us who have been shackled by fear or shame, or enslaved to false ideas and thoughts, it's a gift to help others break free. As I travel the world ministering God's freedom, I am keenly aware of the difference between freedom and bondage—both naturally and spiritually.

When I lie down at night, my life seems far removed from those people who are trapped, afraid, broken, imprisoned, and ignored. Our lives seem worlds apart. I am happily married, with healthy children, living in a safe home, able to come and go as I please. My family and I have food, clothing, shelter, and health care. I have dreams, plans, and goals for my future. I am free.

Yet in ministry around the world, I meet so many people who are living without justice, love, hope, or any promise that their lives or their children's lives may someday get better. I love that every new day—for you and for me—means another chance to make a difference—to help set the captives free.

*Lord, please show me what I can do today and in
the future. Use me to help set captives free.*

WHAT IF?

"I have come that they may have life, and that
they may have it more abundantly."

JOHN 10:10 NKJV

"What if?" That feeling of wondering what would have happened if we'd stepped out in faith and taken an opportunity—one that we now feel slipped through our fingers.

"What if?" That feeling God wants us to experience less and less.

God wants to help us grow in our courage. He wants to set us free from the fear that keeps us settling for a mere existence instead of living "more abundantly." Yes, those of us with a bumpy past may crave normalcy, comfort, and predictability, but being open to taking risks—and even failing—is key to a richer relationship with God as we follow wherever He leads and go wherever He calls. Openness to risk is how we can become braver and live a more abundant life.

It isn't easy to let go of what we know and exchange it for the great unknown. But let's take the risk—together. Let's find comfort in the truth that the unknown is completely known by the trustworthy God we are learning to trust more and more. He promises to go before you and be with you (Deuteronomy 31:8).

*Lord God, I choose to live so that at the end of
this earthly life I have no regrets. Grow my trust
in You as I bravely take the risks ahead.*

HOW FAITH GROWS

Consider it pure joy, my brothers and sisters,
whenever you face trials of many kinds.

JAMES 1:2

Did you just see *joy* and *trials* in the same sentence? Yes, you did. You can trust that your trials bring growth, because God is giving you His strength and expanding you.

Said another way, you *need* storms and trials in your life if your faith is to grow. In fact, faith must be tried to its limits before it can grow *beyond* those limits.

As long as you are on this side of heaven, you can be sure that God is not finished with His work in you or through you. You can be confident that God is continuing to make you more like Jesus—transforming you from timid to an unstoppable champion of faith (Philippians 1:6). His power is at work in you. Your trials are the tools He uses to grow and transform your faith.

James saw trials that come your way as a good thing: "the testing of your faith produces perseverance. Let perseverance finish its work so that you may be mature and complete, not lacking anything" (James 1:3–4). As you face your trials today, you can look forward to a future where you are mature and complete—a finished work in Him.

Lord God, when I go through trials, help me hang tough so
my faith grows stronger and my trust in You is complete.

YOU ARE A LOSTOLOGIST!

"The Son of Man came to seek and to save the lost."

LUKE 19:10

Instead of judging the lost, blogging about the lost, talking about the lost, blaming the lost, avoiding the lost, or ignoring the lost, God has called us to *find* the lost. He's called us to be "Lostologists"!

I love the story of the woman who washed Jesus' feet at the home of Simon—a Pharisee and self-righteous judge (Luke 7:36–8:3). Simon had invited Jesus to dinner, and the woman entered the home and washed Jesus' feet—a sign of hospitality, something Simon hadn't offered Jesus. As she was washing his feet, Jesus looked at the woman but asked Simon, "Do you see this woman?"

How odd. Simon was sitting right there beside Jesus. How could he not see the woman? Yet, Jesus asked, "Do you see this woman?"

How many times do we look but not see? Who do you look at every day, but not see? Who in your world is lost and needs to be seen—and introduced to Jesus?

Let's join Jesus in finding the lost sheep, in sharing compassion. Let's be Lostologists!

Jesus, thank You for seeing me—and saving me. Now help me look and see everyone around me who needs to find life in You.

KNOWING PEACE THROUGH PRAYER

Do not be anxious about anything, but in every situation, by prayer
and petition, with thanksgiving, present your requests to God.

PHILIPPIANS 4:6

I confess: I have lost way too much sleep worrying about things I ultimately couldn't control. Even now, I have to deliberately choose to let go of my anxiety, turn my requests over to God, and trust Him to take care of things. And I know it all happens through prayer.

There truly is a direct correlation between trusting God and praying. Prayer is your way to communicate with the Father, your opportunity to bring before Him your gratitude, needs, and concerns. Sometimes you think you don't have enough time to pray because you have a zillion other things to do. I know that feeling well—and I know that feeling isn't the truth. You and I always have time to pray.

After all, prayer is not limited to a specific location, nor does it need to be done at a certain time. Simply put, prayer is a way of life. When you pray, you are entrusting your needs to your trustworthy God rather than depending on yourself to make things happen. In essence, unceasing prayer is key to getting close to your heavenly Father. With this He brings supernatural peace, lavishing love on you, His beloved child (Psalm 66:19–20). So, talk to Him today. He always loves to hear from you.

I praise You, Lord, for the privilege of prayer—
and for the freedom I have to approach You
anytime from anywhere about anything!

MORE THAN ENOUGH

"Go at once to Zarephath in the region of Sidon and stay there.
I have directed a widow there to supply you with food."

1 KINGS 17:9

God sent Elijah to a region that was in famine—to a widow whose pantry was empty—so she could feed Elijah. Of course, that makes no sense, but God always has a point to make to us.

When Elijah asked the widow to bring him a piece of bread, she replied, "I don't have any bread—only a handful of flour in a jar and a little olive oil in a jug. I am . . . [going to] make a meal for myself and my son, that we may eat it—and die" (1 Kings 17:12).

The widow's natural response was "I do not have." But God knew what she did have—and He is never limited by our lack. He simply asks us to be willing to give Him what we do have.

How do you respond to God? "But, Lord, I don't have the time," or "I don't have the qualifications, talents, gifts, or abilities."

Offer God what little you do have. Then, step out in faith and trust Him. When you choose to put your little into the hands of our very big God, you will always see Him make sure you have more than enough.

Miracle-working God, thank You for calling me to
partner with You in Your work, and thank You for
doing such remarkable things with what I have.

JUNE

Let us then approach God's throne of grace with confidence, so that we may receive mercy and find grace to help us in our time of need.

HEBREWS 4:16

FAVOR IS FOR PURPOSE

The angel said to her, "Do not be afraid, Mary; you
have found favor with God. You will conceive and give
birth to a son, and you are to call him Jesus."

LUKE 1:30–31

When God chose young—and betrothed—Mary to carry, birth, and raise Jesus Christ, the Son of God, it was the greatest honor for any woman in history. But it was hardly an easy assignment. It was, however, incredibly filled with purpose—purpose that required His divine favor.

The future didn't look easy for Mary. She would have to tell her fiancé, family, and friends about her conversation with Gabriel, and she—unlike us—did not know how the story would end. I'm sure that, after the angel left, Mary anxiously wondered if Joseph would leave her, if her family would ostracize her, or if her friends would ridicule her. How could anyone believe her story? It could have cost her everything she knew. Yet she still said yes to the will and purpose of God.

We all want God's favor—but it's much more than everything going our way. To live in the true favor of God, we must be willing to accept His divine assignments and all their ramifications. We must embrace the responsibility, cost, and commitment favor requires. We must be willing to fulfill the purpose of the favor.

Lord, I choose Your purposes—and I thank You
for the favor to complete Your purposes.

AN ANCHOR FOR THE SOUL

[Our God] is the Rock, his works are perfect, and all his ways are just.
A faithful God who does no wrong, upright and just is he.

DEUTERONOMY 32:4

I was on a boat on the Mediterranean Sea when a sudden and rather strong storm arose. The boat was rocking like crazy, but the captain was completely calm. As an experienced sailor who knew storms like this one, he had dropped the anchor. He knew that as long as that anchor kept a firm hold, his vessel—and passengers—would be fine. The captain's confidence in the anchor brought me great comfort.

Of course, this talk about the anchor made me think about our hope in God that is "an anchor for the soul, firm and secure" (Hebrews 6:19). Anchored in the knowledge of God, His promises, His faithfulness, His guidance, and His unfailing love, our souls are secure for now and eternity.

As you journey through this life, waves will get big and winds will blow strong. If your hope is in your possessions, your position, or other people's opinions, you might start taking on water and perhaps even find yourself shipwrecked. But when you are anchored in the Lord, you will weather the storms of life no matter how fierce they get. He will guide you, uphold you, and keep you anchored to Himself.

I praise You, Lord, for You are my Rock, my Fortress,
my Stronghold, and, yes, my Anchor! Thank You
for keeping me secure in the storms of life.

THE SUPREME ACT OF WISDOM

[Jesus] went a little farther and fell on His face, and prayed, saying, "O My Father, if it is possible, let this cup pass from Me; nevertheless, not as I will, but as You will."

MATTHEW 26:39 NKJV

God knows we try to do our best at acting wisely, but we all know that His wisdom is beyond our wisdom (Romans 11:33–36). When we submit to Him, we're submitting to a better plan, a bigger purpose, and a more fulfilling life. After all, He is an all-loving, all-knowing, all-wise, all-just God, whose plans for us could only be good.

Jesus knew that too. With the words "*Nevertheless*, not as I will, but as You will," Jesus submitted to God's perfect will. With that word *nevertheless*, Jesus agreed to die, the sinless Lamb of God, in an act of unsurpassed sacrificial love. And Jesus knew what was coming. The agony. The cost. But then in one powerful word—*nevertheless*—He surrendered all to the will of His Father.

Through that willingness, God saved humanity—including you and me. And He set in motion generations of believers who could walk in great blessing. If He can do all that because of Jesus' "nevertheless," imagine what He can do with your willingness—with your submission to His perfect plan for your life.

Lord, Your wisdom is amazing beyond my ability to comprehend. I submit to Your will in the small details of my day, and in the big plan You have for my life.

A LIVING SACRIFICE

I urge you . . . to offer your bodies as a living sacrifice, holy
and pleasing to God—this is your true and proper worship.

ROMANS 12:1

Sacrificial living—giving up all you are and all you have as an offering to your Father—involves serving others, loving others, putting others before yourself, and living for God's purposes. It's really the ultimate, freeing, most *alive* way to live!

When you act as a living sacrifice, you turn away from self-focus and self-obsession. Suddenly you find yourself more able to live with love, joy, peace, patience, kindness, goodness, faithfulness, gentleness, and self-control (Galatians 5:22–23 NLT). This comes from daily "dying to yourself," which, far from being painful, is more like an old husk falling away. As Jesus put it: "Unless a kernel of wheat falls to the ground and dies, it remains only a single seed" (John 12:24). When the kernel dies, it produces a thriving plant, which in turn "produces many seeds" (John 12:24).

This is the mystery and beauty of living a life like this: the more you pour yourself out in living sacrifice, the more God's love pours into you. You are filled and refilled with the ceaseless, unstoppable, overflowing love of God that spills out into every life you touch.

God, what a privilege to show Your love to this
world! Help me let my old kernel of self fall away, so
I can live a life characterized by Your beauty.

STRENGTHENED BY THE STORMS

I know that my redeemer lives.

JOB 19:25

God grows our faith in good times and hard times, but, truth be told, usually more in the hard times. A faith that can't weather the storms of life doesn't do us much good, but learning to weather those storms requires experiencing them. And God in His mercy promises to be our Redeemer and carry us through.

Job was a man in the Bible whose wife told him to curse God when he lost everything in a cataclysmic series of events. Definitely unhelpful, but certainly understandable.

Job replied to her with godly wisdom: "Shall we accept good from God, and not trouble?" (Job 2:10). With the storm raging around him and undoubtedly within him as well, Job nonetheless landed on "I know that my redeemer lives" (19:25).

Maybe you have found yourself facing circumstances that seem unfair, or loss that seems unbearable. I know that your pain is real and should never be minimized—and it may never be understood. That's why our Redeemer lives—and despite how painful today may be, He will not let us be tested beyond our strength (1 Corinthians 10:13). He longs to build you up and set you free. He longs to carry your cares and sustain you (Psalm 55:22).

Lord, I know that You live. You are my Redeemer.
Help me to cling to Your wisdom in hard times
and keep hope in Your ultimate deliverance.

A LOVE LIKE THAT

We know that in all things God works for the good of those who
love him, who have been called according to his purpose.

ROMANS 8:28

Life will eventually turn every person upside down and inside out. *When*, not
if, your world is turned upside down, know that you will be sustained. No disaster is too devastating for God to reach out with His loving hand and comfort
you—and, unimaginably, make it work for His purposes.

A grown child loses her way, a marriage crumbles, sickness ravages,
financial disaster leaves you with nothing—these things are common to
humankind. But God's love can bring us through any emotional earthquake
like these and through any shakings that we experience. Jesus' sacrificial, saving, supernatural love can lift us out of betrayal and hurt. It can deliver us
from any mess. Love like that can release us from every prison of fear and
confusion. And love like God's can fill us up until it spills out of us, and we
can't help but speak about it and share it.

Jesus promised, "In this world you will have trouble. But take heart! I have
overcome the world" (John 16:33). Whatever you experience in life, cry out to
Jesus and ask for His love. It will sustain you, strengthen you, and carry you.
When all else is shaken and fails, His love doesn't. And it never will.

*Your love truly is indescribable, Lord Jesus. Show me how
to rest in it, even when my world turns upside down.*

ALL YOU NEED

God is able to bless you abundantly, so that in all things at all times, having all you need, you will abound in every good work.

2 CORINTHIANS 9:8

It's a message we see throughout our culture: "You can have it all!" It's an appealing thought that easily can compel us to seek after all we want. But there's so much more for us than this unattainable goal. For real fulfillment in life, our pursuits and dreams should result from our seeking first the kingdom of God and His guidance for our lives, trusting Him to give us all we need when we need it.

When you receive from God *all you need* rather than striving on your own for *all you want*, you will know peace. You will be free from stress, anxiety, and too many hours at work. When you choose to put God first in your life, He will provide all that you need in order for you to do what He created you to do. When you are doing the good works God planned for you, you will fulfill your purpose—and always have all the time, energy, and resources you need to do those works.

Seek God first today, and He will bless your life abundantly, for your good and His glory.

Thank You, Lord, for guiding me and providing all I need, and blessing me beyond what I could want or expect.

GOD'S PLAN

They asked each other, "Were not our hearts
burning within us while he talked with us on the
road and opened the Scriptures to us?"

LUKE 24:32

In your times of heartache and disappointment, Jesus won't leave you or forsake you. In fact, He'll walk right along with you as you face your pain.

The two disciples experienced this firsthand after Jesus' crucifixion. Where they once burned with excitement, listening to all His teachings, they now walked away feeling so defeated. *How could God let this happen?* they must have wondered. They had believed that Jesus was the one God had sent to redeem Israel. What a privilege to work for that glorious end. They had been so sure, so committed, so excited. Yet they still were trying to fully grasp that Jesus had been crucified.

As they left Jerusalem, a third man joined them, but they didn't realize who He was. They were lost in their brokenheartedness and deep disappointment. And then, Jesus let them really see Him.

He was right there with them—walking right alongside them—the one who gave them hope that God had a plan, the one who taught them that God would use that crucifixion to redeem the human race. Jesus had not left them. He had not forsaken them. And He hasn't left or forsaken you—and He never will.

When Your plan is hard to see, Lord Jesus,
please show me how You walk with me. Thank
You for never leaving me nor forsaking me.

CALLED AND COMPELLED

---

*You are my rock and my fortress, for the sake
of your name lead and guide me.*

PSALM 31:3

That tightness in your heart. That urge in your soul. When you feel it, you know it: you are drawn, called, and compelled to act on your concern for someone. But how do you know if it's really God calling you?

Personally, when I first was drawn to posters of missing women and children, I wasn't sure about the sudden urge I felt to act on behalf of trafficked women. But as time went on, it became clear that God was interrupting me.

What does God keep bringing to your attention? Stop and recognize His leading. There's no formula for confirming that such a leading is God's voice you're hearing. But if there is a need before you that you can easily do something about, then by all means do it! If the interruption is more significant—one that is potentially life-altering for you—then seek the counsel of your pastor, a spiritual leader, or a trusted friend.

Today, I'm so thankful God added an assignment to my life—a calling. And I believe He wants to do the same with you. All He asks is that you allow yourself to be interrupted—and then He will expand your capacity to accomplish His assignments.

Jesus, thank You for putting Your Spirit in me to lead me. I will keep my heart attuned to You, so I can recognize Your call.

THE BIG PICTURE

Our light and momentary troubles are achieving for
us an eternal glory that far outweighs them all.

2 CORINTHIANS 4:17

Whatever challenge you're facing in life, it probably doesn't seem very "light" and "momentary" to you. Minimizing those troubles or adopting an "it could be worse" attitude likely won't help long-term. The only way to put things in perspective is to reflect on how unthinkably *big* and *great* your God is.

Develop the habit of looking at your problems against the backdrop of eternity—and an eternity of joy, at that. Remember that God is bigger than any opposition, disease, crisis, question, struggle, frustration, hurt, or offense the world and the Devil may send your way. The last time I checked, the Devil was small enough to fit under my feet, and God is big enough to fill the heavens and earth. So wisely look toward the eternal glory of the one you love and trust.

From day-to-day troubles to life-changing issues, all of them—the apostle Paul wrote—are "light and momentary troubles" compared to the eternity of joy God has for us.

Even as you address everyday but essential life stuff, as well as those critical decision points, keep an eye on God's goodness, faithfulness, and eternal glory. He is powerful to overcome any trouble you face.

Lord, I reset my focus on things eternal, on Your
great glory, goodness, and faithfulness. I keep my
perspective balanced on how big You are.

NOT BAD PEOPLE

"A priest happened to be going down the same road, and when he saw the man, he passed by on the other side. So too, a Levite, when he came to the place and saw him, passed by on the other side."

LUKE 10:31–32

Read today's passage again. Nowhere does Jesus say that the priest and the Levite were bad people. But we know from the way Jesus referred to them—*priest* and *Levite*—that they were busy people and religious people. They were focused on staying on schedule, keeping their appointments, and obeying God's commandments. They were so focused that they ended up walking past someone they should have helped.

Busy. Religious. Not bad. But let's ask ourselves the tough question: *When have I been so focused on the people I've chosen to help that I've walked past other hurting people who God put right in my path to help?*

Let's start today being free from the kind of busyness that is really rooted in fear—fear of falling behind or falling short, fear of damaging our reputations, or of letting others down. And let's quit being busy or religious. Let's look past our busyness and seek His heart for people. Then, we can minister as He would minister, out of the overflow of love in our hearts.

Holy Spirit, please give me eyes to see the people around me the way Jesus does, and I'll minister to them the way You would, with love and compassion.

MESSY, BUT FREE

The Lord is the Spirit, and where the Spirit
of the Lord is, there is freedom.

2 CORINTHIANS 3:17

In my early adult years, my life was messy as long as I could remember, and my journey today is still messy at times.

But God Himself called me *daughter* while I was still a mess. God made me feel loved, wanted, and cherished—something I never had experienced before. His calling me *daughter* lifted the shame of abandonment, adoption, and abuse—the shame of being the daughter who never met my parents' expectations for a Greek girl.

Once the shame was lifted, I discovered I had the power to choose to replace my identity as "victim of the past" with my new identity as "daughter of the King." Jesus sets you—and me—free from shame, but then we have to choose to stand up and walk out of our open prison cell, drop off our unlocked chains, and step into the future shame-free.

Of course, this is always much easier said than done, because being set free and walking in freedom are not at all the same thing. Jesus set you free, but you yourself must choose to walk in freedom, relying on His strength, His grace, and His Spirit. Ask Him how to take your steps today.

*Lord, thank You for helping me to be courageous
as I walk into the unknown. I'm privileged to
be Your daughter, even in my mess.*

WIDE-AWAKE

He said to them, "Go into all the world and
preach the gospel to all creation."

MARK 16:15

When Jesus said to go into all the world (Matthew 28:19), He didn't mean to wait until morning, or until you find a spouse, or have raised the kids, or put your house in order, or find a spare weekend. Christ wants us to go into all the world *now*—in whatever way we can. He longs to shake us awake so we will shout out the truth—that human beings are made for eternity and what they decide about Jesus determines where they will spend it.

There are people all around us—at work, in our community, at the businesses we frequent—who are crying out for help, and we have the answer.

Let's renew our commitment today to share the good news of Jesus Christ with the people in our daily path. Let's show them the love and hope of a life in Christ. We know what it is to be lost and then found, hurting and then healed, so we can be passionate and compassionate witnesses to people still lost and hurting. Not tomorrow or when we have life figured out. But today!

*Holy Spirit, show me opportunities to reach the world
one soul at a time. Thank You for giving me boldness
to share what You've given me, wherever I am.*

THE GOD WHO IS FOUND

"Call on me and come and pray to me, and I will listen
to you. You will seek me and find me when you seek
me with all your heart. I will be found by you."

JEREMIAH 29:12-14

I meet Christians all over the world, most weeks of the year, and I learn about so many issues common to all of us. For example, I've learned that a large majority of Christ-followers feel dissatisfied with their spiritual condition—something that can be good if it pushes us to seek more of our loving God. I've also learned other universal insights like:

- New believers are eager to learn more but aren't sure how to get started.
- Some believers are weary because of their busy lives or burned out after lots of hard work that didn't seem to make a difference.
- Others have lost interest in attending a church that they see as irrelevant.
- Most long to know God's power and His presence to a greater degree.
- Many others believe they aren't qualified or gifted enough for God to use them in big ways.

If you feel that something is missing in your spiritual life but it's not on this list, take a few minutes to articulate the problem. Whatever might be dissatisfying to you, God tells you, "Call on Me and come and pray to Me." When we do, He promises, "I will be found by you."

Thank You for this hunger that I'm feeling for You, Lord Jesus.
Please show me where to find You, and lead me as I seek You.

NEW LIFE

Let perseverance finish its work so that you
may be mature and complete.

JAMES 1:4

Healing takes time, and it's easy to get discouraged. Let me share some wisdom I've learned along the way to encourage you.

First, with every step forward I take with God, I discover that His love is deeper than I knew, His forgiveness is more complete than I'd dared to hope, and His grace is richer than I'd ever imagined.

Second, real healing takes time. God revealed to me that I had only put a Band-Aid over some of the wounds from my past: they were not yet healed. But—and maybe this is you too—I had learned to live with the pain, so I didn't realize I was limping. Until I got around some people who were running and God opened my eyes.

Third, sometimes enlisting the help of a counselor is a very wise step. It was for me. I learned that I couldn't write or talk about being healed of shame unless I was willing to stay accountable to the healing process and practice the very principles I was sharing. And let me tell you—sometimes in that process, you need help.

So persevere in healing. God is working out new life in you (Isaiah 43:19).

Thank You, Lord, for the wisdom I can gain from
Your people and Your Word. Please show me
how to accept their help and Your healing.

LOVING YOURSELF

But you, Lord, are a compassionate and gracious God,
slow to anger, abounding in love and faithfulness.

PSALM 86:15

We all know that Jesus wants us to love our neighbors as we love ourselves; it's the second greatest commandment, after all. But how much do you really love yourself?

Do you talk nicely to yourself? I think our self-talk can be very revealing.
Do you take care of yourself?
Do you feed yourself spiritually and physically?
Do you value who you are and what you contribute to those around you?
Are you confident or insecure?

Self-love comes from knowing God-love—an unconditional, freeing love that is offered to us without cost. We can get down on ourselves sometimes because we think we must earn God's love by trying to make ourselves more like Jesus, by behaving well, by doing and saying the right things. But friend, that love is already yours. Christ died to give it to you (John 3:16). He wants you to receive it so you can actually value, respect, and love yourself.

Since it is impossible to offer what you do not have, open yourself to receive God's love so you'll have love to give away. The natural outflow will show others the revolutionary freedom of God's will to heal you and everyone else.

Lord God, please help me to wholeheartedly
embrace Your love for me. Teach me to love myself,
and free me to share Your love with others.

VALUE THE SEASON YOU'RE IN

The revelation awaits an appointed time; it speaks of the end and will not prove false. Though it linger, wait for it; it will certainly come and will not delay.

HABAKKUK 2:3

As the seasons change, you might notice things growing or dying, getting warmer or growing colder, depending on where you live. As things get colder, it's easy to long for warmer, brighter times. Yet if the earth skipped any of the seasons, growth would be limited. So it is for the season of your life right now.

If you're in a season of waiting, of what feels like the fall or winter, and you wish you were in a different time, know that God has more for you to learn.

Maybe it's a lesson in relationships, money management, or cleanliness. For example, if you want an office with a view, then try keeping your current work space tidy. Regardless of your season, allow it to prepare you for the birth of your next season—the one filled with your dreams and God-given purpose. As you continue waiting:

- Recognize and reflect on how far this present season has brought you.
- Ask the question: Is there more to learn here?
- Appreciate the opportunities this season has given you.

And then, keep waiting, trusting that God will bring growth in all your seasons.

Lord, please open my eyes to what You are doing in and around me. I embrace Your teaching and leading in this season.

"WHAT CAN I DO?"

"I am the Lord, the God of all mankind.
Is anything too hard for me?"

JEREMIAH 32:27

Kalli, a forty-one-year-old homemaker and mother of two, assumed it was impossible for God to use her to save lives. God had stirred her heart during one of our A21 Campaign events when she heard about the crushing, billion-dollar business of human trafficking. But she thought, *I'm just one woman. What can I do about this massive global problem?* Yet she stepped out and followed God's leading, and became a volunteer.

That was in 2008. Over the years, she went from a volunteer to a staff member working as a shelter manager, where she gave her phone number to a girl named Katja. *Impossible* for Kalli, a mom and homemaker, to make a difference? Tell that to Katja.

When her life hung in the balance, it was Kalli she called. A driver came and took her to safety. A home was provided where Katja learned to heal. An officer arrested her traffickers. A lawyer won their convictions. Today, Katja is free and home, attending a university—because "just one woman" looked past her *impossible* and took a step forward. She gave God room to allow His infinite *possible* to take over.

Nothing is too hard for Him. Take a step of faith and watch God work through your *impossible* too.

Lord, please give me the courage to step out in Your power
in the face of the impossible. Help me follow Your call!

ONLY YOU CAN BE YOU

Shall what is formed say to the one who formed
it, "Why did you make me like this?"

ROMANS 9:20

When you look around at how others have been shaped and molded, you can too easily forget that God made you perfectly fitted for His purposes. It's easy for our thoughts to be derailed into focusing on not being good enough—not being good-looking enough, happy enough, smart enough, talented enough, eloquent, artistic, creative, holy, fit, thin . . . the list could go on forever. Those thoughts talk us into being dissatisfied at God. "Why did You make me like this?" and we think our lives would be so much better if, if, if.

You are enough. More than enough. Because God made you and He delights in you (Psalm 139:13–14; Zephaniah 3:17). In fact, why waste time trying to be someone else when everyone else is already taken? Find yourself in Christ, in the Word, and discover your purpose—what He has uniquely fashioned you to do—and you will be better at being you! Ask Him to be the one who forms and shapes you more and more into His beautiful vessel. Entrust yourself to Him, and He will gladly help you be the very best *you* that you can be.

Lord, thank You for how You created me. Help me be wise
and look steadfastly at You instead of others, knowing
I am wonderfully made and deeply loved by You.

MADE TO BE YOU

When they measure themselves by themselves and compare
themselves with themselves, they are not wise.

2 CORINTHIANS 10:12

My plan seemed simple enough. Hoping for some relief from all my traveling, I had decided I would become a cookie baker extraordinaire.

To be honest, that goal was a stretch for me, but I wanted to feel normal. I wanted to be like the other moms at my daughter's school and bake treats for the fund-raiser instead of buying something on the way to school. Transitioning into a more typical *mom* life was very appealing. So I carefully followed every single one of the cookbook's instructions, but afterward all I had to show for my efforts were burned cookies and a smoky kitchen. Hardly cookie baker extraordinaire!

Later that night, I distinctly heard the Lord ask me, "Who exactly are you trying to be?" I sat down to spend some time with God so He could help me make some sense out of the last few days—which had been quite busy. He simply reminded me that He had made Christine Caine unique from every other person on this planet and that being unique is okay. In fact, our uniqueness—yours and mine—is His divine design. Sit down with Him and let Him make sense of who you are trying to be, and who you're *made* to be. And then, just be you!

Jesus, please help me learn to celebrate and enjoy
being the unique me You created me to be!

MADE FOR THIS

Do you not know that in a race all the runners run, but only
one gets the prize? Run in such a way as to get the prize.

1 CORINTHIANS 9:24

Before you were born, God chose and marked out a specific lane on the track of life for you. It's filled with your purpose and destiny. That lane has your name on it, and it's designed for your specific race—a perfect one made just for you to run.

God created you, He has positioned you in a certain place in time, and He has given you special gifts and talents for the divine purpose of serving this generation. There are certain things He wants you to achieve while you are on this side of eternity. He wants you loving people with His love. Taking a stand for His moral standards. Boldly sharing the good news of Jesus' death and resurrection for people's sins.

When you stand before God one day and reflect on your race, you will look back on what you did with the time He gave you, the talents He gave you, and the treasure He placed in your hands (Romans 14:12). So evaluate how you're running your race. Make any adjustments necessary, and stay close to Him. Run your race well, because you were made for this!

Gracious Lord, please help me honor You with my life
every day. Guide me in my decisions so I can accept
the good things You have picked out for me.

PARTNERING WITH GOD

Great and marvelous are your deeds, Lord God Almighty.
Just and true are your ways, King of the nations.

REVELATION 15:3

If God wanted to, He could accomplish everything He wanted completed in a display of awesome power. After all, He created the heavens and the earth that way. But today, He chooses to use us to accomplish His new and exciting works with Him.

In the Bible story of God parting the Red Sea so the children of Israel could cross over, God could have slain Pharaoh's army and melted the chariots before they got close enough to His people. But He used Moses instead to stretch out his staff and raise his hands for a miracle and to bring Him glory (Exodus 14).

In the Bible story of Peter walking on water, God could have turned the wild waves beneath Peter's feet into solid rock, but instead He used a miracle to teach us about walking by faith (Matthew 14:22–33).

God's goal in each of those miracles was greater than merely accomplishing a task. He invited people to partner with Him in order to show them His power. He wants His people to see His command over the physical world, recognize the reality of the divine, and worship Him, so we can be transformed by His presence. He lets us partner with Him, so we can know Him more fully, see His amazing works, and say with our ancestors, "Sing for joy to God our strength" (Psalm 81:1).

I am so grateful that You choose to partner with us, God!
Thank You for letting us bear witness to Your glory!

A BETTER PERSPECTIVE

Our citizenship is in heaven.

PHILIPPIANS 3:20

When I travel internationally, I am always interested in learning how citizens of other countries view current world events. The different perspectives never fail to broaden my thinking. I am always glad I considered another point of view.

Similarly, all of us can choose to view every situation in life from one of two very different perspectives: as a citizen of heaven, or as a citizen of this world. The heavenly perspective focuses on the unseen realities of God's presence, power, and sovereignty. The worldly perspective focuses on the seen and the tangible, making possibilities—and hope—limited. God wants us to relinquish our worldly perspective and refocus with a heavenly one.

Changing our perspective isn't always easy. It takes practice to change your default mind-set. But we can start by spending time in God's Word every day. Meditate on the truth it contains rather than on your current circumstances. Immerse your mind and memorize verses so you can quickly recall His truths during difficult moments and challenging seasons.

Jesus has freed you, has given you His Holy Spirit, and offers all the wisdom of Scripture to keep you grounded in the perspective of your eternal home.

Thank You, Lord God, for the truth and the hope I find in Your Word and for its heavenly perspective of my earthly life.

DETERMINING GOD'S PERFECT WILL

Then you will be able to test and approve what God's
will is—his good, pleasing and perfect will.

ROMANS 12:2

In today's scripture, Paul promises that we will be able to test and confirm the "good, pleasing and perfect will" of our God. If you're like me, you're saying, "I'll take it! Of course I want to know the will of God! After all, isn't doing His will the reason we are on this planet?"

Before Paul makes this promise, though, he directs us to live our lives for God and be transformed by the renewing of our minds (vv. 1–2). When your thoughts are fueled by God's Word, they inevitably become governed by His truth. That is how you become internally transformed, healed, and guided.

If you were wondering how to live like a citizen of heaven while you are on this earth, that transformation is the key. It will have an immeasurable effect on your words, actions, and responses to what comes your way. You will find yourself looking at situations from a heavenly perspective and reacting accordingly. Even lovelier, you'll find yourself looking at people with God's gracious and compassionate eyes. It's amazing what a godly, Spirit-guided response can do for a seemingly hopeless situation or relationship.

Let the wisdom in God's Word transform your heart and mind, and you'll find yourself growing closer to His loving will.

Lord Jesus, I want to know Your will and live in
it. Please renew my mind with Your Word!

YOUR SPECIAL ASSIGNMENT

For he chose us in him before the creation of the
world to be holy and blameless in his sight.

EPHESIANS 1:4

No matter how little you may think you have to offer, *you* have special gifts and an assignment for God's kingdom. He wants to use you for something wonderful.

When Josiah was eight years old, he became king of Israel—and he reigned thirty-one years (2 Kings 22:1). He had a special assignment foretold hundreds of years before his birth (1 Kings 13:2). That assignment was to rid Israel of idolatry and to renew his people's covenant with God. The Bible says that Josiah did what was right in the sight of the Lord and walked in the ways of David (2 Kings 22:2). Josiah fulfilled his purpose, and he was pivotal in restoring the house of God, as well as respect for His Word and opportunities to worship the one true God.

God has made each of us just as purposeful. He wants us to do for our generation what Josiah did for his: use our gifts for His glory and to build His kingdom. It's wise to discover God's specific purpose for your life by seeking Him, reading His Word, and searching your heart for the gifts and passions He has placed there. Remember: He chose you before the foundation of the world (Ephesians 1:4), and He will equip you.

Creator God, please show me what You designed me to do for Your kingdom. I want to fulfill Your special assignment for me.

OPEN EARS

"My sheep listen to my voice; I know them, and they follow me."

JOHN 10:27

Google. Wiki. E-books. Print books and papers. Facebook. Podcasts. YouTube. The billions and billions of pages on the Internet. Our world will make more information available in the next decade than has been discovered in all human history. If we were to start reading, watching, and listening right now and continue for 24 hours a day, 365 days a year, we would never catch up with everything being produced.

We live in a very noisy world—full of external voices. Who knows how many voices—helpful or not—we have in our heads? With all these voices (and pardon the graphic illustration), be sure you are regularly removing the wax from your spiritual ears, so you can accurately hear God's voice.

How do we do this? The book of Proverbs gives us some wisdom: "If you accept my words and store up my commands within you, turning your ear to wisdom and applying your heart to understanding—indeed, if you . . . search for it as for hidden treasure, then you will understand the fear of the LORD and find the knowledge of God" (2:1–5). Make His voice the loudest in your head today!

Jesus, my Good Shepherd, I long to hear Your voice.
Please help me seek—and never miss—Your divine
wisdom like treasure, so I can be close to You.

A TRUE FRIEND

At that time Mary got ready and hurried to a town in
the hill country of Judea, where she entered Zechariah's
home and greeted [her relative] Elizabeth.

LUKE 1:39–40

When Mary heard God's promise that she would give birth to the Messiah, she wisely went to be with a friend—one who would speak life, hope, faith, and blessing over her and her child. She stayed with her cousin Elizabeth for three months. There Mary was protected, provided for, and loved as our promised Savior grew in her womb.

When God gives us a promise, it normally begins in seed form just as the baby Jesus did—and what we do with that seed is crucial. As we plant it in nutritious soil and water it daily with faith, we also rely on the people with whom we share those dreams and promises. Wisely chosen friends can offer us support that's invaluable to the unfolding of our dreams.

Just like Mary ran to Elizabeth, surround yourself with people of faith and prayer, people who believe in you, who will encourage you, and who are committed to helping you run your race well. Whether through church, from your family, or by some other blessed connection, ask God to fill your life with true friends, for His glory.

Lord, please bless me with true friends—and help
me be the kind of friend who supports, prays,
encourages, and loves with Your love.

RUNNING FREE

I consider my life worth nothing to me; my only aim is to finish
the race and complete the task the Lord Jesus has given me—
the task of testifying to the good news of God's grace.

ACTS 20:24

Many times, the apostle Paul referred to life as a race. The author of the letter to the Hebrews did as well, calling believers to lay aside "every weight" and "the sin which so easily ensnares" (Hebrews 12:1 NKJV). These weights—whether they are sin or other obstacles—keep us from running our race well.

The weight might, for instance, be the fact that you consistently hang out with the wrong people. Or maybe you have reached a plateau in your Christian life and don't know how to get unstuck. Reluctance to accept any faith-stretching challenge may be weighing you down, keeping you from growing in your faith.

You don't need to be carrying extra weight. Make it a practice to regularly look at your life, see where you can shed weight, and cast off anything that is slowing you down.

*Lord God, please help me to let go of each weight I'm
carrying, and show me how to run a race that will honor You.*

DAUGHTERS OF GOD

"See, I have engraved you on the palms of my hands."

ISAIAH 49:16

When I watch my husband, Nick, interact with our daughters, I am often moved to tears by his tenderness, love, delight, generosity, protection, and provision. Nick is not at all a detached father; he is not aloof, distant, or rigid with our girls. Rather, because he loves them, he is involved in every aspect of their lives.

The most wonderful aspect of Nick's love for the girls is that it's *unconditional*. He does not expect the girls to do anything to earn his affection. He is head-over-heels in love with them for who they are. His devotion to them bursts from his loving heart—and that is *exactly* how God the Father loves us! It's such a blessing for me to see in my husband's love for our daughters a reflection of God's love for us—His beloved daughters.

He has your name engraved on His hand, and He wants to be part of every aspect of your life. In light of that great love, know that you can enter boldly into God's throne room of grace, full of joy and expectation. No matter what your earthly father was like, you can dare to open up to receive the head-over-heels love of your heavenly Father today!

God, You are my loving Father. Thank You for loving me unconditionally, for caring about every aspect of my life.

REACHING FOR THE FUTURE

Always be zealous for the fear of the LORD. There is surely a
future hope for you, and your hope will not be cut off.

PROVERBS 23:17–18

Every one of us has a yesterday, a past. For some of us, it's filled with wonderful memories. For some of us, maybe nondescript events. But if your past is like mine, it's filled with pain. And God wants all of us to let go of our past and walk into our future with Him.

The apostle Paul taught us a powerful truth when he wrote that he forgot what was behind and strained for what was ahead, for what God had for him (Philippians 3:13–14). Paul was determined to let go of everything that was in his yesterday (good, bad, nondescript) so that he could freely reach forward into his tomorrow. He understood that where we are going is much more important than where we have been.

Today, take steps to courageously and intentionally let go of your past. Better than erasing your past, denying it, outrunning it, or escaping it, choose to deal with it so it no longer defines your future. That means facing it and forgiving others. It's taking ownership and embracing all the seasons of it—whether good or bad—so God can use it for a good future. I'm so thankful for what He's done with mine.

*Lord God, please give me guidance for dealing
with the past so I am free to enjoy the present
and embrace the future You have for me.*

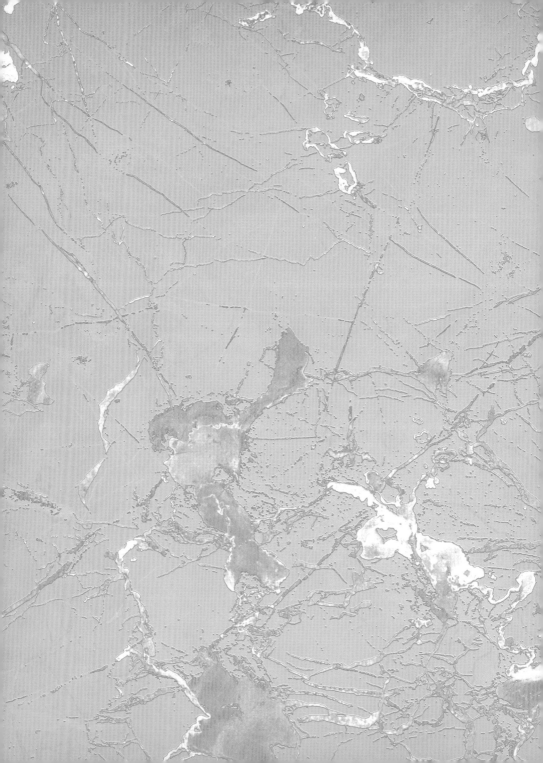

JULY

Above all else, guard your heart,
for everything you do flows from it.

PROVERBS 4:23

CHANGE YOUR FUTURE FOR GOOD

"I know the plans I have for you," declares the
LORD, "plans to prosper you and not to harm you,
plans to give you hope and a future."

JEREMIAH 29:11

Today's verse is one of the most comforting, life-giving, and truth-telling in the Bible. It gives you so much hope for your tomorrows—and courage for dealing with your yesterdays.

When you choose to deal with the wounds and the pain of past rejection, hurt, betrayal, offenses, abandonment, abuse, mistakes, regret, and failures, you take away the power they wield in your heart, your mind, and your life. You acknowledge God's good and hopeful plans for your future. Free of the blame game, you can bravely embrace the pain of the recovery process so you can move on.

So when you find yourself thinking about, talking about, and listening to conversations about a negative "back there," instead remember God's promises and change your thoughts and words. Speak about all the good things that God has for you today and in your future. After all, His plans for you are for good and not for evil; they are plans to prosper you, not to harm you.

You cannot change the past, but as you deal with it and move on with God's help, you can change the future.

Lord, I accept Your good promises for me. Thank
You for giving me the bravery to accept healing
and to walk into the future You have for me.

STRENGTHENED AND EMPOWERED

I pray that out of his glorious riches [the Father] may
strengthen you with power through his Spirit in your inner
being, so that Christ may dwell in your hearts through faith.

EPHESIANS 3:16–17

God is transforming you into the image of Christ. He's making you more Christlike. He's even more committed to the process than you are—and that's okay. All God wants you to do is to keep showing up. To be ready and willing for Him to use you in the world.

When Christ dwells in you, you are taken out of yourself and beyond your very real limitations. When asked to give of yourself to others, you may think, *I don't have enough to give, I don't know what to do*, or *I'm not qualified for this*. That may be true for you, but definitely not for God. All you need to do is just show up and be faithful. And as you follow His lead, you'll be transformed, and you'll witness His unstoppable power.

He will continue to make you more like Jesus as He expands your impact on your world. Embrace this mystery of Christ in you, and you'll find yourself choosing to love the lost, the hurting, and the forgotten with your words and actions. You'll find yourself being used by God to transform the world around you.

God, help me "to grasp how wide and long and high and deep
is the love of Christ" (v. 18). Thank You for empowering me!

FAITH FOR TODAY AND TOMORROW

"Do not worry about tomorrow, for tomorrow will worry
about itself. Each day has enough trouble of its own."

MATTHEW 6:34

A quick glance at the headlines can make me wonder how people go through life without the Lord. Without Him in my life, I'd be overcome by worry. Maybe that's the positive side of daily trouble: these things can get us relying on God and walking in faith again.

We will always need Him as we face troubles like injustice, hurting people, shattered relationships, disease, and natural disasters.

We will always need God's wise guidance as well as His protection.

We will always benefit from the Lord's wisdom for nurturing our marriages and raising our children.

We will always be required to step out into the unknown.

We will always need boldness to stand for our faith among family members, friends, neighbors, and coworkers who need Jesus.

Each day has plenty of troubles, and each one is an opportunity to turn to the Lord, to choose faith in the day-to-day, and to call out for His guidance. As you do, He will lovingly come near to you and give you direction and peace in your worries (John 14:27).

*Lord, I turn back to 24/7 dependence on and communication
with You. Thank You for guiding and loving me
through today's troubles and tomorrow's worries.*

GIFTS WELL USED

If your gift is prophesying, then prophesy in accordance
with your faith; if it is serving, then serve; if it is teaching,
then teach; if it is to encourage, then give encouragement;
if it is giving, then give generously; if it is to lead, do it
diligently; if it is to show mercy, do it cheerfully.

ROMANS 12:6-8

What is your spiritual gift? The list you just read is just the beginning; for instance, you might have gifts of encouragement, hospitality, and administration. Whatever your giftedness, life becomes richer as you invest in others by coming alongside and serving them.

Life becomes more exciting when you start to see how your giftedness and calling fit perfectly within the Lord's strategy for reaching the lost, telling the gospel, and sharing His love. When you use your gifts, you are playing your role in God's plan to impact the world around us.

If you step up and run your race, exercising your gifts, who could hear about Jesus who otherwise might not? Who might receive freedom from being hungry—or enslaved, impoverished, or hopeless? And who could be transformed by God's healing touch and redemptive power?

When you have identified and readied your gifts, ask God to guide you and use you wherever He needs you. He will empower you (1 Corinthians 12:11).

Lord God, help me discover and use the good gifts You've given me. It is my joy to live in Your plans and power!

BY DESIGN

God said, "Let there be lights in the vault of the sky to separate the day from the night, and let them serve as signs to mark sacred times, and days and years."

GENESIS 1:14

Have you ever stopped to think, *Why am I doing everything I'm doing? Is this really God's will for my life, or is it just what I think I'm supposed to do?*

Questions like these can wake us up. They can shake us out of living by default instead of according to God's design. The symptoms of a life lived by default are mechanically going through our days, probably feeling unsatisfied and unmotivated, and doing what everyone else is doing. God has planned so much more for us.

Time is sacred. Let's throw off the default life and learn to spend it wisely and well. Let's prayerfully take an inventory of where our time goes and how that aligns with God's plans. We always have the one true God to guide us—the one who lovingly formed us and numbered our days (Psalm 139:15–16).

Lord, please help me to be a good steward of the days You bless me with. I want to live joyfully in the sacred time You've appointed for me.

TASTING GOD'S GOODNESS

Taste and see that the LORD is good; blessed
is the one who takes refuge in him.

PSALM 34:8

Confront your fears today. I know it can feel risky, but I promise you that God is with you. Let these verses cause faith and trust to rise up in you:

- He promises to be your light in the darkness and your strength (Psalm 21:1; 27:1).
- He reminds you not to be dismayed, because He will help you and hold you (Isaiah 41:10).
- He tells you to be of good courage because He will never leave you nor forsake you (Deuteronomy 31:6).
- He exhorts you to be strong and courageous (Joshua 1:6).
- And He delivers you from your troubles and doubts and fears so that you may taste and see His goodness (Psalm 34).

When you look bravely at your fears, you are poised for God to free you from any fear that constrains you. When He does, your world becomes bigger. Your life opens wide to the possibilities and even the miracles that He has for you. And your heart is more open to serving God—in His power and by His grace—despite any risk involved. Taste and see that He is good. Know that you are blessed as you take refuge in Him.

Lord, I choose to be strong and courageous. I exchange
my fears for faith in Your goodness. I take refuge in You.

CREATED IN THE IMAGE OF GOD

I praise you because I am fearfully and wonderfully made;
your works are wonderful, I know that full well.

PSALM 139:14

So many of us identify ourselves by what we do for a living. "I *am* a teacher. I *am* a doctor. I *am* a caregiver." Even if we're proud of all those good things we do, God reminds us that *who* we are is so much more than what we do—good or bad. We are made in His image, and that is as good as it gets.

We also *do* things we're not proud of. Adam and Eve disobeyed God ("I *did* a bad thing") and felt shame ("I *am* bad"). They set a pattern none of us are immune to. The apostle Paul said it plainly: *"All have sinned and fall short of the glory of God"* (Romans 3:23). We *all* do—and say and think—things that fail to honor God and others. But here's where God wants to remind us of *who* we are.

Scripture doesn't give us a message of shame, even if like Adam and Eve we fall tragically short. Instead, the Bible says that you are *"fearfully and wonderfully made."* That you are created in the image of God (Genesis 1:27).

Nothing we can do will change our value or our worth in His eyes.

Lord, may I find my value in Your love for me—a
love You offer despite my shortcomings. I am
so grateful to be made in Your image.

THE STRENGTH TO DO WHAT IS RIGHT

"Have you eaten from the tree that I
commanded you not to eat from?"

GENESIS 3:11

"Did you eat that last cookie?" "Did you take your sister's toy?" A little child might say, "No, not me," even as she wipes the crumbs from her face, or as he hides the toy behind his little back. That behavior is expected of such a small one—and many parents make these into teaching moments. But as we grow older, we learn to take responsibility and own up to our actions. It's a mark of maturity to rely on honesty rather than denial, on reality rather than blame. And it's a mark of God's grace.

Adam and Eve took the kids' way out in Genesis, blaming and denying. But God, like a loving parent, knew what had happened and used it as a teaching moment—the first and most crucial one in history. From Adam and Eve we learn what guilt should do for us. It serves as a signal that we need to turn away from our out-of-line behavior and return to the Father who loves us.

So when you get that hand-in-the-cookie-jar feeling, remember to take responsibility for your actions before God. It's not easy to confess, but it's the first step in accepting God's miraculous forgiveness.

Lord, please grow me in honesty and maturity.
Give me courage to do what is right and to take
responsibility so I can know Your forgiveness.

NUMBER YOUR DAYS

Teach us to number our days, that we may gain a heart of wisdom.

PSALM 90:12

Our days are ordered differently, but I'm guessing we both have routines. We probably eat breakfast, lunch, and dinner. We may conquer laundry, grocery shopping, and vacuuming. Orchestrate homework, dance, and sports. Get everyone to church, youth group, or Bible study. These are good things, necessary things. And routines can be so helpful. But when they become a rut, we may need to evaluate how we're spending our time.

Today is truly one of a kind. It won't be repeated. Our days are numbered, ordered by God. And we have a specific purpose we are called to embrace and fulfill in those numbered and ordered days.

Before you were born, God had a plan for your life, an assignment that matches your gifts and your heart (Psalm 139:16). This unique role you have in the body of Christ may take courage and strength you don't have right now, but that's by design. God wants us to work *with* Him even as we work *for* Him, and He will carry us through our days.

"Teach us to number our days." What a beautiful way of saying . . .

Teach us to see our days as You do, Lord, and to use them wisely to fulfill all the purpose You placed inside of us!

EMBRACE YOUR PLACE

You have searched me, Lord, and you know me.

PSALM 139:1

In the race we're called to run, God never throws away a runner. He never disqualifies us from the race for any reason. There aren't even any insignificant lanes, unimportant legs, or second-rate positions. Every runner is important, as is every lane, every leg, and every position we find ourselves in as we run our race.

God not only has a specific place for you, but He also has perfect timing when it comes to moving you along your track. He has searched you and He knows you—and He's growing you in this leg of the race. May that hope keep you running today when you're tempted to leave the race or simply stand on the sidelines for a while. Resist those feelings of inferiority that might disconnect you from the purposes God has in mind for you, or that could distance you from Him. Follow close to Him, and you'll never go too fast or too slowly.

Boldly embrace your place. It is important and significant. God's plans are good, and He is glorified when you trust that His purposes for you are guided by His will and His timing.

Thank You, Lord, for knowing me and placing me at this point in my race. Help me follow You wherever I need to be.

GOD'S CHOICE FOR KING

The Lord said to Samuel, "Do not consider his appearance
or his height, for I have rejected him. The Lord does not
look at the things people look at. People look at the
outward appearance, but the Lord looks at the heart."

1 SAMUEL 16:7

God sent His prophet Samuel to the family of Jesse to anoint the king who would succeed Saul. And the Lord's choice absolutely defied our human logic. Samuel looked at Eliab, Jesse's firstborn son, saw his impressive appearance and size, and assumed Eliab must be God's choice. God said no, so Samuel considered the next son, and then the next, and the one after that, until finally he asked Jesse, "Are these all the sons you have?" (v. 11). That is when Jesse called his youngest—David—in from the fields where he was tending the family's sheep.

From a human point of view, this last-born son was the least qualified for the throne. But the Lord said to Samuel, "Rise and anoint him; this is the one" (v. 12).

What has God called you to do? Whatever it is, no matter your age or stage in life, you are full of potential and great purpose. The Lord looks at your heart, just as He looked at David's. And He has equipped you with every good thing for doing His will (Hebrews 13:21).

*Lord, thank You for looking at my heart. Help
me know and embrace Your calling for me!*

DIVINE DELAYS

Not only so, but we also glory in our sufferings, because
we know that suffering produces perseverance;
perseverance, character; and character, hope.

ROMANS 5:3-4

For the past several years, I have flown several times a week, most of the year. And I would love to say every flight is an easy trip. But you and I both know—especially if you fly a lot too—that your schedule is subject to all kinds of potential interference. Whether it's long lines going through security, weather delays, chasing down lost luggage, waiting on maintenance to repair a plane, or the flight crew arriving late, anything can happen.

Through all the unexpected delays I've experienced—including spending the night on the floor of an airport—I've learned patience and perseverance. Neither of these qualities is my strong point, but God is always faithful to use our circumstances to strengthen the areas where we are weak. He is so faithful to use whatever is at hand to grow us, to keep us on course, and to get us to our destiny. And if we get off course, He's faithful to help us make an adjustment and get headed in the right direction again.

As you walk through today, let any divine delays strengthen you. Let them challenge your thinking and mature you. Let them keep you on the right course to reach your destiny.

God, I know that You orchestrate my path, and You're
there in delays and schedule upsets. Please grow me
and stay with me as I stay flexible this season.

BLESSINGS SHARED

Suppose a brother or a sister is without clothes and daily food. If one of you says to them, "Go in peace; keep warm and well fed," but does nothing about their physical needs, what good is it?

JAMES 2:15–16

One of the most moving experiences of my life was visiting the refugee camps in recent years on the Macedonian border during the greatest move of people since World War II. Millions of people from Syria and other Middle Eastern nations were pouring into camps. As our A21 team spread the word about the dangers of human trafficking, I was so moved by what those people had been through. They'd left everything behind, and some had lost family members along the way. And here they were, dependent on others for basic necessities. Our team supplied water stations made from shipping containers. A place to shower, wash, and get a drink.

What do you need today? I hope you are blessed beyond measure—and willing to share with others. If you're not, I know God sees you and He cares about you. Just like He cared about all those refugees.

Jesus has sent us into the world to be His hands and feet to people everywhere. He expects us to give to others because when good people—when Christ-followers—do nothing, injustice thrives.

Lord, please show me how to become a channel of Your grace in this world of need. Show me where I can demonstrate Your love and justice.

RUNAWAY TRAIN

Whatever is true, whatever is noble, whatever is right, whatever
is pure, whatever is lovely, whatever is admirable—if anything
is excellent or praiseworthy—think about such things.

PHILIPPIANS 4:8

It happens to all of us. We suddenly realize what we're thinking and wonder, *Wait, how did I work myself into such a state?* Maybe you're angry again. Frustrated, lonely, disillusioned, heartbroken, anxious, fearful, defeated. You hopped on a train of thought and it took you to a place you don't want to be. Well, I have some good news: you can hop right off that train and catch a different one.

That's right. Our thoughts, like a train, take us somewhere. And sometimes it's a bullet train to a dark place. But we have the power to manage our thoughts. We have a choice about whether or not to follow the train of thought we're on, or change trains so we don't end up where we do not want to be. Thank God, there's a way to change trains and jump tracks!

Over the years, I've learned to renew my mind to what God's Word says so I don't just think the thoughts that pop into my head. I've learned to think about what is true, noble, right, pure, lovely, admirable, excellent, and praiseworthy. Thoughts that can bring healing and peace and keep me on a better track.

Lord, as I renew my mind with Your Word, I
choose new thoughts that reflect Your truth.

GO TO THEM

"But a Samaritan, as he traveled, came where the man was;
and when he saw him, he took pity on him. He went to him."

LUKE 10:33–34

Maybe you've experienced this situation: You're looking at a very familiar passage of Scripture and you see something you had never noticed before—something that speaks directly to what you're dealing with right now. That happened to me once when I was reading Jesus' story of the good Samaritan.

The story begins, "A certain man went down from Jerusalem to Jericho, and fell among thieves, who stripped him of his clothing, wounded him, and departed, leaving him half dead" (v. 30 NKJV).

That's when it struck me: How many people today are in situations just like this man's? Hurt and wounded in different ways, people are lying on the side of the road for so many different reasons—abuse, addictions, imprisonments, loss, famine, disease, people broken by injustice, and people stripped of their dignity, identity, and self-worth.

Then I read: *He went to him.* I read the entire story again, slowly . . . and scales fell from my eyes.

I had always thought of myself as the good Samaritan. Now God was asking me if I would really *go to* the wounded, leaving behind my fear of the heaviness of their situations. He invites you, too, on a journey toward going, giving, and loving, free from fear and full of compassion.

Thank You, Lord, for Your Word that speaks to me
and Your Spirit who transforms my heart.

REST UP

God blessed the seventh day and made it holy, because on it
he rested from all the work of creating that he had done.

GENESIS 2:3

When you are weary in body, mind, or soul, you *must* have rest. God specifically gives you rest time to recharge and reinvigorate yourself—He even made a sabbath rest His loving command.

Weariness can steal your passion and leave you depleted and ineffective—so you must actively take care of yourself. Take a short rest inventory: Are you getting the sleep you need? Are you taking a sabbath? Are you being drained by entertainment or are you spending too much time catching up on social media? Sometimes we're weary because we don't know how to say no. You can't do everything that everyone asks you to do. Or perhaps you are driven to control what is not yours to control. Relinquish what is not yours to carry, and rest awhile.

Rest is just as important as nourishment or exercise in keeping a healthy body and soul. Whether it's in prayer, sleep, silence, solitude, or just turning everything off and sitting with Jesus for a while, take advantage of His healing rest today. As He said to His disciples, "Come with me by yourselves to a quiet place and get some rest" (Mark 6:31).

God, thank You for making rest Your loving command.
Please show me how to recharge with You.

GOD'S HEALING JUSTICE

Do not take revenge, my dear friends, but leave
room for God's wrath, for it is written: "It is mine
to avenge; I will repay," says the Lord.

ROMANS 12:19

Forgiveness is a gift God gives us to free us. It's a powerful tool to free our own hearts.

For years I thought that forgiving meant I was letting my abusers off the hook or approving of their actions. But my refusal to forgive them was only hurting me. My failure to forgive wasn't affecting them at all! That's why the old saying goes that failing to forgive is like ingesting poison and expecting the other person to die.

Unforgiveness harms only you, and the damage can be considerable. Unforgiveness can affect you emotionally, psychologically, physically, and even spiritually. It keeps you stunted, isolated and alone, and bitter. That's not the way your loving Creator intended for you to live. For your own good, freedom, and healing, Jesus said, forgive the person who keeps sinning against you, even if you have to do it again and again (Matthew 18:22). God's justice is more powerful than any amount of your anger could be. Forgive, because Jesus has forgiven you. When you do, you'll experience the freedom Jesus provided for you.

*Lord, You have forgiven me of so much. Thank You.
Now I freely extend that forgiveness to others—
even those who have hurt me deeply.*

TRUST FALL

The LORD is my strength and my shield; my heart trusts in him, and
he helps me. My heart leaps for joy, and with my song I praise him.

PSALM 28:7

A "trust fall" is an exercise where you close your eyes and fall backward into the waiting arms of another person. As frightening a feeling as that is, that's exactly how much I want to trust God. I want to fall without hesitation into His arms every day—something I think we have to challenge ourselves with in every area of our lives as we walk out our freedom.

Do you, for instance, trust God enough to believe that He is at work in your present relationships? To persevere under the pressure of your responsibilities? To remain faithful and patient in this season, no matter what you are dealing with? Risking trust in every one of these scenarios is what falling into His arms really looks like:

"Yes, Lord, I will fight for the survival of my difficult marriage."

"Yes, I will remain honest through this bad financial situation."

"Yes, I will offer forgiveness in an attempt to repair this broken friendship."

Trust your heart to God. Fall back into His arms and feel the solid embrace of your Strength and Shield.

*Lord, thank You that You are at work according
to Your perfect timing. I trust in You more
today, my Strength and Shield.*

BETTER THAN "BUT"

Moses said to the Lord, "Pardon your servant, Lord. I have
never been eloquent, neither in the past nor since you have
spoken to your servant. I am slow of speech and tongue."

EXODUS 4:10

Read that verse again. Can you believe that Moses, a great father of our faith, started out this way? Three verses later he said to almighty God, "Please send someone else" to talk to Pharaoh about letting God's people leave Egypt (v. 13). But God had much bigger, better plans than Moses could have imagined.

When have you said something similar to God about what you know He's called you to do?

- "But, God, I don't know enough about the issue."
- "But, God, I'm not skilled enough to get involved."
- "But, God, I already have enough on my plate."
- "But, God, I have a family."
- "But, God, it's too dangerous."

But, God . . . Spend a few minutes with God thinking about why you might be responding this way. Ask Him to transform your heart and guide you, as He guided Moses, into the freedom that comes with embracing His plan.

> Lord, please forgive me when I answer Your call with
> a "but," and lead me onward into Your good plans.

HITTING THE WALL

I have fought the good fight, I have finished
the race, I have kept the faith.

2 TIMOTHY 4:7

My friend Kylie is a marathon runner. She has told me that, without exception, she hits "the invisible wall" (a condition of sudden fatigue and loss of energy) in every single race she runs. No matter how much she trains and even though she knows the moment is coming, hitting that wall is never any less painful than when she hit it before. Having run more than a dozen marathons, though, Kylie now knows that if she just keeps running, she will get past that wall.

Maybe you've hit the wall in your journey of faith. Suddenly—and for whatever reasons—you don't feel that you can go on. I want to encourage you to keep going with small steps. You don't always have to be charging forward at a hundred miles an hour, and you don't need to set your sights on conquering the next hill.

Instead, just take the next little step, even if it's a shuffle. Sometimes all you can do is place one foot in front of the other, and let that be okay. Let God carry you. He is already close by your side.

Thank You, Lord, that when I hit a wall, I just need
to put one foot in front of the other and be carried
by You. You have unlimited grace for me.

GOD QUALIFIES YOU

The Lord did not set his affection on you [Israel] and choose
you because you were more numerous than other peoples, for
you were the fewest of all peoples. But it was because the Lord
loved you and kept the oath he swore to your ancestors.

DEUTERONOMY 7:7–8

Those God calls, He qualifies—including you, me, and Bible heroes like Moses and Gideon. They were far from qualified when they first started out.

God chose Moses to tell Pharaoh to let His people go (Exodus 3–4). Frightened, Moses insisted that he was not eloquent and that this powerful leader wouldn't listen to him. When Moses finally did as God told him to, God was clearly with him, sending plagues, parting the Red Sea, and providing food, water, and clothing for forty years.

God referred to Gideon as a "mighty warrior" and told him to save Israel from Midian (Judges 6–8). But Gideon was hiding from the enemy, and he couldn't imagine how God could use a coward like him to fight for his people. God promised He'd be strong where Gideon was weak, and He enabled Gideon, with only 300 soldiers, to defeat the Midianite army of more than 135,000 (Judges 8:10).

God chooses the unlikely to do the unimaginable—and He always qualifies those He calls.

Lord, how amazing that You choose the unqualified—
like me—and make me strong to do the unimaginable.
Thank You for the power of Your redemptive love!

NOTHING TO LOSE

[The four men with leprosy] said to each other, "Why stay
here until we die? If we say, 'We'll go into the city'—the famine
is there, and we will die. And if we stay here, we will die. So
let's go over to the camp of the Arameans and surrender.
If they spare us, we live; if they kill us, then we die."

2 KINGS 7:3-4

I love the attitude of these guys! These four lepers had been relegated to the absolute bottom level of society because of their disease. But these lowest of the low in society's eyes—nobodies with no rights—decided to take action.

Aware they had nothing to lose, they looked at each other and said, "Why are we sitting here until we die?" What a great question!

However dire the circumstances of life become, choose the lepers' attitude: if you feel you're just sitting around waiting to die, so to speak, consider taking a course of action instead. After all, what have you got to lose?

The lepers headed into the Syrian camp, and they were amazed to discover that God had gone ahead of them and performed a miracle. Maybe if you get up from where you are sitting, perhaps focusing on your problems, and take a risk on God, He just may do something miraculous on your behalf. I believe He will.

*Lord, I refuse to sit and do nothing. I choose
to get up and step out in faith, trusting You
to perform miracles ahead of me.*

TRUSTING HER TRUSTWORTHY LORD

Mary said: "My soul glorifies the Lord and my
spirit rejoices in God my Savior."

LUKE 1:46–47

When Mary was given news of God's life-changing favor, she sang a song. That song included so many fear-fighting, faith-building elements that it certainly must have strengthened her heart for what was to come (Luke 1:46–56).

Humble and willing, Mary accepted her divine assignment with faith. She responded to the angel's message with thanksgiving and praise. In the face of any fears she might have had, she glorified God, proclaimed His goodness, and celebrated His faithfulness to her and to His people.

In her song of praise, Mary reminded herself of amazing things her trustworthy God had done for her people through the generations. She trusted that He would be every bit as faithful to her. She knew God was worthy of her trust, so she entrusted her future—her very life—to Him. And as the months unfolded, Mary kept her eyes fixed on the Author of the Promise who she carried in her womb.

What a beautiful example of how to build faith and trust in our great God. Great is His faithfulness! Great is His love for us! He *is* completely trustworthy!

Lord, thank You for Mary's example. I choose to live with joy
and hope, confident in Your great design. I love You, Lord!

THE SPIRIT'S AWESOME POWER

"The Spirit of the Lord is on me, because he has anointed
me to proclaim good news to the poor. He has sent me
to proclaim freedom for the prisoners and recovery
of sight for the blind, to set the oppressed free."

LUKE 4:18

My husband, Nick, is a whiz with computers and technology. I am a dinosaur, and that's fine with me. But when I get frustrated with some software on my laptop, he always helps me figure it out so I can accomplish so much more than my natural skills allow.

That's exactly how the Holy Spirit operates in our lives. He is our "Helper." And He enables us to reach out beyond ourselves and help others. With Him, we can accomplish unthinkably more than our skills allow. We don't possess the power of the Holy Spirit just so we can have a peaceful Christian life. That is great, but if we stop there, the Holy Spirit inside us is a little like my laptop without Nick's help—not operating up to full power.

Open up your heart and let the power of the Holy Spirit move within you to do all He's called you to do—to proclaim freedom to others in bondage, to help the blind see, and to set the oppressed free. In His hands, you'll be able to accomplish far more than you ever could on your own.

Lord, I allow Your Holy Spirit to work freely in me and through me to bring hope and truth to hurting people.

STRENGTHEN YOUR CORE

Love the Lord your God with all your heart and with all your
soul and with all your mind and with all your strength.

MARK 12:30

Jesus identified our spiritual core muscles as the heart, the soul, and the mind. These three muscles enable us to love God wholly and completely. But do we have to exercise them so we can be spiritually healthy and strong?

Let me explain it this way: A body builder wouldn't go to the gym week in and week out and focus only on building his biceps. He knows that without an exercise routine that develops his body as a whole—not just his biceps—his other muscles would develop unevenly, or even atrophy. Similarly, we should focus on strengthening and growing *all three* muscles that make up our spiritual core, or we risk growing stagnant, complacent, and lukewarm. Spiritual fitness, on the other hand, will help us deal with life's challenges and be ready to respond with a strong heart, soul, and mind.

Keeping spiritually strong is no different from keeping physically strong. We need to work out our physical core muscles regularly. We need to work out our spiritual core muscles every day. Showing love to others, praying, and studying God's Word are three ways we can do that and start today!

I want to love You, Lord, with all that I am, with my
heart, soul, and mind. I will strengthen them so I
can be spiritually healthy and serve You well.

OUR FIRST LOVE

I hold this against you: You have forsaken the love you had at first.

REVELATION 2:4

I remember when Nick and I first fell in love. He truly captured my heart. I longed to be with him as many hours of the day as possible. And we would literally—and joyfully and unselfishly—do anything for each other. And we still would!

In the same way, when we were first saved, we felt that "in love" feeling. Jesus completely captured our hearts, and we were overcome with wonder at His love, grace, and mercy. Everything we learned was fresh, and we loved spending time in His presence, reading His Word, and worshiping in His house. In every message we heard, God seemed to be speaking directly to us. We were keenly aware of His presence with us and His hand guiding us. Our earnest desire was to be with Him and become like Him.

But over time, we grew up and maybe grew familiar with His great love—in a way that makes us less responsive than we once were. I believe it's time to rekindle that first-love feeling with God and allow it to take us to the next level in our walk. God loves it when we reignite all the fire He placed in our hearts!

Jesus, I renew my commitment to You with the wonder I felt when I first met You. I never want to forget Your amazing love!

BATTLING EVIL

"Break camp and advance into the hill country of the Amorites."

DEUTERONOMY 1:7

Moving forward in our lives always takes great strength and courage. It requires us to challenge ourselves to interrupt our existing ruts—and to take risks. Whether it is stepping into a new level of leadership or a new relationship, we can't get to where we are going by staying where we are.

God in His great mercy always calls us to progress into our future so we don't overstay in the wrong place. He gives us steps and an action plan—just like He did for the children of Israel when they needed help advancing to the promised land:

"The LORD our God said to us at Horeb, 'You have stayed long enough at this mountain. Break camp and advance into the hill country of the Amorites; go to all the neighboring peoples in the Arabah, in the mountains, in the western foothills, in the Negev and along the coast, to the land of the Canaanites and to Lebanon, as far as the great river, the Euphrates'" (Deuteronomy 1:6–7).

There was a beautiful land ahead for the children of Israel filled with mountains, foothills, rivers, and a coastline—perfect for flourishing. They just had to step out in faith.

There's so much good ahead for you! So risk the next move and step into your future. Break camp.

Lord, thank You for promising to provide direction to me as I get up and go on to the next good thing You have for me.

GOD'S INTERRUPTIONS

Keep on loving one another as brothers and sisters. Do not forget to show hospitality to strangers, for by so doing some people have shown hospitality to angels without knowing it.

HEBREWS 13:1–2

When has someone shown you unexpected hospitality? Maybe it was a compliment when you were down on yourself, a gift of support when you were having trouble with bills, or even just a word, smile, or small act of kindness when you most needed it. What would happen if we interrupted our days more often to do the same? And what if we greeted each interruption with "Lord, what do You want to do here?"

Sometimes we miss these God interruptions. Insecurities, awkwardness, and schedules can keep us from responding to interruptions God has prepared. So resist that urge and make a habit out of the following:

- Speak an encouraging word to someone in line with you.
- Acknowledge a cashier or waitress by name. That person is not your servant.
- Make eye contact when you talk to people.
- Respond patiently to people's rudeness.

Allow God to continually soften your heart so that it beats for what His heart beats for—people. As you stay close to Him, you will start to see what He sees and love as He loves.

Lord, show me when You are sending an interruption and giving me an opportunity to love with Your love!

TREASURED PROMISES

Keep me as the apple of your eye; hide me
in the shadow of your wings.

PSALM 17:8

To be the apple of someone's eye is to feel fully confident in that person's love and devotion for you. That's how God feels about you—but it may be something hard to grasp.

To transition from not being sure of His devotion to living overjoyed in His love is a process—but one that is well worth the time and energy.

Here are some steps in the process of transformation that can help you:

- Immerse yourself in God's Word: make time every day to read Scripture. Memorize verses about God's love for you. Meditate on those words. You will find life in them.
- Pray His Word. For example, you could pray Psalm 17:8: "Father, I'm so grateful that I'm the apple of Your eye. You hide me and protect me in the shadow of Your wings."
- Learn God's promises—and personalize them. Trust God that He will keep them.

Truth that you internalize from God's Word will build your confidence in His love for you and help you develop *unshakeable* faith you can stand on when life's inevitable storms strike. God's promises can become a lifeline for you to hold on to. And His faithfulness to you and His presence with you will be like a life raft that protects you from being overwhelmed by crashing waves.

I am the apple of Your eye. Thank You for loving
me and transforming me through Your Word.

HE WHO PROMISED IS FAITHFUL

By faith even Sarah, who was past childbearing age,
was enabled to bear children because she considered
him faithful who had made the promise.

HEBREWS 11:11

God will often wait until a situation is impossible before He works a miracle. I'm guessing that, like me, you look at your circumstances—at your bank accounts, your education, your physical body, your gifts, your connections—and decide a promise cannot be fulfilled because it is not naturally possible. But your infinite God can go way beyond the finite options you can imagine!

If God has said He will do something, then He will be faithful to perform it whatever your natural circumstances. Sarah was already "past childbearing age" when she conceived Isaac. It was biologically impossible for a woman over ninety to have a child. Only when Sarah came to the place of yielding the situation to God, choosing to trust He would be faithful, did the miracle occur.

Just because *you* cannot do something doesn't mean *God* cannot. After all, when something is no longer possible and God turns up, then only He can get the glory. Don't let impossibility quench your faith. Instead, allow it to fuel your faith! Look beyond your circumstances to your completely loving, faithful, and powerful God. He who promised is faithful.

Lord, please show me how to look beyond my circumstances to You, for whom nothing is impossible! How exciting to live in anticipation of what You are about to do!

A GIFT FOR YOUR GOOD

The fruit of the Spirit is love, joy, peace, forbearance, kindness, goodness, faithfulness, gentleness and self-control.

GALATIANS 5:22–23

Self-control is not something we hear a lot about in our culture. We're often pressed to embrace excess, charge it to a credit card, go all out, or throw caution—and other people—to the wind in pursuit of our dreams and aspirations. Yet the Bible teaches that self-control is both the hallmark of a real Christian and a natural by-product of living God's way.

Self-control is a fruit of the Spirit. The list—love, joy, peace, patience, kindness, goodness, faithfulness, gentleness, and self-control—offers a sharp contrast to the characteristics of an unstable world. Without self-control, people are liable to do whatever they like whenever they feel like it. Without self-control, we are easily prompted to wrong actions by our emotions and natural self-centeredness.

In order to honor Jesus, we must rely on this vital spiritual resource. God provides self-control so that we can more easily make choices that both benefit us and honor Him. Believe me: it will save us a lot of pain in the long run!

Holy Spirit, help me to be sensitive to Your guidance
and willing to follow Your lead. Today I choose to yield
to the fruit of the Spirit, especially self-control.

AUGUST

Your word is a lamp for my feet,
a light on my path.

PSALM 119:105

THE ONE WHO SENDS YOU

The LORD turned to [Gideon] and said, "Go in the strength you
have and save Israel out of Midian's hand. Am I not sending you?"

JUDGES 6:14

When the Lord chose Gideon to lead Israel into battle against the Midianite
army, he answered, "O my Lord, how can I save Israel?" (Judges 6:15 NKJV).
Good question! He couldn't—but God could.

Gideon felt inadequate and unqualified. He mentally was stuck on his
limitations. Gideon wasn't even convinced that God was on his side. But God's
choice was not based on Gideon's faith, courage, strength, or experience. *God*
chose to use him, send him, and work wonders through him despite all of
Gideon's shortcomings.

Are you like Gideon? Are you focused on what you are not rather than on
who God is? We often think we are just being realistic or humble when we list
our limitations, but contrary to what you might think, we actually are being
prideful. If we focus on what we cannot do or who we are not, we are really
saying to God, "My limitations are greater than Your power and strength."

When you feel inadequate for the assignment God gives you, choose to
believe that He is faithful to do the very thing He has set Himself to do in and
through your life—no matter how impossible, no matter how wonderful.

*Lord, when You next give me an overwhelming assignment,
may I welcome it as an opportunity to see You work.*

DAUGHTERS AND AMBASSADORS

God was reconciling the world to himself in Christ, not counting people's sins against them. And he has committed to us the message of reconciliation. We are therefore Christ's ambassadors. . . . Be reconciled to God.

2 CORINTHIANS 5:19–20

What's your "job title"? Mom? Sister? Wife? Boss? Employee? Minister? Entrepreneur? When you read today's verse, are you thinking, *Ambassador? Another hat to wear!* Relax.

First, you won't be doing this all alone. Jesus said, "You will receive power when the Holy Spirit comes on you; and you will be my witnesses" (Acts 1:8). God promises His presence and power to be with you. But notice something else.

The power is not for *doing* the witnessing but rather for *being* witnesses. That's great news for us *do*ers. We don't work ourselves into a frenzy in order to *do* witnessing. Instead, we have the pleasure of witnessing to others when we are most authentic in our relationship with Jesus. It's more natural that way. Just *be* before you *do*.

To be ambassadors and witnesses for Christ, we bear witness to the truth of His Word in the way we live. More than any words, programs, or doctrines, your life is a platform from which you proclaim the love of God to others. So *be* with your powerful God today, and embrace another job title He gives you: freed and forgiven woman of God.

Holy Spirit, thank You for empowering me to be Your witness and ambassador. Show me how to be with You.

STRENGTH FOR TODAY

The LORD is the everlasting God. . . . He gives strength
to the weary and increases the power of the weak.

ISAIAH 40:28-29

I'm guessing that—like me—you weren't awake very long this morning before you were mentally rehearsing the list of things you have to accomplish today. Just thinking about all our responsibilities, commitments, and obligations can exhaust us even before we've had breakfast. Thankfully, we also can start our day with the words from Isaiah: the Lord will give us strength! This truth is reiterated again a few verses later: "Those who wait on the LORD shall renew their strength" (v. 31 NKJV).

It looks to me as though we receive God's strength as we "wait on" Him, if we commit our days to Him, trust Him for what's ahead, and rely on Him every step of the way. In other words, if you are willing to be utterly dependent on God, He *will* enable you to do all He has called you to do.

May this truth put a smile on your face as it does on mine. As you begin a day of being a wife, mother, cook, chauffeur, personal shopper, or "whatever it takes" person, make an effort to take a break and consciously wait on God. He will renew your strength and make you "mount up with wings like eagles" (v. 31 NKJV).

Lord God, I'm so grateful that waiting on You will mean
strength for today. Thank You for increasing my power!

THE GOD OF THE IMPOSSIBLE

Jesus looked at [His disciples] and said, "With man [salvation]
is impossible, but with God all things are possible."

MATTHEW 19:26

"It's impossible that he will be saved."

"It's impossible for that stronghold to be broken."

When I hear, "That's impossible," about anything, I think to myself, *Fantastic! Impossible is where God starts.*

Because our God is the God of the impossible, the seemingly impossible is not a barrier to what He wants to do in our lives or what He wants us to do for Him. If you are open, God will equip you to serve Him no matter how impossible anything may seem. After all, God blessed the gospel efforts of fishermen, a tax collector, a doctor, and many more—and two thousand years later, we are the fruit of their labor! He did the impossible through their lives.

Whatever you are facing today—a presentation, a relentless schedule, or a spiritual hurdle—refuse to let *impossible* make you sit down and not even try to do what He wants you to do in this world. Refuse to let impossible discourage you from cooperating in the transformative work God wants to do in your heart and through your life. After all, what's impossible with man is *always* possible with God.

Lord, I am so grateful that You achieve the impossible.
Show me how to stay open to Your amazing possibilities.

HE WILL SHOW YOU

The Lord had said to Abram, "Go from your country, your people
and your father's household to the land I will show you."

GENESIS 12:1

In my early years of ministry, I became a woman with a mission. My pastor had entrusted me with a new and big responsibility: I was to open a youth center.

I was scared and excited, and I decided to put into practice what I'd been reading in God's Word and hearing preached. I would approach this project as a step of faith. I would enter this unexplored territory the way Abram left his country—without a map or itinerary, not knowing where I was going. My daily prayer time took on a new focus: *Dear God, please show me what to do.*

What a change! The old Christine would have relied on her own strengths and resources, however limited both were. But that old Christine was shrinking, as *Christ in me* was growing larger. I was now willing to admit my weakness and ask God and others for help. I was daring to take a step of faith, confident it would lead to another and willing to begin God's on-the-job training. I was learning a new lesson: *rely on God's power, not your own.*

I believe He wants you to live out that lesson as well. It's one more way you build *unshakeable* faith.

Lord God, I want to rely on Your power
today rather than my own.

WISDOM FOR THE RACE

Those who hope in the LORD will renew their strength.
They will soar on wings like eagles; they will run and
not grow weary, they will walk and not be faint.

ISAIAH 40:31

The annual review. The self-assessment. They're ways of making sure we are clicking along smoothly in life goals. In the same way, it's wise to self-assess the running of our race for God. From time to time, we need to evaluate how we're doing and ask for His help. These questions will get you started:

- Am I running my race in *my* lane, answering the specific calling God has for *me*?
- Am I lacking direction, not really knowing where I'm going?
- Am I in my lane but distracted, looking around to see how others are doing?
- Have I completely stopped running, overcome by discouragement, disillusionment, and disappointment, and feeling hopeless?
- Have I become a spectator in the grandstand, watching the race when I should be running?
- Have I been sidelined by a sin and the resulting guilt and shame?

What knowledge about yourself have you gained from this evaluation? Knowing where you are—even if it isn't where you want to be—is so important on this race. Ask God to help you to be honest with yourself, hopeful in Him, and open to wisdom about how to improve your race. Then you can soar.

Lord God, please provide me wisdom for running this race of life, and renewed strength so I can "run and not grow weary."

SUPER-HEARING

[Jesus] called out, "Whoever has ears to hear, let them hear."

LUKE 8:8

Some voices in our lives are unmistakable, like when we were kids and one of our parents called us in from playing. We knew that voice as soon as we heard it.

In the same way, when my girls were young, we could be at a playground filled with kids, noisy with laughter, talking, and, yes, crying. But if one of my daughters called for me, I was able to discern her call instantly no matter how many screaming, excited children were sharing the playground with us. When my Cattie or Sophia yelled for me, I could hone in on her voice and respond immediately. That kind of "super-sense" comes from spending time with a person—and it's amplified by love.

We all have this ability to hear certain voices, don't we? I remember thinking at those playgrounds, *I wish I had this kind of ear for Jesus' voice!*

Throughout God's Word, He tells us to constantly keep an ear inclined for the voice of the Spirit. Tune your ear—and heart—to hear His divine voice by spending time with Him, reading Scripture, memorizing it, praying, and worshiping. Develop your senses by sitting with God in prayer. He wants you to hear His voice even more than you do!

> Lord God, I do want to hear Your voice! Help
> me hear Your call no matter what's going on,
> and give me strength to do Your will.

SPIRITUAL FORCES

Our struggle is not against flesh and blood, but against the rulers,
against the authorities, against the powers of this dark world
and against the spiritual forces of evil in the heavenly realms.

EPHESIANS 6:12

Knowing that you have an Enemy is one thing; finding yourself face-to-face with that Enemy is another. Whether you feel it or not, you are in a spiritual battle. Yes, you are ultimately "more than conquerors," but there is still a fight to be fought on a daily basis (Romans 8:37).

Prepare yourself with this knowledge: the Enemy does not want you to walk with the Lord, trust Him for what's ahead, or love people with His love. That's why when you say yes to God, you may go from running with the wind to running against the wind.

Trials and storms come. Obstacles rise up. Challenges multiply. And the Enemy comes at you hard. Why? Because he wants your spiritual life to grow stagnant and your influence in this world to diminish. Yet if you fight and draw on God's power, you can have an unbelievable impact on eternity! Yes, you must fight, but you don't battle alone. Lean on God in prayer, community, and His Word. "Do not be afraid or discouraged. . . . For the battle is not yours, but God's" (2 Chronicles 20:15).

*Thank You, Lord, that You arm me for battle
and You enter the battle with me. Thank You
that, ultimately, the victory is Yours!*

AUGUST 9

OUR TRUST-BUILDING GOD

I will say of the LORD, "He is my refuge and my
fortress, my God, in whom I trust."

PSALM 91:2

Trust building is a process. But you don't have to go the journey alone. *God knows how to grow your trust.* He knows how to both sow seeds of trust and nourish them. He knows how to repair trust when it's been broken and how to restore trust when it's been lost. God is in the trust-growing business.

And what does God use to grow it? Exactly what the Enemy uses to try to keep us from trusting. God uses our fear to grow our trust. So when you come face-to-face with fear, remember this: you are looking at the very next place God wants to build your trust (Joshua 1:9).

So how do you cooperate with God in this trust-building journey? You put more faith in what you do know about God than in what you don't know about the future. You walk in obedience, acting as if you trust God even if your trust is waning. Your heart just may follow once you see Him come through in His will.

As Peter advised, "Humble yourselves, therefore, under God's mighty hand, that he may lift you up in due time. Cast all your anxiety on him because he cares for you" (1 Peter 5:6–7).

Thank You for being a trust-building God. Please help
me to see fears as places where You want to build my
trust, and to remember how much You care for me.

THE POWER OF PLANNING

Do not despise these small beginnings, for the
LORD rejoices to see the work begin.

ZECHARIAH 4:10 NLT

God wants you to live a life of meaningfulness and significance. But a successful life won't happen by accident. Each of us must be intentional about the choices we make in relationship to our dreams—particularly the ones God plants in our hearts. We need to set goals to ensure we are moving toward an intended target, rather than letting our lives just happen.

People who live taking life as it comes have no strategy or infrastructure to help them realize their God-given dreams. And because of that, they most likely won't see their dreams fulfilled.

God wants you to have goals. Only a succession of small, daily, measured steps can take you into the future you envision. Yes, you need God's favor, anointing, and opportunity, but He also gave you an intellect to plan out ideas, strategies, and goals. Measurable steps.

So ask yourself: "What future do I see for myself, my family, my relationships, my work, my finances, and my ministry?" Then, write out goals to achieve those dreams. Begin to take small, incremental steps forward. As you do, one day you'll find yourself standing in your dream, living out God's epic plan for your life!

*God, thank You for small beginnings—and great
endings. I look forward to taking steps toward
my goals, trusting You in every season.*

YOUR LIFE-DEFINING LORD

At three in the afternoon Jesus cried out in a loud
voice, "Eloi, Eloi, lema sabachthani?" (which means
"My God, my God, why have you forsaken me?").

MARK 15:34

You can know in your head that God has your good in mind and that He can redeem any situation, yet you can still feel hugely disappointed and deeply despondent when something goes wrong. Your head tells you God is trustworthy—but your heart tells you He's not even there. Yet Jesus is there— His love is true, even if it doesn't *feel* true.

Maybe your children move away and never call. Colleagues betray you. The one you've prayed to find Jesus never does. People disappoint you. You disappoint yourself, and at times you feel that God Himself has let you down.

In these places of deep disappointment, remind yourself of those things about God that you know to be true, though they might not *feel* true at the moment. Remember that the valley of death through which you are walking truly is a shadow, and that shadow does not define you or your life. Jesus does. With Him, "weeping may stay for the night, but rejoicing comes in the morning" (Psalm 30:5).

Lord, Your power and love are so much greater than
any disappointment I could experience on this earth.
You are my Comfort and my Hope. I trust You.

HELPED AND UPHELD

Because you are my help, I sing in the shadow of your
wings. I cling to you; your right hand upholds me.

PSALM 63:7–8

Pure joy is not our natural response when we face challenges like betrayal, illness, financial stress, or an unexpected tragedy. Especially in seasons where it seems that we're being hit by one thing after another. Yet those of us who know the Lord can face bad news and the worst situation with great hope.

Wherever trials come from—our own brokenness, poor choices, someone else's choices, a flood, earthquake, tornado, or simply because we live in a fallen world—we can take heart. Whatever the trial, we can choose to trust our sovereign Redeemer, all-good, all-loving, ever-present God. There is no surer Source of hope. Even when we are hurting and grieving—by trusting in Him and entrusting our very lives to Him—we can be hopeful and even joyful.

Why? Because as trials test our faith, those trials reveal where we can grow, and that insight is key to our future. God always seems to first change us and then our circumstances. And that process begins with trusting Him and trusting that He upholds us through everything we face.

Lord, I put my trust in You. Thank You for being my help. I cling to You, and I know that You uphold me today in all I face.

DISPELLING DOUBT

God chose the weak things of the world . . .

1 CORINTHIANS 1:27

I want to talk about an empowering subject today. Something that will really get you pumped up and ready to take on the world. Let's talk more about your weaknesses. Yes! Believe me—in God's view, your weaknesses are cause for a real, hopeful sense of joy. Your weaknesses are His strengths in the making.

The world may tell you to keep these things hidden inside where you can easily ignore them, forget about them, or hide them from others. The world may tell you to be ashamed. Yet when you reveal all your weaknesses to your loving God—when you acknowledge them—you'll see God doing His transformative work inside you, and you'll see those weaknesses rooted out and replaced with His strength.

Today's verse encourages us that "God chose the weak things of the world to shame the strong." When we hide our weaknesses from God and ourselves and pretend to be strong, we are putting on a pointless act. Our human strength is nothing compared to the unlimited, loving, gracious strength available to us from our Father. Hiding our weaknesses is unfounded, when He is waiting to fill us with His loving power and show us His strength.

Of course, Lord God, I don't want to look full-on at my weaknesses, but I know doing so is worthwhile. Help me keep my eyes on the end result as You refine my character and faith.

SAVED AND TREASURED

The Lord himself goes before you and will be with
you; he will never leave you nor forsake you.

DEUTERONOMY 31:8

God created you. God chose you as His. He loves you. So when you feel alone,
remember these truths:

- *God is always with you.* God never leaves you, forsakes you, or betrays
  your trust. Whatever circumstances you encounter, God is always
  there with you.
- *He calls you by name.* He knows you intimately, by your name: "Do
  not fear, for I have redeemed you; I have summoned you by name; you
  are mine" (Isaiah 43:1).
- *He gives you a fresh start.* Not only does God give you a fresh start
  in life by making a way for you to be born again, His mercies are
  new every morning. Yes, He wipes away the mess of your past and
  gives you hope for the future, for your eternal future (Romans 8:2).
  When you confess your sin, recognize Jesus as the One who took the
  punishment for your sin, and ask Jesus to be Lord of your life, then
  God forgives your sin, cleanses you, walks with you on this earth, and
  will welcome you into your eternal, heavenly home with Him (John
  3:16).

What wonderful love is this! You died for my sins. You
know me more intimately than anyone else does. And
You will always be with me! Thank You for fresh starts!

HEALED, REDEEMED, TRANSFORMED

If anyone is in Christ, the new creation has come:
The old has gone, the new is here!

2 CORINTHIANS 5:17

If life is hard, and you seem to be facing one thing after another, I have good news for you: *it's not you*. And you aren't unlucky, beset, or cursed. Life is hard—naturally—for everyone. We are flawed, imperfect people, surrounded by flawed, imperfect people, living in a broken world. That might not sound like good news on the surface, but fortunately, that's not the whole story.

God is at work transforming you into a strong Jesus-follower who spreads grace and acts in His strength to build up others. It's a constant process, revealing His power. So, for instance, the next time you get hurt or face a storm in life, bring it into God's light and have hope in His healing strength.

Camp on the truth that God is sovereign: He has a plan for you, and at some point He just might have you ministering to people who are going through what you've been through. In His power, He makes you new and brings you up out of the past and into His future.

*Thank You, Lord, for the healing, redeeming,
transforming work You continue to do in my life.
And thank You for Your power to make me new.*

THE WHITE SPACE

Great is our Lord and mighty in power;
his understanding has no limit.

PSALM 147:5

"What do you see?" my psychology professor asked as he projected a picture of a small black dot in the middle of a very big white screen. We all responded immediately: "A black dot." I was excited, thinking, *If all the questions are as simple as this one, this course is going to be easy!* But then he asked again. "What do you see?"

Confused, we repeated back to him, "A black dot!" When he finally gave us the answer, it was a lesson I'll never forget: "You were all so focused on the little black dot in the center of the screen that none of you noticed the dominant image on the screen: the large white space covering the screen top to bottom, left to right." Suddenly it was obvious. We had chosen to focus on the black dot, so that's what we saw.

When we choose to focus on our weaknesses or trials, that's all we see. But God's power is at work in the overwhelmingly large white space around us. When we focus on the vastness of God's mighty power and amazing work on this planet, we'll start to see His work in our lives.

*Lord, I want to focus on what You are doing
instead of the little dots of my life. Please
give me new vision to see You at work!*

TOUGH BUT GOOD

O Lord my God, I cried out to You, and You healed me.

PSALM 30:2 NKJV

Sometimes the wisdom that is hardest to hear is the most helpful. So, I'll tell you the truth: there are no quick fixes for emotional pain. Accepting that wisdom prepares us to work patiently and persistently through the healing process—and to never give up.

Maybe the scar tissue around my heart is similar to yours. Haunting memories can last for decades—and immobilize us. Our hearts, broken in an instant, can keep us from loving for years. Old, harsh words can still echo in our hearts. So many experiences can injure us, keeping us from stepping out, risking, moving ahead, loving, and letting ourselves be loved. But that's not the end of your story.

Of course you want God to heal you quickly and painlessly. Like physical healing, though, the healing of your heart can take time. On top of that wisdom, remember this—healing can and does happen: your Great Physician is faithful and good.

Lord God, please give me patience with the healing
process, strength for the hard work I need to do,
hope for the freedom that will come with wholeness,
and complete faith in You, my Healer.

LOVE CONQUERS FEAR

Dear friends, since God so loved us, we
also ought to love one another.

1 JOHN 4:11

Do you feel fear when it comes to connecting with God's people? Maybe it's the feeling of vulnerability, or maybe you've been hurt by other Christians. Whatever it is, don't let fear keep you from one of the biggest blessings of our faith: the love of a Christian church family.

Whether your fear is subdued or strong, rational or irrational, fear freezes you—in whatever area it consumes. For example, you won't walk up a steep hill to see a beautiful sunset because of your fear of heights. You can't bring yourself to go to the party because of your fear of crowds. You don't join that Bible study because you fear having to read aloud.

When you let fear run your life, you close yourself off from anything that might hurt you or make you uncomfortable, including opportunities to know God's love through the love of His people. "Perfect love drives out fear" (1 John 4:18). And one place we can experience godly love is in community with other believers. So if you're feeling fear of connecting, take it as a cue to say *no* to letting life pass you by, and *yes* to love. Risk loving in community again.

God, I choose to receive all of Your love, because
perfect love casts out all fear. I want to engage
fully in the life You've planned for me!

STOPPING THE FEAR THIEF

No one has ever seen God; but if we love one another,
God lives in us and his love is made complete in us.

1 JOHN 4:12

God calls us to serve. But maybe because you fear being rejected—even by a stranger—the homeless person on the street never receives the hope you could share. You don't consider a mission trip because you fear the unknown. You don't befriend the mother at your son's football practice who drinks every night because she has no one to talk to.

God doesn't want fear limiting our influence in these ways. He wants us free so we can love and serve others freely. He doesn't want us to let fear make us languish and feel alone, broken, and unfulfilled, never experiencing what God created and called us to do.

He doesn't want the Enemy using fear to steal our purpose from us: "The thief comes only to steal and kill and destroy" (John 10:10). Plain and simple, fear is a thief. It robs us and others.

Jesus has promised us, "I have come that they may have life, and have it to the full." By resisting fear and trusting God, we can live to the full and have the privilege of showing God's love to everyone we meet.

God, I resist fear and embrace faith. I want to share Your love with everyone I meet today.

RISE AND SHINE

"Tell us," [the disciples] said, "when will
this [end of the age] happen" . . .
"About that day or hour no one knows, not even the angels in
heaven, nor the Son, but only the Father."

MATTHEW 24:3, 36

Do you know what it's like when you have to get up, but you just keep hitting snooze until, all of a sudden, your morning is gone! When it comes to sharing the gospel, it's time for us to rise and shine. The world is too dark for the church to keep hitting snooze.

Each time we become sidetracked or indifferent about sharing the gospel, it's like we are choosing snooze and allowing the world to linger in darkness longer. Every single day brings open doors for us to extend love, grace, mercy, truth, and justice through holy living, acts of kindness, and words of life. But only when we are awake can we seize these opportunities to be light-bearers in this world.

Let's commit to not hitting snooze anymore, or else we might sleep through the very reason we were sent into the world. Once the day is gone, it's gone—and no one knows when Jesus will return. So, go into your part of the world today and spread the hope-filled gospel of God's great love. Rise and shine, and Jesus will shine through you.

Jesus, I choose to wake up and spread Your
gospel of love today. Help me be alert and
seize every opportunity to shine for You.

JUST FOR A SEASON!

There is a time for everything, and a season for every
activity under the heavens . . . a time to weep and a time
to laugh, a time to mourn and a time to dance.

ECCLESIASTES 3:1, 4

God has carefully designed every season of your life to be a vital step in your journey. With that heart-knowledge, you can find greater joy in the seasons of laughter and greater purpose in the seasons of weeping. And you can live every season with passion, whether or not you fully understand God's plan.

After all, sometimes God is doing a deeper work in you than you realize. He may be preparing you for the season that follows. He may have you sowing seeds for a future harvest of believers. Or, the Lord may be helping you develop greater faith.

Some seasons are more enjoyable and some, more difficult. Some seasons bring droughts while others bring floods. Some seasons bring mourning, and others, joy—and both are necessary. Whatever is happening in this season of your life, embrace it. Pour yourself into whatever God is doing during this season because, after all, it's only for a season. At the end of your life, you'll be able to see, "He has made everything beautiful in its time" (Ecclesiastes 3:11).

*Loving God, as You guide me through one
season after another, please help me embrace
each one as Your design for me.*

PLACED IN YOUR SPHERES

The entire law is fulfilled in keeping this one
command: "Love your neighbor as yourself."

GALATIANS 5:14

Look around your world. Consider the different spheres of influence in which God has placed you. It is no coincidence who your neighbors are, who you work with, or who your kids play soccer with. God has you in each of those places, in the lives of those people, on purpose. He wants you to be His light, to pass on the baton of faith—and He has uniquely equipped you to fulfill your assignment.

Passing the baton of faith is as simple as taking time to invest in people's everyday lives just as Jesus did. It's finding a way to turn normal, inconsequential moments into eternal moments. Traveling with a co-worker on business? During your time waiting in the airport, share a recent answer to prayer. Shopping with a friend or getting a cup of coffee in the office break room? Casually talk about a Bible verse that struck you or a life concern you're praying about. Make sharing life an opportunity to share spiritual truth. Always be listening for the Spirit's leading, and you'll see more and more opportunities to be His light.

Lord, there is no greater act of loving my neighbor than sharing the gospel. Thank You for showing me how to take advantage of every opportunity in my sphere of influence.

REFRESHED AND STRENGTHENED

The LORD . . . said, "Get up and eat, for the journey is too much
for you." So he got up and ate and drank. Strengthened
by that food, he traveled forty days and forty nights.

1 KINGS 19:7-8

It can take just one message—one tweet, phone call, comment, note, text, or social media comment—to reduce us from a high to a low. It's one of the Devil's favorite tactics to distract us and control us, but with God's help we can bounce back.

In today's verse, the prophet Elijah had just routed 450 prophets of Baal and seen God perform a great miracle of victory. Yet, in the next scene, it only took one threatening messenger from the evil queen Jezebel to send him running for his life, cowering in fear. He curled up under a tree and prayed to die. But when he fell asleep, an angel came and revived him: "Get up and eat, for the journey is too much for you" (v. 7).

Sometimes one small message from the pit of hell can pull you out of the fight. You run and hide, deflated. But when you call out to the Lord, He will refresh you, heal you, and strengthen you. He will get you back on course to fulfilling your destiny.

Lord God, protect me from the messengers
of this world who bring me down. I run to You
to renew my soul and strengthen me.

SOFTHEARTED

"I will give them an undivided heart and put a new
spirit in them; I will remove from them their heart
of stone and give them a heart of flesh."

EZEKIEL 11:19

As I allowed the Lord to heal my heart from past hurts, I noticed growth in my faith, my strength, and my courage. I realized I had made a change: Instead of constantly trying to protect myself by controlling every detail of my life, I was now—bit by bit—giving myself over to the Lord. A hidden supernatural, divine exchange was occurring. God was replacing my clogged, hardened heart with a heart of flesh—and healthy hearts foster healthy, fruitful lives and healthy, nourishing relationships.

That exchange began subtly. But over time, God transformed me from a person with a wounded heart to one who began to have the capacity to help others. After all, only free people can truly free people.

What God has done in my life and in my heart, He can and will do in yours. Let Him replace the hardened or calcified heart with a beating, loving, fully functioning healthy heart. Let Him help you share your story so God can tell someone that freedom is truly possible. Let Him use your past hurts to build new, stronger compassion for others.

Redeemer God, how beautiful that You transform our
pain into wisdom and strength. Show me how to share my
"heart of flesh" with the people You've placed in my life.

HUMILITY AND COURAGE

Humble yourselves before the Lord, and he will lift you up.

JAMES 4:10

I remember some of my first few jobs—working in a donut shop, then later at a grocery store. They definitely were not glamorous jobs! But they played a valuable role in teaching me responsibility and accountability—and humility.

Most first jobs do that. They teach us valuable skills we use later in life. Even King David had some early not-so-fun jobs. He tended sheep. Then he became Saul's private musician and armor-bearer. Not the most prestigious role for a future king, but this exercise in humility gave David a real-life education.

David even became an errand boy, charged to carry lunch to his brothers who were fighting the Philistines on the front lines of a battle. And then, God used David's position as a delivery boy to introduce him to the giant Goliath.

By the time David killed Goliath, God had used all of his first jobs to equip him with the skills, strengths, and courage to take out the giant. In the same way, God is using the here and now to prepare you for your future too. So humble yourself, because everything you're learning now He will use to help you fulfill His call on your life.

God, I humble myself before You, trusting that
You will lift me up at the right time.

CHOOSE JOY

Though there are no sheep in the pen and no cattle in the stalls,
yet I will rejoice in the LORD, I will be joyful in God my Savior.

HABAKKUK 3:17–18

Joy and happiness are not the same thing. Happiness is based on circumstances; joy is based on God. Happiness is rooted in positive emotions; joy is a fruit of the Spirit (Galatians 5:22–23). No matter what is going on in our lives, God longs to give us joy through the power of His Holy Spirit.

Once, when I lost a baby—between having my two girls—absolutely nothing about that loss made me happy. Not then. Not now. Yet God cared for me in that moment. As He had in every other painful event in my life, God met me in my sorrow—and He walked me through it. He didn't leave me stuck because He had something good ahead to show me—joy.

Joy isn't a cheap imitation of happiness. It's something much more. Think of happiness as candy; think of joy as medicine. When your heart is sick, when the pain seems unbearable, you want medicine—not sweets.

Because of God's good medicine, I could heal. I had lost something precious, and everything around me seemed dead, but God was still good. Joy in the midst of pain was the medicine I needed.

You are my strength, Lord. Thank You for
Your joy that heals me and frees me.

LIVE WHAT YOU BELIEVE

---

*What good is it, my brothers and sisters, if someone
claims to have faith but has no deeds?*

JAMES 2:14

Nineteenth-century philosopher John Stuart Mill reportedly said that Christians seem to have an amazing ability to say the most wonderful things without actually believing them. Ouch. What prompted that? I'm guessing it's the wide gulf between how so many of us live and what we claim to believe.

We Christians make amazing claims about the power of the gospel of Jesus Christ to transform lives, communities, and nations. Imagine if you lived with such radical faith that this power was evident to all. Imagine . . .

- the conversations you would have that you don't.
- the acts of kindness you would do that you skip.
- the places you would go that you avoid.
- the generosity you would give that you hold back.
- the forgiveness you would extend that you can't muster.
- the prayers that you would pray that you put off till later.
- the people who would be reached who now aren't.

Why not choose to live every moment today as if you truly believe what you profess to believe? Your faith, lived actively, would demonstrate these amazing things, because an amazing God would be acting through you.

*Jesus, show me the gaps between what I say I believe
and how I live—and help me close those gaps. I want
to effectively show Your amazing gospel truth.*

GOD'S GRACE IN BATTLE

You armed me with strength for battle.

PSALM 18:39

Understanding that God is light literally changed my life. I finally understood that a God without any darkness is a God who has nothing to hide from me. He cannot hurt me, and He will not hurt me. Unlike broken people, He does not have a dark side, so I can completely trust Him. His light enables me to walk through dark places with confidence that the darkness will not last forever. I no longer need to cover up, hide, or try to escape reality. I no longer need to shrink back from whatever God uncovers, no matter how painful, because I know that what He reveals is for my good—for my healing and freedom.

Yes, I will have to battle darkness in this life (2 Corinthians 10:3–5). But the God of grace battles with me and for me. He helps me do what I need to do: make wise choices, focus my thoughts, pray fervently, trust in Him.

God wants the revelation of His bright light to flood your soul. Let this same understanding that freed me free you. I know that you can trust Him. He is good. He does good. He is for your good.

And He will never leave us to fight alone (Deuteronomy 31:6).

Thank You, gracious Lord, for the light of Your presence when darkness falls and the battle rages. Thank You for fighting for me and for equipping me every day.

PROMISES KEPT

Let us hold unswervingly to the hope we
profess, for he who promised is faithful.

HEBREWS 10:23

God is faithful to keep His promises.

God gave Abraham and Sarah the son He had promised (Genesis 21). God led His people out of Egypt and into the promised land just as He said He would (Exodus 14). And God sent His Son, our Messiah, as the perfect sacrifice for our sins (Genesis 3:15). The list of promises fulfilled can go on and on.

Think now about the promises God has spoken to you. And all the times He kept His word. When, for instance, have you seen Him bring beauty out of ashes in your life? Or sensed His love in a dark time? When have you been quiet before the Lord and been reminded that He is God, that He is good, sovereign, loving, and wise? And when have you found His grace sufficient for you in challenging seasons with your friends or loved ones?

Whatever God has promised you—that word you hold dear and pray over frequently—He will be faithful to you.

Lord, You have always graciously kept Your promises
to Your people. May I always remember Your great
faithfulness to me in matters both big and small.

LETTING GO

Cast all your anxiety on him because he cares for you.

1 PETER 5:7

Control is something we often grasp for in order to stabilize our lives. When Nick and I were first dating, and long before I was free, he helped me realize that I tried to control so much—including where we ate, what we did, and when we left.

It seems silly, but it was a learned response to protect myself—and it was rooted in fear. I had somehow bought into the belief that if I could control all the scenarios in my life, and in the lives of those around me, I would be safe. Safe from what? Who knows. Whatever I was afraid would happen if I gave up control.

But the truth is, God is in control—and we should just let Him be God in our lives. Just as I had learned to control, I learned not to. I quit trying to manipulate people or circumstances, and instead, I learned to pray and cast all my cares and anxieties over on the Lord.

God truly cares for you, so cast your cares on Him. Let Him free you from all the stress, anxiety, worry, scheming, and fretting. Trust God—and how much He cares for you.

Lord, I cast all my cares over on You. I trust You and will stop controlling everything and everyone around me. I believe that You care for me.

WHAT ARE YOU LOOKING AT?

Keep your eyes on Jesus, who both began
and finished this race we're in.

HEBREWS 12:2 The Message

Drivers keep their eyes on the road. Lifeguards keep their eyes focused on the water. Babysitters keep their eyes on the children. What do you keep your eyes focused on in your day-to-day life?

In Hebrews, God calls us to keep our eyes on Jesus. Yes, easier said than done. Life's hardships can loom large and block our vision of everything else. I am grateful that, even during the most difficult seasons, the Spirit has prompted me to keep my eyes fixed on Jesus. Doing that has helped me to believe that God was using those tough times to make me more like Jesus. I learned to embrace the season—sometimes a little unwillingly, but at least to some degree!—rather than resist it or try to somehow avoid it.

I haven't been perfect at this. At times, I've chosen to focus on the pain, the frustration, or the challenge instead of on Jesus. But let me assure you, nothing good came out of camping on the hurt or the situation. Trust me, it's so much better to keep your eyes on Jesus regardless of the circumstances—and watch Him perfect your faith.

Spirit, please teach me to keep my eyes on Jesus when life is calm so that it's a good habit by the time the storms come. Thank You for perfecting my faith day by day.

SEPTEMBER

––––––––––

Let them give thanks to the Lord
for his unfailing love
and his wonderful deeds for mankind.

PSALM 107:21

CHOOSING TO TRUST

"Do not let your hearts be troubled. You
believe in God; believe also in me."

JOHN 14:1

Think back to the last time you confronted a tough situation you could do nothing about. How did you respond? Those times can be so overwhelming. Often, we collapse, become anxious, mourn, and grieve. We can feel overwhelmed.

And yet, Jesus tells us to not let our hearts be troubled; therefore, we must be able to learn how to not let our hearts be troubled over situations we can do nothing about. Jesus' words "Do not let" imply that you can take an active role in letting or not letting your heart be troubled. To choose the latter, remind yourself of God's sovereignty and goodness. Read Job 38–41 to remember how great and powerful God is, and then your situation may not look so big. Pray to God, who can solve and fix what you can't. Call on the Holy Spirit to be your Comforter, to be your help in this time of need. Consider making this your prayer: "Lord, I do not see You and I do not understand what You are doing, but I am choosing to trust You."

Whatever is happening in your life today, you can choose to trust. Take steps today to "let not your heart be troubled," because your Savior is with you.

Almighty God, please help me find peace in remembering the storm is not big to You. Please help me choose to trust You today and always.

CHOSEN FOR A PURPOSE

I pray . . . that you may know . . . his incomparably great power
for us who believe. That power is the same as the mighty
strength he exerted when he raised Christ from the dead.

EPHESIANS 1:18–20

God has called you for a kingdom purpose, and nothing can disqualify you. Consider these legends from the Bible who chose to serve His kingdom purposes despite characteristics that should have disqualified them:

- Noah got drunk (Genesis 9:20–27).
- Sarah was impatient (Genesis 16).
- Abraham was old (Genesis 17:1; 24:1).
- Jacob was a cheater (Genesis 25–27).
- David had an affair (2 Samuel 11–12).
- Jonah ran away (Jonah 1:3).
- Peter had a temper (John 18:10).
- Paul persecuted believers (Acts 8:3; 9:1–2).
- Martha was a worrier (Luke 10:40–41).
- Thomas doubted (John 20:24–26).

God had a purpose for each of these people. He chose them. He called them. He qualified them. And He empowered them. And He does the same for you and me. Whatever limitations you perceive, go and serve in God's name. Lean into a limitless God and see where He takes you. It will be the ride of your life.

Lord, I'm so grateful that Your power is greater than my own human limitations. Make me effective for Your purposes.

THE SECOND MILE

"If anyone forces you to go one mile, go with them two miles."

MATTHEW 5:41

I remember going to a store ten minutes before closing time only to be told by the clerk that she was closing early, and that I would have to come back the next day to make my purchase. Clearly, that woman did not own the business! If it had been her store, she would have been pleased to have a customer and stayed open as long as it took.

But because the store was not hers, she had no desire to go the extra mile. She simply performed the bare minimum requirements to keep her job. Her attitude was, "How little can I do and still be paid?"

Aren't we all like that sometimes? To live a life based on how little you can do is to lead a little life.

When we are truly devoted to a person, dedicated to a ministry, or invested in a cause, we undoubtedly develop a "whatever it takes" attitude and a "second mile" commitment.

There is a better, more God-honoring way for you to live, because great churches, ministries, families, marriages, friendships, and businesses are never built in the first mile. They are built on the second. So ask God to give you strength to go the distance.

Holy Spirit, when I feel like stopping at the first
mile, please give me strength and energy to
honor the Lord by going as far as it takes.

THE COAT *AND* THE SHIRT

"If anyone wants to sue you and take your
shirt, hand over your coat as well."

MATTHEW 5:40

Your life becomes bigger and richer when you live bigger—when you live more generously, more joyfully, more graciously, more selflessly. Life becomes bigger and richer when, as Jesus put it, we give away both our coat *and* our shirt. Our God provides more than enough, so we don't have to live small and clutch at what we have.

After all, God has not called us to live a life that asks, "How little?" but "How much? How far? How big? How wide?" Our God is able to do far greater than anything we can ask or imagine. So let's not think in minimums. Let's live big lives of faith as sons and daughters of our limitless God.

An ordinary life is lived in the first mile, but an extraordinary life happens only when you are willing to go the second mile. So don't just do what is asked. Instead, choose to go above and beyond the minimum requirements so that you can have maximum impact for God's kingdom and His glory. Always be willing to give your shirt *and* your coat!

Lord, I want to live in anticipation of what You will do through me and how You will be glorified! Please show me new opportunities to give away my coat or go that extra mile.

SLOW DOWN AND SEE

Jairus, a synagogue leader, came and fell at Jesus' feet,
pleading with him to come to his house because his
only daughter, a girl of about twelve, was dying.

LUKE 8:41–42

If there ever was a time for Jesus to hurry, getting to Jairus's house was one of them. But a lot of things happened along the way, and Jesus took those opportunities to teach us that life is as much about the journey as it is about the destination.

First, on Jesus' way to save the dying girl, the crushing crowd made it hard for Him to move quickly. Then, there was a courageous and desperate woman who needed a healing touch—so Jesus stopped to heal her. By the time Jesus arrived, Jairus's daughter had died, but that wasn't the end of the story: Jesus raised her to life.

How encouraging to realize that more than one miracle occurred that day—because Jesus wasn't in a hurry.

We citizens of the twenty-first century are busy, which means we are pretty much always in a hurry. In our rush, we often fail to enjoy the journey. We miss out on blessing people and being blessed by them. So, let's slow down today. Let's really see the people around us today. As we do, we may just see a miracle or two.

Lord God, I slow down my pace so I don't
miss the people You've put in my path. I want
to be sensitive to Your leading today.

FEAR, TRUST, REPEAT

I sought the Lord, and he answered me; he
delivered me from all my fears.

PSALM 34:4

If you are learning to trust God again—in spite of your fears—I'll definitely vouch for Him. God is good and God does good because good is who God is.

As you face your fears one by one and work through them with your Father, don't be ashamed of being afraid. Basically, the life in Christ you signed up for is a lifetime, three-step process of fear, trust, and repeat. This cycle of growth is at the heart of building *unshakeable* faith.

The children of Israel went through this cycle many times on their way to the promised land. In the face of terrifying odds, they had to trust that God would protect and defend them—over and over again. With each new encounter with fear, He was teaching them more faith and more trust—and so He is with us. The next time you face a fear, see it as a teacher and your gateway to more trust. If you have to forgive someone who has hurt you deeply, decide to trust that God will work in your heart. Pressing through a fear like that each time you encounter one, and choosing to obey despite that fear, is how you grow.

*Jesus, help me take this cycle one step at a time,
toward the goal of more fully trusting You.*

HE WALKS WITH US

---

*Surely I spoke of things I did not understand,
things too wonderful for me to know.*

JOB 42:3

Our friends, Maria and her husband, Dimitri, were stunned when Peter, their fourteen-year-old son, was diagnosed with stomach cancer. These faithful servants prayed earnestly and diligently for God to heal Peter, as did we. But Peter's healing did not come this side of eternity.

"Where is your God now?" some mockers asked. "If He is so powerful, so good, why didn't He heal your son?"

Why indeed?

No explanation ever will satisfy us, and our deepest questions will go unanswered. But Maria and Dimitri didn't try to answer those difficult questions. Instead, they determined to walk down that road of disappointment and heartbreak *with Jesus*. They did not understand why this tragedy had occurred, but they decided to continue to trust God. They chose to keep on believing His promises and resting in His good and wise love for them. They decided to look for other heartbroken travelers on this journey of life, so they could introduce them to the Savior who would walk with them.

God didn't give Maria and Dimitri answers, but He did give them His presence. If your heart is hurting with unanswerable questions, know that Jesus wants to walk through this with you, too, comforting you and loving you in ways beyond your understanding.

*Lord, I can't begin to understand Your ways, but thank You
for Your presence with me when I am asking, "Why?"*

THE PACE OF YOUR JOURNEY

The plans of the LORD stand firm forever, the
purposes of his heart through all generations.

PSALM 33:11

"What is happening when nothing seems to be happening? What is God up to when there is no evidence of Him answering my prayers or moving me along in my journey?"

God is always preparing you for what He has already prepared for you. The point of this journey is who you will become on the way, not just the destination where you will arrive.

We live in a world that rushes everywhere and knows very little about journeying. As Christians, we are often infected with that same virus. We want God to act in our lives *now*, and we become impatient if we don't see any evidence of Him moving (or if He isn't moving as fast as we want Him to). If that's how you're feeling now, take a moment to consider what God has been doing in your life. Look at events in the context of your whole journey.

How has He changed you? Who has He placed in your path? What have been your struggles, and what growth has resulted from them? As you look back, open your heart to Him and His timing. Trust His pace. Trust His plan.

Lord, You are wise, and You are sovereign. Change my heart
so I can remain in step with Your perfect pace and plan.

SHARE YOUR HEALING

I will give thanks to you, Lord, with all my heart;
I will tell of all your wonderful deeds.

PSALM 9:1

Whatever you've been through, your healing journey is of value to the people in your life. Today, I encourage you to identify the women around you and closest to you, and make these resolutions to keep the healing going.

- Refuse to pass down or pass around—with actions or words—any shame, guilt, and brokenness.
- Live as you hope your daughters will live because yours is the life they will emulate.
- Ensure that they see God working through women.
- Instill in those you come alongside a sense of responsibility—that although they can't control what has happened to them, they can control their response from this day forward. They can choose God's truths over the lies of the Enemy, abide in God's Word, and live free.
- Help them see that their lives count before God and that they have tremendous potential.

Inspire your sisters and daughters—natural, adopted, or spiritual—to live confident in the love of their Redeemer God. They are your companions on this healing journey.

Lord, thank You for Your healing goodness. I want to share it with the ones I love—please show me how!

UNLEASHED

[God] created them male and female and blessed them.

GENESIS 5:2

I talk to women all over the world, and many have bought into the lie that we are the second sex, that we do not matter *as much* as men, and that we are not gifted *as importantly* as men. If this is the story running in the background of your life, I want you to know: you are not *less than*.

Women from all walks of life have confided in me their own struggles with this kind of shame—from CEOs to sales clerks, from ministry leaders to stay-at-home moms. A shocking number of us struggle with the *less than* lie.

Woman, God created you on purpose, for a purpose. He did not make a mistake when He made you a woman. You were predestined, predetermined, and preordained to be who you are—a divine creation. God carefully and by design placed gifts and talents within you, and He has called you to activate them and use them to influence others for His glory.

Share your light, reach out to others, and never be stopped by the idea that you should shrink back, be quiet, limit your horizons, or temper your ambitions. The world needs what God has deposited in you. He does not want you to be restricted by any limitations—but rather He intends to unleash you and all your potential into your kingdom purpose.

God, thank You for creating me intentionally.
Help me live and love without limitations.

FOLLOWING WHOLEHEARTEDLY

"Because my servant Caleb has a different spirit and follows me wholeheartedly, I will bring him into the land he went to, and his descendants will inherit it."

NUMBERS 14:24

When Nick and I got married, we committed 100 percent of our hearts to one another—we were wholehearted. If we had entered our marriage only half-heartedly, we would have set ourselves up for trouble. We knew that the only way to make our marriage work was to invest our *whole hearts* in it, and that has returned dividends of love over the years.

Your wholehearted commitment to God will fuel your passion for your faith, for the spiritual disciplines, and for every other aspect of your spiritual life. When you are completely sold out to Jesus, you won't merely be fulfilling a Christian obligation. You will genuinely love others, the church, reading your Bible, praying, giving, and serving. You will love what God loves and desire to do what He wants you to do. You will be wholehearted.

That's how Caleb was. He was one of the spies Moses sent to check out the promised land—and because he was wholehearted for the next forty years as they lived in the desert, he and Joshua were the only two from the original three million who entered the promised land. That's the power of being wholehearted!

Lord Jesus, please bring me back to Yourself
and show me how to live and follow You
wholeheartedly, so I can know Your love.

THE TRUTH ABOUT GOD'S LOVE

See what great love the Father has lavished on us, that we should be called children of God! And that is what we are!

1 JOHN 3:1

For more than a decade, I immersed myself daily in God's Word, and I memorized countless verses about God's love for me. I desperately needed His love. And when I read about how much He loved me and that He had a plan, a purpose, and a place in His family for me, I soaked it up. That truth was water for a parched soul. It helped reconstruct my broken heart. I meditated upon God's words of love. I pondered them and prayed them. I found life in them.

And when storms came, those promises about God's unconditional love held me. And I experienced this truth: *When you believe God is who He says He is, when you choose—in faith—to hang on to Him and His Word, His truth sets you free.* The truth you store up in silence comes back to you during the storm, and like a life raft, it lifts you away from the fears and disappointments that would otherwise pull you under.

Today, soak up His Word. When you abide, or stay faithfully, in His Word, He abides in you, providing peace and reassurance of His love for you.

Lord, fill me with knowledge of Your love, and help that knowledge travel from my head to my heart. Make it grow there, so I remember Your goodness when storms come.

LOOK AND SEE

"See, I have delivered Jericho into your hands,
along with its king and its fighting men."

JOSHUA 6:2

If there's one key to watching the walls in your life fall and moving forward in freedom, this is it: *believe the truth of God's Word over the facts of your circumstances.* That means looking to God, and not at everything around us. Only then are we able to see what's going on from His perspective.

When God rallied the Israelites for battle, He spoke the words in today's verse—and they always make me smile. I picture the Israelites looking at each other with puzzled expressions: "*See*? See *what*? All I see is a wall! I don't see deliverance!" God was calling them to see not with their physical eyes but with eyes of faith. He wanted them to see that even though the situation was impossible, He would give them the promised victory.

For your promised victory, search God's Word for instructions. Follow His instructions, whether or not they make sense, whether you will look courageous or crazy. What matters is doing what God says—and remembering that He is faithful to do what He has promised (Hebrews 10:23).

*Lord, please give me eyes of faith that see Your
promises fulfilled instead of my impossible
circumstances. Give me ears that hear Your
instructions and a heart willing to move forward.*

BE WITH GOD'S PEOPLE

"Blessed are those who mourn, for they will be comforted."

MATTHEW 5:4

When you are hurting, isn't home the best place to be? And not just our physical home, but also our church—our spiritual home. I encourage you today to take your pain—no matter how raw you feel—to the house of God, to the family of God.

I know firsthand how impossible that might sound. I dreaded going to church the first Sunday after Nick and I lost a baby. But what I remember most is not how awful it was to tell the news again and again, but rather how incredibly loving and warm our church family was. As they gathered around Nick and me in our grief, we were able to lift our eyes off our circumstances and see God's lovingkindness. Because of their love, in time, we were able to begin hoping again—and God gave us Sophia.

And in the years since, I have run to my sisters to encourage them, to inspire them, to tell them of God's faithfulness. Because I know His love and healing personally.

I know God will use His people in your local house of worship to help you. You were meant to help each other: "How good and pleasant it is when God's people live together in unity!" (Psalm 133:1). Go home and be with God's people—your family. There, He will heal you.

Thank You, Lord, that Your love for me becomes
more real to me through Your people.

AMAZING LOVE

I pray that you, being rooted and established in
love, may have power . . . to grasp how wide and
long and high and deep is the love of Christ.

EPHESIANS 3:17–18

If you need a light in the darkness today, ponder God's amazing love for you:

- As He knit you together, He loved you (Psalm 139:13).
- Before you could choose Him, He chose you (John 15:16).
- When you were broken, bitter, and blaming, He made you whole and showed you the sweet taste of forgiveness (Psalm 103:8–12).
- When you had no hope, He became your hope (1 Peter 1:3).
- When you were too busy with the cares of this world, He interrupted you to show you what is eternal (Psalm 90:4).
- When you were lost, He found you, rescued you, and showed you that His mercy and justice will prevail (Luke 15).
- When you were disappointed, He taught you that disappointments can bring you to appointments He ordained (Romans 8:28).

Then, in His ultimate act of love, Jesus owned the cross—He made a way for us to be with God. Now you are empowered to know His love and bring His hope to a world desperate to know Him.

Lord God, Your love is overwhelming. Show me
how to share Your light in the darkness.

GETTING BACK ON COURSE

Then the LORD sent a great wind on the sea, and such a
violent storm arose that the ship threatened to break up.

JONAH 1:4

When you're off course and headed the wrong way in life, God always provides a way back to Him—and sometimes spectacularly. For Jonah, after he'd bought his ticket, boarded the ship, and sailed for Tarshish, God sent a storm and a big fish.

Jonah's disobedience jeopardized the lives of the ship's terrified crew. They made it through the storm, but Jonah found himself in the belly of a fish. From there the wayward prophet made a critical shift: he cried out to God. In places of great frustration or when we feel trapped with no way out, God often does His greatest work in us. In such cases, He brings us to a place where we finally stop running long enough to be still and hear His voice.

The word of the Lord came to Jonah again, and he chose his purpose. If you have been running away from the will of God, let this be the moment that you decide to stop running and return to Him. Today is a good day to get off the boat that is taking you the wrong way and get back on the course God has for you.

Gracious God, please show me the ways I am heading in the
wrong direction. I want to get back on Your course for me.

A HEALTHY HEART

Since, then, you have been raised with Christ, set your hearts
on things above, where Christ is, seated at the right hand of
God. Set your minds on things above, not on earthly things.

COLOSSIANS 3:1-2

Your physical heart muscle pumps and regulates your blood flow. That blood carries oxygen and nutrients throughout your body. If you exercise that muscle with cardio workouts and feed it healthy nutrients, it grows stronger. But let it languish and feed it junk food, and you know what happens: the arteries get clogged, and the muscle grows weak.

The same is true of your spiritual heart. It is the seat of your passions and the essence of who you are. What happens if you let your spiritual heart languish and you feed it junk food, the "earthly things" that do not satisfy? It also gets clogged, grows weak, and sends toxicity pumping throughout your life. But it's not too late to help an unhealthy heart.

Your loving God brings healing and freedom to all! He gives you good things to feed your spiritual heart—His Word, His guidance, love, prayer, practices, and wisdom. So "set your mind on things above," and feel your heart beat stronger with His love.

*Lord God, thank You for the healing work You have done
in my heart, for making it soft toward You. Keep me
focused on things above, so it stays healthy and strong.*

STRONG IN SPIRIT

The child [John the Baptist] grew and became strong in spirit; and
he lived in the wilderness until he appeared publicly to Israel.

LUKE 1:80

For centuries God's people have practiced spiritual disciplines as ways to be aware of God's presence and to become "strong in spirit." For you, spiritual disciplines can be concrete steps toward a stronger spiritual life. Among the many ways to become "strong in spirit" are these disciplines:

- Absorbing God's Word
- Praying
- Fasting
- Reading Christian books
- Being planted in a life-giving local church
- Listening to biblical teaching
- Worshiping God regularly
- Being in community with other strong believers

Sound doable? The frantic pace of twenty-first-century life leaves little time for spiritual concerns. But you weren't built to focus on the finite, temporal aspects of life while losing sight of the eternal and spiritual aspects. Your soul longs to get away from the distractions and to silence the distracting voices. So make time and space to grow "strong in spirit." After all, your spirit is eternal. Why not make it as strong as it can be?

Lord God, I pray for more understanding of
spiritual disciplines. Please give me guidance
in where and how to practice them.

BEAUTY INSTEAD OF ASHES

[The LORD has sent me] to bestow on [the brokenhearted]
a crown of beauty instead of ashes, the oil of joy instead of
mourning, and a garment of praise instead of a spirit of despair.

ISAIAH 61:3

Sometimes you can find yourself so blinded by disappointment that you can't see Jesus walking with you through your heartache. You probably aren't thinking that things will get better. But Jesus *does* walk with you through disappointment and despair—and He has hope for you in the process. Why? Because He loves you. And He wants to reassure you and show you that God has plans for you beyond your disappointment (Jeremiah 29:11).

When you face disappointment, be honest. Look to your healing Lord for His promises of beauty, joy, and a praising spirit. You can pray, "Lord, I don't understand why all this has happened. But I do know You want me to keep walking, to keep looking for You and the beauty You'll bring from these ashes."

It could be helping someone who is dealing with hurt and heartache. It could be something else beyond your imagination. But hold fast to the promise: God will be with you, and He will bless you as He lifts you up.

Lord Jesus, Your promises are a balm to my soul.
Show me more how You bring beauty from ashes.

THE MARATHON OF LIFE

Let us draw near to God with a sincere heart and with the full assurance that faith brings, having our hearts sprinkled to cleanse us from a guilty conscience and having our bodies washed with pure water.

HEBREWS 10:22

Marathon runners are consistently—if not constantly—in training. Maybe you've seen them bounding down your roadways, or you might even be one yourself. These long-distance runners understand that training for that race is essential. In addition to strengthening their physical capacity to run that distance, training also prepares them to deal with any possible obstacles and hindrances they might encounter along the way.

We Christians must constantly be in training as well. Every day we need to make the effort to do the things that will determine our capacity to run the race of life and prepare us to know how to deal with possible obstacles and hindrances.

Think about your training program and whether it will get you where you want to be. Reading the Bible, praising and worshiping God, and asking Him to attune your heart to the Holy Spirit are among the disciplines that strengthen believers. Faithfulness—every day, some days more and some days less—will yield amazing results as you run the marathon of life for your Lord.

Lord, help me be faithful in discipline with the
end goal in mind: building unshakeable faith
and fulfilling Your purpose for my life.

CALLED AND FATHERED

You are the body of Christ, and each one of you is a part of it.

1 CORINTHIANS 12:27

You are irreplaceable. Indispensable. Unique. Chosen. Valuable. You are a gift from God.

But if you don't feel that way, keep moving through the process of renewing your mind from what you have believed to embracing God's truths. Meditate today on just these two and see what a difference it makes:

- *God called you.* God created you for a purpose. The big purpose—the Great Commission—is to share the news of His love with others (Matthew 28:16–20). You, however, have a very specific, personal, and unique role in that effort. God designed and created you for that role, and He will equip you to fulfill it.
- *He is your Father.* You may know and love your earthly father, or you may not know your biological dad. But you can know your heavenly Father, and He loves you more than you can perceive. In fact, He wants you to know Him; He wants to be in relationship with you. He has made Himself known to us as our *Abba* Father (Galatians 4:6).

You are called, and you are not alone. Your heavenly Father is walking you through the process all the way to freedom. All the way to being who He created you to be.

Thank You, Father, for loving me with an unconditional, never-ending love that brings healing, transformation, hope, and joy!

GROWING GENEROSITY

In everything I did, I showed you that by this kind of hard work we must help the weak, remembering the words the Lord Jesus himself said: "It is more blessed to give than to receive."

ACTS 20:35

Think about your many blessings: maybe it's your marriage, family, education, career, house, car, friends, health, spiritual well-being, or church. As your loving God generously pours His blessings into your life, remember that those blessings are not the end of the story. They're not the climax. They're the beginning of a new story: *being* a blessing and expanding your world.

God wants to bless you so that you can be a blessing to others. If the blessings were an end in themselves, then ours would be a pretty self-absorbed, self-indulgent story—and a short one. But passing on those blessings makes us more fruitful and effective for Him. If the point of our whole story is to become more like Jesus—and it is—then our blessings are a lesson in giving, in generosity.

A generous person's world gets larger and larger, so the more generous you are with your finances, possessions, time, knowledge, and skills, the larger your sphere of influence and impact will be. Believe Jesus when He says that it truly is more blessed to give than to receive. Then try it and see!

Lord, everything I have is from You. May I be a wise and generous steward, sharing freely and happily all that You have entrusted to my care.

TRAINING YOUR FOCUS

Through [Jesus] then let us continually offer up a sacrifice of
praise to God, that is, the fruit of lips that acknowledge his name.

HEBREWS 13:15 ESV

If you're a problem solver, it's likely you can easily spot a lack. Sometimes what we do *not* have, who we are *not*, and where we have *not* yet arrived stand out like glaring red lights, telling us where to train our focus. The challenge here, my friends, is to put those *nots* where they belong—far behind the things we *do* have in Christ. Focusing on what you do have may take more effort, but that exercise is well worth the effort.

Today make a list of all that you have to be grateful for. Far from a mere mind trick or positive thinking, this practice will help you appreciate what you have right where you are—and then you will experience God's grace, peace, and contentment. Savor those quiet moments with your Lord.

Today, try developing the daily habit of giving thanks to God for all the blessings, opportunities, and answered prayers *before* you go to Him with all your needs—and that is definitely not our natural inclination! Have hope that your focus can be retrained, because you really can choose to focus on the good things.

God, I retrain my focus and learn to see the good in my
life first, because Your powerful Spirit is transforming
me. Thank You for making me more like Jesus.

VANQUISH YOUR ENEMY

"No weapon forged against you will prevail, and you
will refute every tongue that accuses you."

ISAIAH 54:17

Perhaps you've never had an actual weapon wielded against you. Maybe you're blessed to have never known a disastrous false accusation. But let me tell you why this verse is still relevant to you: You have an Enemy who is alive and well and busy and effective in the twenty-first century. He will never hesitate to launch an attack against you. But God is on your side, and *nothing* can hinder His plan for you as long as you do not give up.

Your battle is spiritual (Ephesians 6:12). Maybe you're feeling under attack even now and are wondering how you will manage. But take heart. You will never know what you're capable of in God's strength if you run away from trials and avoid obstacles. Pushing ahead and fighting the battle despite the wavering of your faith will actually build your faith and dependence on God.

So place your trust in Him, and know that God is with you and that He is at work in you. His strength will see you *through*.

Lord, thank You that You fight with me and
for me every single day. Show me where my
battles are, and how to fight back!

FACE YOUR GIANTS

The LORD is my strength and my defense;
he has become my salvation.

EXODUS 15:2

What are the giants in your life? Sin you haven't forgiven yourself for? Memories you can't shake? Shame because of what you've done or because of what was done to you? As scary as it sounds, facing those giants means both freedom and growth.

So when a giant comes crashing into your mind or heart, consider it an opportunity to run into the arms of God. Maybe it is an opportunity to confess, repent, and receive the gift of forgiveness—or to extend it. A giant will always be an opportunity to celebrate that you are loved inexhaustibly by your heavenly Father.

Then, standing strong on the truth of God's love, face the giant. Rely on the Holy Spirit to be your Defender. Find strength in Him. Speak to yourself words of truth about God's great love for you. Be confident that He can and will bring good things even out of your challenges and pain. God will complete His perfect work in you (Philippians 1:6).

He wants you to be free from those giants, and He will strengthen you in the process!

Lord, I want to be free from my giants, and I know I need
Your help when I face them. Thank You for the courage,
wisdom, strength, and deliverance You provide.

COME NEAR TO GOD

Come near to God and he will come near to you.

JAMES 4:8

Years ago, when I was in Bible college, I was able to spend two or three hours a day praying and studying the Word. After graduating, I stepped into full-time ministry . . . and then I got married . . . and then I had kids . . . and then . . . and then . . . and then . . . Once life happened, it became harder and harder to spend time with God. I bet life happened to you too.

We know in our heads that spending time with God is the most important thing we can do in a twenty-four-hour period. And we know how hard it is to make that happen—and I say *we*. I'm not here to condemn or make you feel guilty. I'm here to offer words of freedom: disregard legalism, find what works for you in this season of life, and don't feel guilty about whatever you land on! There is no correct formula for drawing near to God—not a time of day, not a place in your home, not a formula of any kind. So do whatever you need to do to walk closely with Him.

Be creative. Be free. Just make time with your heavenly Father, so you can find the strength, wisdom, peace, direction, and joy to help you navigate this season of life.

Lord God, thank You for coming near to me as I draw near to You. Show me the best way to spend time with You now in this season of my life.

WILLING TO GO

I heard the voice of the Lord saying, "Whom shall I send?
And who will go for us?" And I said, "Here am I. Send me!"

ISAIAH 6:8

When God wants to send you somewhere, He does not ask, *Are you capable?* He simply asks, *Are you willing?* That's a profound difference, and it takes a profound amount of pressure off you and your abilities. God can do wonders with willingness.

Maybe you have seen an ad about the plight of starving children in Africa. Or read about people trafficked around the world. It may be natural to wonder, *What difference could I possibly make?*

Focusing on our capabilities can stop a good work before we even start. And how ironic that we often pray for God to use us for His purposes—and then when He answers our prayer, we respond with a list of all our inadequacies. He knows about all our inadequacies and calls us anyway.

Reconsider what God is asking you to do. Are you willing? Isn't He powerful enough to fill in the gaps where your capabilities end and His limitless abilities begin? When you feel called, respond with willingness, and He will get you to your destiny.

I yield my heart to You, Lord. I want to do
what You have called me to do, trusting You
to make me capable when I say yes.

MIGHTY AND MAGNIFICENT

These are but the outer fringe of his works;
how faint the whisper we hear of him!

JOB 26:14

Expansive. Heart-stopping. Limitless. These words and more could be used to describe the night sky, sprinkled with endless stars. As we stand beneath it, like tiny specks, it's easy to agree that the God we serve is mighty and magnificent. He created this world; He sustains this world; He redeems this world—and He has created you to play a unique part in His redemption story.

Our big God is not aloof or distant; He is ever-present, loving, compassionate, and longing to be in an intimate relationship with you. Furthermore, He has the infinite ability to solve any problem, to heal any memory, to reconcile any relationship, to forgive any sin, to stretch any budget, to feed every mouth, to clothe every body, to free any captive, to break any habit, and to cure any disease. If you truly believe that God has the power to create and sustain the universe, then absolutely nothing in your life is beyond His power to mend, heal, or restore.

You really can live a wide-open, expansive life that reflects His might and magnificence, His mercy and love. Tonight, go look outside at the night sky, the outer fringe of His works, and be encouraged: nothing is impossible for our Creator God!

I find such comfort, God, in Your might and Your
magnificence around me, in me, through me,
and beyond me. Nothing is impossible!

YOUR VITAL CONTRIBUTION

"You will be my witnesses in Jerusalem, and in all
Judea and Samaria, and to the ends of the earth."

ACTS 1:8

Taking the gospel to the ends of the earth—to every single living person—sounds like a tall order. Is it even possible in our lifetime? Let me share some encouraging math.

Statistics vary, but let's just assume that there are two billion Christians on earth today. If there are eight billion people on earth, and every one of us reached three or four people in our community for Christ—can you imagine how quickly the world would come to know about Christ? Think about what might happen if we each took seriously our mandate to transform our communities by being salt and light (Matthew 5:13–16). We could achieve in one week what the greatest preaching evangelist could not possibly achieve in a lifetime. Can you see the urgency here?

Even so, we still have a long way to go. Sharing the gospel around the world will require each and every one of us to do our part. Only then will the church be able to fulfill this God-given mandate. You count, and your contribution to this holy effort matters. Don't minimize the vital part you play in helping share the gospel to the ends of the earth, with those who have not yet heard it.

Help me, God, to play my part as Your witness where You've placed me. Show me how and where to share Your love!

TIME FOR A NEW LENS

If the Spirit of him who raised Jesus from the dead is living in
you, he who raised Christ from the dead will also give life to
your mortal bodies because of his Spirit who lives in you.

ROMANS 8:11

If you wear glasses, you know that a change in lenses radically alters the way things look to you. The same is true for your spiritual glasses. When you look at your future through the resurrection lens of hope instead of the shamed or hurt or less-than lens, you will see possibility, hope, and purpose. You will no longer have to accept shame as your lot in life. You will be able to move past your past—and live a transformed life.

Choosing that resurrection perspective will alter how you see everything.

"I can't escape the images of the abuse or the sound of the cruel voices" *will become* "God sustained me through the abuse of my past and is healing my brokenness so that I might offer hope to others."

"I come from a long line of addicts and feel doomed to be the next" *will become* "I am freed from addiction. God is breaking the generational chain of addiction and beginning a new heritage of sobriety for my children and grandchildren."

Put on your resurrection lens today, and see how your view of the past changes your future.

God, I look through the resurrection lens of hope so
I can confidently walk with You into the future.

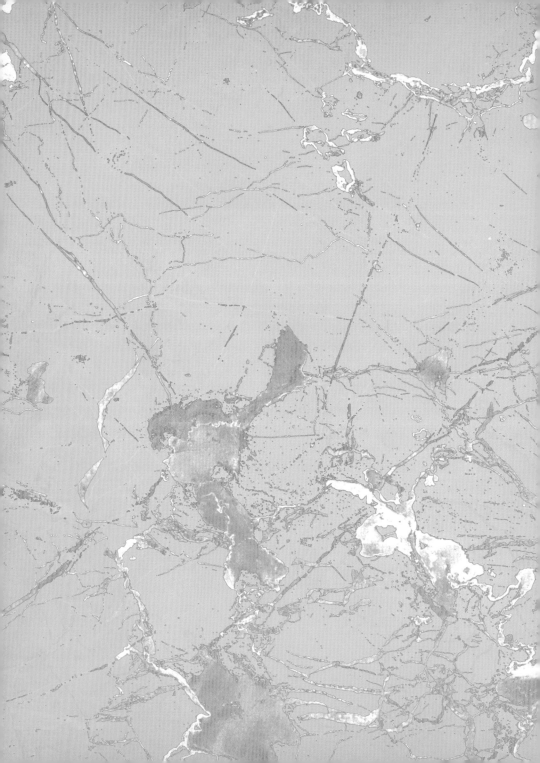

OCTOBER

My son, pay attention to what I say;
turn your ear to my words.
Do not let them out of your sight,
keep them within your heart;
for they are life to those who find them
and health to one's whole body.

PROVERBS 4:20-22

LEAVING BEHIND, MOVING AHEAD

I will walk about in freedom, for I have sought out your precepts.

PSALM 119:45

Here is the simple but profound truth: you cannot go where you are going without leaving where you have been. So ask yourself, "What must I leave behind in order to serve God with my whole life?" God is looking for runners who, like Paul, will say, "Whatever were gains to me I now consider loss for the sake of Christ. What is more, I consider everything a loss because of the surpassing worth of knowing Christ Jesus my Lord, for whose sake I have lost all things. I consider them garbage, that I may gain Christ" (Philippians 3:7–8).

Imagine the freedom you will experience when you are willing to lose that garbage! Think about running unhindered as you do the work God calls you to do! Toss away the old junk from your past—and eliminate any way to get it back. Commit yourself to Jesus Christ and His cause, and step out in faith.

Do you want God to do something new in your life? Then logic tells you to stop doing the "same old thing." Do you want God to change your circumstances? Then seek change in your life. As you walk in freedom, God will take you to new and freedom-filled places.

Lord God, I want to drop my old junk and be unhindered in my walk with You! Thank You for the freedom and newness You bring.

LIGHTER SHOES, LIGHTER HEART

He put a new song in my mouth, a hymn of praise to our God.
Many will see and fear the LORD and put their trust in him.

PSALM 40:3

The shoes that competitive sprinters wear when they train are often heavier than their race shoes. When they switch out—when they throw off those heavier shoes—they run more easily and much faster.

It's a good strategy for runners—and for us. Are you ready to let go, are you ready to throw off—completely and once and for all—everything that weighs you down and holds you back? You don't need to hold on to sins that you have confessed, mistakes you have made and learned from, and wounds that God is healing. Let go. Put an end to that way of living. An ending, it turns out, is the perfect place for a new start. And for a new, lighter pair of shoes.

God promises that the plans He has for you are for good and not for evil, to give you a future and a hope (Jeremiah 29:11). Why live weighed down by the past when His promises are propelling you into your future? Unburden yourself of all that hinders and cast it all away so you can praise God with a brand-new song and trust in Him!

Lord, please help me to let go of the weights
I've been carrying. I want to use that freedom
to praise You wholeheartedly!

GODLY AMBITION

Whoever pursues righteousness and
love finds life, prosperity and honor.

PROVERBS 21:21

Our culture encourages us to act on ambition—and this is not necessarily a bad thing! We just need to know the difference between godly ambition and selfish or worldly ambition. One grows God's kingdom, and one feeds our flesh. Check your ambitions against this list and make those adjustments that keep you pursuing God's good ways:

GODLY AMBITION	SELFISH AMBITION
Is initiated by God	Is driven by self
Is about advancing the kingdom	Is about building a personal empire
Honors others	Competes with others
Is loyal	Is opportunistic
Is others focused	Is self-focused
Is content with anonymity	Wants the spotlight
Prefers others	Uses others
Longs to please God	Pleases man
Prioritizes obedience to Christ	Will compromise to advance
Loves people	Leverages people
Thinks of the next generation	Indulges this generation alone

One kind of ambition destroys, and the other brings life and love beyond your own lifetime. As you pursue your ambitions, constantly evaluate and bring them before God to be tuned to Him. It will lead to something greater than anything you can imagine on your own!

Lord, I set my heart to please You and pursue
Your godly ambition for my life. Thank You
for showing me Your perfect path.

DEFEATING GIANTS

This day the LORD will deliver you into my
hands, and I'll strike you down.

1 SAMUEL 17:46

"What if" questions can be launching pads of faith, or they can hold us back in fear. Whatever your "what ifs" are, you can change them from a sign of fear to a sign of faith.

Fear asks questions like these: *What if no one comes? What if there is not enough money? What if I fail? What if we lose everything? What if my friends walk away?*

Faith asks questions like these: *What if hundreds of young people come and surrender their lives to Christ? What if we are approved for the loan? What if my coworker says yes to coming to church? What if that business deal works? What if I get a degree?*

Faith questions rise up in our hearts when we place our confidence in God—when we trust in Him more than we do our insecurities. When David killed the giant Goliath, he didn't think about how big Goliath was. He only thought about how big his God was! That's why he could declare in confidence, "This day the Lord will deliver you into my hands."

So *what if*—starting today—you choose to put your faith in God? What if you start asking all of your questions with a faith perspective? If you do, you'll defeat all of your giants!

*Lord, I choose to retrain my thinking and start
asking questions of faith. Thank You for helping
me reframe my perspective starting today!*

LIFESAVING MEDICINE

The law of the LORD is perfect, refreshing the soul. The statutes
of the LORD are trustworthy, making wise the simple. The
precepts of the LORD are right, giving joy to the heart. The
commands of the LORD are radiant, giving light to the eyes.

PSALM 19:7–8

God will give you the power to exchange any of the Enemy's lies for His unchanging truth. But what is your role in this process? What do you need to do in cooperation with God to trade wrong thinking for God's thoughts?

As you are already doing by reading this devotional, continue to start each day by filling your mind with the Word of God. Remind yourself of what God says about you and what the pages of Scripture say about Him. When you are armed with the truth of His Word, you will be better able to stand strong against any fears, negativity, or lies that the Enemy hurls your way.

If you're not yet convinced of the value of opening your Bible before your day gets going, consider this analogy: if you needed kidney dialysis every day to stay alive, you would do it, right? I urge you to consider studying the Word just as important. The Word will keep you on God's path and help you know joy, hope, and peace, whatever comes your way.

Lord, thank You for Your Word. Please make me
hungrier for the Scriptures—and to consider them
as crucial to my health as life-saving medicine.

THE ROARING CROWD

Therefore, since we are surrounded by such
a great cloud of witnesses . . .

HEBREWS 12:1

I had joined the 219.4 million Americans tuning into NBC for their coverage of the Olympic Games in London in August 2012. And it was turning out to be the most watched Olympic Games in history! Team USA was about to run the relay race, and as the camera scanned the passionate crowd that filled the Olympic stadium that day, today's verse flew into my mind. *Did this compare with the great cloud of witnesses watching us?*

Hardly! On your race, you are surrounded by a "cloud of witnesses"—all the believers who have come before us and will come after us. The passionate, roaring crowd in the stadium and watching remotely that day was but a shadow of what we experience. And more importantly, the combined passion of all those Olympic witnesses pales in comparison to the passion for us and for our salvation that motivated Jesus to die on the cross, go to the grave, and be resurrected—just for us.

It is that passion living on the inside of us that calls us to run— unstoppable—the race God has designed for us. So run your race with joy! And think of the crowd surrounding you!

Lord, today, when I remember all Your saints, let me
draw from the tremendous joy and passion that drives us
toward You. It all comes from You and ends with You!

DON'T LOOK BACK

---

*One thing I do: Forgetting what is behind and straining toward
what is ahead, I press on toward the goal to win the prize
for which God has called me heavenward in Christ Jesus.*

PHILIPPIANS 3:13–14

Wherever you are on your healing journey today—keep yourself in a healthy place by staying mentally and emotionally in the present moment or thinking about the future.

These two options are far wiser choices than spending any time rehashing old injustices. Ruminating over what cannot be changed only leads us to emotionally revolve around the past. As the apostle Paul coached us in today's scripture, there's far greater reward in thinking about the future.

I had to learn how to focus on the future—and it didn't come easily. I had to mentally stretch and strain "to take hold of that for which Christ Jesus took hold of me" (Philippians 3:12). I had to realign my thoughts with the brand-new life Jesus gave me now here on earth and what would be in eternity with Him in heaven. What a glorious future to look toward and take hold of!

As you move forward in Christ's healing, open your eyes to the present and to your glorious eternal future. It will fuel you with hope as you press on toward the goal.

*Lord, I forget what lies behind and I press on. I
press forward toward all that You have for me.*

THE BEST WAY

You have laid down precepts that are to be fully obeyed. Oh,
that my ways were steadfast in obeying your decrees!

PSALM 119:4–5

God's Word is a vital part of my daily life. If I'm not writing down verses to memorize, then I'm listening to a message or reading a book or studying a passage. I do everything I can to keep God's Word going into my heart.

When we first become believers, we need its guidance for how to live. For example:

- God tells us how to behave with sexual purity, to keep us from diseases, broken hearts, damaged emotions, and wounded souls (1 Corinthians 5:11).
- God encourages us not to covet other people's things because He knows we will never be truly happy until we are content with what He has already blessed us with (Exodus 20:17).
- God teaches us to tithe because He wants us to remember that all we have is His and that we are to be involved in His work in the world (Malachi 3:10).

Without the Word of God to guide our lives and shape our perspective, we would remain self-absorbed and self-indulgent. We would remain people who do what is right in their own eyes.

God's Word is His gift to you and me. As you continue to open His book daily, thank God for helping you learn to live His way.

You established Your laws, Lord, for my good. Show me
the truth in Your Word, and help me apply it to my life.

GOD'S THOUGHTS

How precious to me are your thoughts, God!

PSALM 139:17

One of the most important lessons I have discovered is that nothing is as powerful as a mind made up. It has the power to control the way your day—as well as your life—goes. We really don't have to think every train of thought that pops into our minds. Just like a real train, we can jump trains and even jump tracks. We don't have to let the train control where we go mentally and emotionally.

We have the power to control what we think. And consequently, we have the power to control who we become, because we are what we think, whether or not we choose to learn how to consciously control our thoughts: *"As he thinks in his heart, so is he"* (Proverbs 23:7 AMP).

How crucial it is for you to manage your mind and feed it daily with the thoughts of God from His Word. Learn to manage your mind, so your mind doesn't manage you. As you hop on trains of thought, pay attention to your destination today. Jump tracks and change trains every time you need to. Consciously choose the trains that take you to God's precious and life-giving thoughts.

Lord, I choose to think on whatever is true, right, pure, lovely, admirable, excellent, and praiseworthy, just like Philippians 4:8 says. I choose my train of thought.

FORWARD, NOT BACKWARD

Wouldn't it be better for us to go back to Egypt?

NUMBERS 14:3

More than once the children of Israel lost focus of how bad life had been when they were slaves in Egypt, and they wanted to return to the land of their bondage. Moses contended with them over and over—with taking the slave out of slavery, but more importantly with taking the slavery out of the slave.

And aren't we the same way? How easily we forget how bad our former enslavement was when the wilderness season grows too dark, becomes too hard, and lasts too long. Maybe we forget how hard it is to be enslaved by taskmasters like shame, secret hurts, grief, and lies. How easy it is to slip back into our old patterns and start yearning for the old and familiar—even though we know none of it was good for us.

Because we're human, it's always easier to default to our old behaviors than to work on forming new ones—just like the children of Israel did. But remember: this is not a drive-through breakthrough. The Lord is leading us through the wilderness to get to freedom, so we can emerge better and stronger because of our time with Him there.

Lord God, I want to be permanently free. When I start yearning for the past, help me stay close to You. Help me trust You for the future beyond the wilderness and stay focused on my freedom.

"FEAR NOT!"

"Do you love me?"

JOHN 21:15

Jesus asked Peter this question three times—and three times Peter answered yes. Jesus was emphasizing that loving Him was what really mattered. When we're afraid, He asks us the same question: *Do you love Me?*

When Jesus asks us, He is also saying, "Then turn your fear over to Me. Replace that fear—that I did not give you—with the love, power, and sound mind that I have given you [2 Timothy 1:7]. Know that My presence is the antidote to your fear. Hold fast to Me in faith."

Jesus knew that in this world we would be afraid, and we would doubt. That's why we read *Fear not* again and again in the Bible—365 times, one for each day of the year. God knows that sheer willpower will not enable us to conquer our fears, but His love—and His grace and a sound mind and courage—can and will. But know this: courage is not the absence of fear; it's the will to persevere in the face of fear. As you make that choice—as you see the dangers—remember *Fear not.*

When Jesus asks, "Do you love Me?" say, "Yes." And rest in that love. Let it move into every corner of your heart. As you do, fear will have to move out.

For Your presence with me, Your love, Your power, the sound mind You've given me—thank You, Lord!

WALKING WITH GOD AND EACH OTHER

The eyes of both of them were opened, and they realized they were naked; so they sewed fig leaves together and made coverings for themselves.

GENESIS 3:7

Transparency. Vulnerability. Authenticity. These are the ways God meant for us to relate to Him and to each other. Yet this kind of emotional "nakedness" can be frightening, especially if we're afraid of how others—or even God—will respond.

That's why Adam and Eve sewed those leaves together. Their first instinct was to hide from God when they realized they had sinned. The Word says they were naked and afraid of how He would respond. And we all have been hiding ever since. But that beauty of transparency, vulnerability, and purity is still available to us. God wants you to trust Him with openness, honesty, and your true self. He wants you whole—in your spirit, in your soul, and in your body. He wants your mind healthy and your heart fully alive to Him.

So bring all of yourself to Him. Share the depths of your heart—and let Him heal every facet of you. Risk telling Him everything—everything He already knows.

Lord Jesus, thank You that I can be completely vulnerable with You. Show me when I'm "sewing fig leaves" to cover myself, and lead me toward honesty and a loving connection with You today and every day.

GOD'S TIMING FOR GOD'S PLAN

Pharaoh said to Joseph, "I hereby put you in
charge of the whole land of Egypt."

GENESIS 41:41

Joseph was a man in the Bible whose life story has so much to teach us. Being thrown into a pit by his brothers, sold into slavery, and wrongfully imprisoned would make anyone feel pushed to the edge with bitterness and resentment. But what a lesson in God's redemption and the beauty that can come out of initial disappointments.

Any dreams or goals Joseph might have had were undoubtedly shattered throughout his treacherous journey. Yet Joseph did not lose hope. In God's timing and according to God's plan, Pharaoh met Joseph and placed him "in charge of the whole land of Egypt."

What a turn of events! A miraculous turnaround that's just like God—just like what He wants to do in your life. As you move forward, like Joseph, decide ahead of time that you will not allow disappointments to derail your journey of faith. Even if things haven't turned out as you had hoped and prayed, know that God loves you, and His good plans for you are still unfolding. I believe future God appointments await you on the other side of your disappointments—just like they did for Joseph.

You know my heart, God. Even so, I am glad I can be
honest with You when I feel let down. I believe for divine
appointments on the other side of my disappointments.

A HEALTHY ENVIRONMENT

"I am the vine, you are the branches; he who abides
in Me and I in him, he bears much fruit."

JOHN 15:5 NASB

Years ago, before Nick and I married, I had to step out of the environment of family dinners. I love my family, and they love me, but they could not understand why I was "becoming a nun," which was how they saw my Christian work! Because of their criticisms, I left dinners feeling deflated and depleted. I soon recognized that, for my dream to survive, I had to limit my exposure to their disapproving comments.

This was a very painful choice, but for a season it was vital. As my dream grew, family dinners no longer were a threat. In fact, everyone's criticism eventually grew into encouragement, and now we are closer than ever!

What dream has God put in your heart? And what environment is tearing it down? For you, it may be going to a certain bar or club or joining in on the lunchroom gossip. Perhaps it's spending time with certain family and friends. Whatever it is, if it takes you away from fulfilling your purpose, have the courage to walk away for a time for the sake of your dream. Protect your dream until it's strong enough to stand up anywhere. Ask God to lead you toward more positive environments, where your dream can flourish.

Lord, please give me discernment as I choose to make
a life where the dream You gave me can grow.

THE PROMISE OF POSSIBILITY

We should go up and take possession of the
land, for we can certainly do it.

NUMBERS 13:30

What are you going to take possession of? Perhaps it's greater freedom from the past. Perhaps it's a new calling, a new adventure. Whatever it is, I invite you to imagine this "possession" as if you've already achieved it. That's what two of Israel's leaders, Joshua and Caleb, did in the desert.

Instead of looking only at fortified cities like Jericho and its intimidating walls, and strong people like the giants of the land, Joshua and Caleb kept their eyes on God, who was bigger and stronger. Rather than being distracted by all that looked impossible, they saw all that was possible. They fixated on God's promise: a land of plenty for His people. Joshua and Caleb could see it, feel it, and taste it. That's why they told Moses, "We can certainly do it."

Joshua and Caleb knew that the God who had performed miracles for the children of Israel would absolutely take them into the promised land. They were confident that God—who was the same today, yesterday, and tomorrow—was more than sufficient (Hebrews 13:8). Put your faith in God's promises today. Go in and possess your land, confident that God will deliver it all into your hands.

*Lord, thank You for Your promises. I place my confidence
in You, believing I possess everything You've shown me.*

IDENTITY CHECK

"I no longer call you servants, because a servant does not know his master's business. Instead, I have called you friends, for everything that I learned from my Father I have made known to you."

JOHN 15:15

Who are you really? We all wear so many hats—mom, wife, sister, friend, co-worker, leader, innovator, activist, minister. But what we do is not who we are. And who we are is what God wants us to continually stay in touch with.

I've compiled a short list of who you really are. As you go about your day, hold these truths close to your heart. Read them out loud in first person to really let them sink in, and even consider carrying this list around with you. Memorize it and meditate on it until you think first of who you are and not what you do:

I am a child of God (John 1:12–13).

I am saved by grace (Ephesians 2:8–9).

I am alive to God and dead to sin (Romans 6:11).

I am sanctified (John 17:19).

I am a new creation (2 Corinthians 5:17).

I am a royal daughter (1 Peter 2:9).

I am reconciled to God (2 Corinthians 5:19).

I am free (John 8:36).

I am justified (Galatians 2:16).

I am chosen (Ephesians 1:4).

God, I'm so grateful for the ways You remind me of who I am. I meditate on them, letting them sink into my heart so I can remember them when my identity is tested.

CHOOSING WORSHIP

Ascribe to the LORD the glory due his name; worship
the LORD in the splendor of his holiness.

PSALM 29:2

I don't know what giants you're facing, but I *do* know that God is bigger than any situation you could ever face. (Read that sentence again!) Problems that seem overwhelming can look quite small in light of God's greatness.

When faith-shakers arise—when crises or challenges come—boost your ability to see God's hugeness by *worshiping Him.* Regardless of your circumstances, declare God's greatness, praise His goodness, and celebrate His faithfulness. Even though your circumstances may not change immediately, your heart may now know hope, and your perspective on both the present and the future includes God. Choose to look up to the Lord and into His Word.

When you look to your great and glorious and trustworthy God, those life situations are less likely to steal your peace. Whatever the size of your challenge, He is bigger. Your loving God wants the best for you, and He is at work doing something you cannot yet see—something that will amaze you when all becomes clear.

Lord, when faith-shakers come, please remind
me how big You are. I look ahead expectant of
all the good that You are accomplishing.

PROTECT YOUR IDENTITY

Take the helmet of salvation, and the sword of
the Spirit, which is the word of God.

EPHESIANS 6:17

A friend of mine went through the awful ordeal of being a victim of identity theft. She encountered nothing but frustration when she couldn't use her credit cards or access her money. Since then, she's taken all necessary precautions to protect her identity!

In the same way, it is crucial we do all we can to ensure that we protect our identity in Christ. The Bible teaches us, *"The thief does not come except to steal, and to kill, and to destroy"* (John 10:10 NKJV). That's why it's so important to remember who God says you are! If we're not careful to take the steps designed to protect our blood-bought identities—like memorizing and hiding God's Word in our hearts and minds—then while we're busy trying to forge our own identities, we run the risk of the Enemy stealing our true identity from us.

Just as we go to great measures to protect our credit cards, bank accounts, and documents, let's also ensure that in our pursuit of having and doing it all, we don't lose our true identity: who we are in Christ (which is unchanging). Fight for your identity today by remembering who He says you are.

*God, I want to live in my true identity. Help me keep
who You say I am foremost in my mind and heart!*

THE NECESSITIES

For our boast is this, the testimony of our conscience, that we
behaved in the world with simplicity and godly sincerity.

2 CORINTHIANS 1:12 ESV

What everyday things can you *absolutely* not live without? Your phone? A cup (or two or three cups) of coffee? Here's a freeing fact: you can live with so much less than you think you can!

I learned that when my hand cream and hairspray were confiscated in an airport, and then, when I hopped off the plane three thousand miles later for a speaking engagement, my bags had been lost! I was mortified that I'd have to speak in my track suit and sneakers, flaky-handed, and flat-haired. But when I began preaching, the Spirit of the Lord moved, and I forgot all about it. God was what was important, and He was there in power! He still did everything He was there to do, and it was a joy.

To live effectively, let's master the art of simplifying our lives. Of all our supposed necessities, loving God and loving others are the only two we *absolutely* can't live without (Mark 12:28–31). Everything else is a nice bonus, but God is the one who empowers us to do His work—not hair spray or coffee. And we can depend on Him to always provide, to always come through.

Lord, teach me how to simplify my life, so I
can remember what is important to You.

TAKE A BREATH

The Lord replied, "My Presence will go with
you, and I will give you rest."

EXODUS 33:14

Busy, busy, busy. We are always so busy. We feel driven by the urgency of everyone else's needs and demands—from our kids to our families to our jobs. But we can't go on that way indefinitely. Take time today to pause and ask yourself: *What things in my life can I replace with time for me in order to recharge and breathe?*

I have found that the greatest gift I can give to my family and co-workers is a healthy me, and the only way I am able to do that is to take time to recharge my soul and spirit. I have to be very disciplined to set aside time for just me, and then use that precious time wisely!

Personally, I enjoy a bike ride, a walk on the beach, or a good book. For you, it might be sitting in a comfy chair, sipping a cup of coffee, and resting. It might be putting on your running shoes and going for a jog in the park. Or listening to music, gardening, cooking, or simply sitting on the porch, watching the sunset. Whatever refreshes your soul, take time today to recharge and regroup. You'll find relief from mental confusion, emotional outbursts, and physical exhaustion if you simply stop, breathe, and lean in to the presence of God.

God, please teach me how to breathe
and rest today. I lean in to You.

THE ACTUAL AND THE POSSIBLE

"Before I formed you in the womb I knew you,
before you were born I set you apart;
I appointed you as a prophet to the nations."

JEREMIAH 1:4–5

When we're young, people talk a lot about our potential. Teachers often tell parents their children are not living up to all their potential. They see so much in children and want them to flourish. But as we grow older, we tend to lose this "potential" mind-set. No one encourages us to keep developing. Well, I have news for you: you still have potential—and it can still be fulfilled. There's much more on the inside of you to be developed and expanded.

Potential is the difference between what is actual and what is possible—the unexposed ability, reserved strength, unused success, dormant gifts, hidden talents, and latent power that lies within each one of us.

All of creation—including you—possesses the hidden ability to accomplish even more for the kingdom than we do today. In us right now are the seeds to be all God has destined us to be—all that He's created us to be. So, let's look to Him and ask Him to develop all that He placed within us. Let's live up to all our potential—and fulfill all the purpose God called us to live.

God, You have so much planned for me. I want to
grow into the person You made me to be!

ASK GOD ON A DATE

You, God, are my God, earnestly I seek you.

PSALM 63:1

Without sounding too sacrilegious, I venture to say that God wants to date you! I believe He wants to spend time with you and dream dreams with you and plan an amazing life together. And, I believe He wants you to get to know Him better—and to grow closer to Him. So, if you were to start dating God, where would you go? Why not try:

- going for a walk with God before burying yourself in your daily demands.
- chatting with Him as you drive to work (completely ignoring the people staring from the car next to you).
- taking God on a shopping trip. (He'll be very honest about how big your thighs look in skinny jeans.)
- inviting God out for coffee. (He is well known for leaving His coffee untouched, which means you always get a second cup!)

Seriously, though, time spent getting to know God in our day-to-day activities increases our intimacy with Him. And He loves to respond to our questions, our heart-cries, our musings when we ask to spend set-apart, designated time with Him. He loves to keep His promise to us: "Come near to God and he will come near to you" (James 4:8).

God, I want to spend time with You and get to know You better. Please meet me for a quiet moment together today!

YOU ARE WORTH FAR MORE

"Are not five sparrows sold for two pennies? Yet not
one of them is forgotten by God. Indeed, the very
hairs of your head are all numbered. Don't be afraid;
you are worth more than many sparrows."

LUKE 12:6-7

Years ago, our gracious God took my heart—that had been broken and made
to feel so unworthy—and healed it and made me whole. Then, because I was
willing to take one step . . . and then another . . . and another, God used me
to come alongside those who were suffering—alongside people who have been
flattened by life.

Do you see the beauty of this design? The very thing the Enemy used to
try to destroy my life is the thing that God has used to help others. And that's
what God wants to do with your life too.

He can heal every hurt and turn your scars into points of connection in
a ministry that draws people to Jesus. He knows the worth of each one of us,
and as He heals us, He connects us to Him and to each other. He knows you,
loves you, and values you. How great that your past need no longer define you
or your future.

I thank You for choosing to love me and heal me, Lord.
And thank You for redeeming my life to help me connect
with hurting people who need to meet Jesus.

THE FUTURE OF THE CHURCH

I will build my church, and the gates of Hades will not overcome it.

MATTHEW 16:18

The future of the church is bright! Every time I stand in a stadium filled with young people desperate to worship and eager to change their world for Jesus, I am inspired with hope for the future. The greatest days for the church are ahead of us, not behind us—because there is a generation of young people marked by God for greatness in a brand-new way.

Hebrews 11 tells us all about the giants of faith in the Bible, and what they did "by faith." Paul did this not to make us think that things were so much better in the old days, but to remind us that *we also* are part of this heritage. God is not up in heaven worrying about the economic, social, or political state of our world, or the challenges we face. No! He is "building his church"—so aggressively that not even the gates of hell can prevail against it! And we are working with him, as co-laborers ushering in the lost, and so will the Christ-followers who come after us.

Through Jesus, we have the victory. Through Jesus, we have the ability and strength to endure. Through Jesus, we join our ancestors in telling the next generation about how very great our God is. And in His power, the best is yet to come.

Lord, bless this generation! Thank You for placing us on this earth to build Your church and to encourage those who come after us, until You finally come.

LEARNING TO LISTEN

> "Go. I am sending you to Pharaoh to bring my
> people the Israelites out of Egypt."
>
> **EXODUS 3:10**

When Christians find themselves wandering in the "wilderness," there comes a point when they ask themselves, *How in the world did I wind up here?* If you're in that place, listen for God's voice. You just might hear God calling you to your next assignment.

Take Moses' story, for example. Moses was a Hebrew baby adopted by the daughter of Egypt's pharaoh. Moses spent his first forty years in Pharaoh's palace, brought up like royalty. Then, God stirred within Moses the desire to help his people, who had been the Egyptians' slaves for more than four hundred years.

One day, Moses saw an Egyptian mercilessly beating a Hebrew slave. Enraged, Moses killed the Egyptian. To escape Pharaoh's wrath, Moses fled to the desert land of Midian, where he remained for *four decades*—until God spoke: "Go. I am sending you to Pharaoh."

Moses spent 14,600 days in that desert. Occasionally, while watching over his flock, he must have wondered, *How in the world did I wind up here?* The Bible doesn't say much about what Moses did during those forty years, but he must have honored God and learned to recognize His voice. When God suddenly showed up on day 14,601, He revealed Moses' assignment: to free His chosen people from slavery.

> Lord God, thank You for making my
> assignment very clear to me.

YOUR METAMORPHOSIS

As obedient children, let yourselves be pulled into a way of life
shaped by God's life, a life energetic and blazing with holiness.

1 PETER 1:13–16 THE MESSAGE

One of my favorite books when I was a child was *The Very Hungry Caterpillar*.
In the story, that little insect eats and eats! He consumes everything from
apples to cupcakes. And once he's finished eating and is twelve times his
original size, he enters a cocoon to sleep things off. The best part of the book
is the final moment when my little friend turns into a stunning butterfly. It's
a beautiful story of the transformation process we know as *metamorphosis*.

I believe, as Christians, we too go through a metamorphosis. As we abide
in the word, it's as though we're spinning our own spiritual cocoon—a hidden
place where an unseen work takes place. It's where we're transformed from
the inside out into the image of Jesus. It happens slowly over time, as we allow
the Word to shape our thoughts and change our lives. The final result is a
complete transformation—an external manifestation of an internal process.
It's our own metamorphosis into who God created us to be, fulfilling all that
God has called us to do.

So, the next time you read your Bible, think of the hungry caterpillar and
all that you are destined to become.

Lord Jesus, thank You for growing me in the
safety and wisdom of Your Word. Thank You
for how it changes me, inside and out.

RECOVERY TIME

A person's wisdom yields patience.

PROVERBS 19:11

Once, on a wipeout down a ski slope, I ruptured major ligaments in my knee and needed emergency surgery. When the doctor took that first post-op look, he warned me that my leg would look abnormal due to the swelling. Still, I was shocked.

"Don't panic," he said. "This is perfectly normal, given the trauma of the surgery. Give it time, and your leg will return to normal. I should warn you, though, that the pain of the recovery will be much greater than the pain of the injury." Not what I wanted to hear.

When life hurts us, we want the quick fix, instant newness, wholeness completely restored. We want God to take care of the problem—yesterday.

But most of the time, damage to the heart doesn't happen overnight, and neither does its healing.

Sometimes, wounds seem to heal over, but then we realize they were never cleaned well enough, and the infection was merely hidden. Other times, scar tissue remains that influences how life in general and relationships in particular are unfolding for you. Total healing might require that we go deep into painful places, so I encourage you to rely on the wisdom of patience. He *is* healing you.

Lord, please give me patience with the healing process. I'm so grateful You will sustain and encourage me during my recovery.

SUPERNATURAL WOMAN

Charm is deceptive, and beauty is fleeting; but a
woman who fears the Lord is to be praised.

PROVERBS 31:30

You don't have to be a superwoman; you just need to be supernatural! In Proverbs 31, a picture is painted of such a woman—an excellent wife and mother who worked diligently, provided food for her family, rose early, was an entrepreneur, dressed immaculately, helped the poor and the needy, and was wise, kind, strong, and dignified.

Simply reading about this Proverbs 31 woman can make us feel tired and stretched to capacity. Rather than motivating us, she potentially only serves to remind us of how much we are not doing. However, I see this woman not as a superhero but rather as an inspiration.

In the midst of a normal life, she discovered a secret—the God factor—and came to realize she didn't need to be superhuman at all, but supernaturally empowered by the Holy Spirit. Through His strength, wisdom, and endurance, she was able to have and do her "all"—as God defined it. And He defines it differently for each of us.

God wants us all to live an abundant life, one where we fulfill all the purposes and plans God created for us to fulfill. One where we fulfill all the potential He placed inside of us.

God, I want to do it all, but I want it to be Your
all. Please show me how it can be done!

TRUTH VERSUS FEELINGS

"Heaven and earth will pass away, but my
words will never pass away."

MARK 13:31

Your heart may insist that God created you and loves you, but that doesn't stop your mind from punching away with thoughts like, *What's wrong with me? I never seem to do anything right!*

It's an age-old war—of truth versus feelings—but there can be peace!

When there is a fight between your heart and your head, the best thing to do is read God's Word and remind yourself of who God says you are. Soaking in the promises of His love, acceptance, and delight in you will slowly quiet those condemning voices—and renew your mind. Those negative blows can give you an overwhelming sense of worthlessness and rejection, because that is what the lies of the Enemy do to us. They beat us down and try to knock us out.

It's God who will always lift us up. It's always God who will help you get it all right!

I am God's child (1 Peter 1:23).

I am God's workmanship (Ephesians 2:10).

I am the light of the world (Matthew 5:14).

I am a doer of the Word and blessed in my actions (James 1:22, 25).

I am firmly rooted, built up, established in my faith, and overflowing with gratitude (Colossians 2:7).

Jesus, when my feelings assail me, please draw me
back into Your love. Imprint Your Word on my heart,
and keep me coming back to it again and again.

WE ARE CHOSEN

"You did not choose me, but I chose you and appointed you
so that you might go and bear fruit—fruit that will last."

JOHN 15:16

For years, I didn't know I was adopted. But after I found out, and began to share freely the journey God had taken me through, I began to realize that my story connected with so many others. It was actually a gift I could share to help others. I realized that because I knew that I was chosen by God—despite being left unnamed and unwanted in a hospital—I could help others discover that they too had been chosen by God, regardless of the circumstances of their lives.

I remember when I read "unnamed" on my birth certificate for the very first time. That may have been what the hospital staff believed, but God's word said differently: *"Before I was born the LORD called me; from my mother's womb he has spoken my name* (Isaiah 49:1).

Regardless of our start in life, you and I are chosen. Named. Wanted. Nothing about my birth—or yours—was random or accidental. I was born for this time—and so were you. So as we step out into our day, let's help others discover the wonder of how they are chosen too. Let's bear fruit that will last by sharing our stories of God's great love.

*Father God, thank You for choosing me—and letting
me help others know they are chosen too.*

FAITH IN THE FACE OF FEAR

"Do not fear, for I have redeemed you; I have
summoned you by name; you are mine."

ISAIAH 43:1

Sometimes, when we take a risk in faith, the very thing that frightened us—and almost paralyzed our future—becomes amazing. Perhaps it was reaching out to a new person, performing onstage, or interviewing for a new job. If fears are keeping you from experiencing the extraordinary today, remember that God can work, despite your fear, to make miracles happen—especially when you step out in faith.

As we fix our eyes on Him, we see His love, we taste His power, and it feeds us. It helps us grow stronger—so strong, in fact, that we find every bit of strength we need to soar above and beyond any fear holding us back. When we keep our eyes on Him, He takes us out of the constraints that otherwise bind us in fear.

In this freedom, our world and our lives are enlarged, and the possibilities for the miraculous are increased. We achieve the impossible by focusing on the God with whom all things are possible. We bring healing and hope to the broken and hopeless. We go places we never imagined, because He frees us from fear—for our good, and for the good of others too!

Lord God, thank You for working with me past,
through, and despite my fear. Show me where facing
fear in Your power will move me forward.

NOVEMBER

But the plans of the Lord stand firm forever,
the purposes of his heart through all generations.

PSALM 33:11

A GOOD CHOICE

Enter his gates with thanksgiving and his courts with
praise; give thanks to him and praise his name.

PSALM 100:4

What are you thankful for today? Maybe you've had a good week. Maybe you have enough money to pay your bills. Maybe the kids behaved like angels, cleaned up the house, and paused to ask, "Mom, how *are* you today? May I make you a cup of tea?"

Give thanks for those blessings—even though finding something to be thankful for *isn't* a condition of entering the Lord's gates with thanksgiving and His courts with praise. We aren't supposed to wait to enter until something nice has happened to us. We're to thank Him every moment of every day!

Regardless of what is going on in our lives, thankfulness is a choice. We can *decide* whether or not we will enter God's presence with a thankful heart, with gratitude based not on what is happening to us but on who God is. And He is a good God—always, in countless ways.

So, whether things are going well—or not—let's give God thanks for every little thing we can today. Let's choose gratitude as our attitude. Let's honor God in everything we say, praising His holy name.

*Lord, I enter Your gates with thanksgiving today,
Your courts with praise. You are a worthy God, and
I am so thankful for all You've given to me.*

DEVELOP YOUR WILDERNESS SKILLS

Give thanks to the Lord of lords: His love endures
forever. . . . to him who led his people through
the wilderness; His love endures forever.

PSALM 136:3, 16

When you hear the word *wilderness*, what do you think of? Starry nights to commune with God in His beautiful creation? Or bugs, sleeping on the ground, and no running water? For Christ-followers, a wilderness can mean a time of testing and a season of growth. If you're in the wilderness today, rest assured that your guide is none other than Christ Himself.

Every follower of Jesus goes through several wilderness seasons in life. Each time the experience exposes how vulnerable, how defenseless, and how small we are in this big world and vast universe. But God is always doing something in us. The wilderness is no mistake in navigation. It is the path to freedom that God has chosen for His people to go through. In the wilderness, God's love becomes more strongly rooted in our hearts.

Still, none of us ever goes looking for the wilderness. Instead we feel thrust into the unknown, and we sometimes get lost as we wander. During your wilderness times, know that God will change your thinking as He transforms you. He will not let you be lost or forgotten as you follow Him wherever He leads you.

Since the wilderness brings me more strength
and understanding, Lord, help me follow
where You lead, even into the unknown.

REPLACE AND RENEW

"Keep this Book of the Law always on your lips; meditate on it day and night, so that you may be careful to do everything written in it. Then you will be prosperous and successful."

JOSHUA 1:8

Almost four thousand years ago, people started writing down what would become the Bible on sheets of papyrus. It's incredible to think of the way that holy book has multiplied since then! You can find scores of translations and commentaries. You can purchase workbooks and attend Bible studies. You can download apps and listen to messages. It's nonstop access.

God is and always has been serious about getting His Word to you. Take time to read it, listen to it, and study it to set your course and stay on track every day. I write Scripture verses on Post-it notes and place them on my bathroom mirror or by the kitchen sink or around my computer.

Knowing who you are in Christ is key to the choices you make each day. And knowing your identity in Christ requires knowing God's Word, something that happens only when you read it, meditate on it, and study it. Only then can you apply its truth to your life. Ingrained old thought patterns won't be ousted overnight. But, step-by-step, replacing your thoughts with God's thoughts will change the course of your life for the better.

Thank You for Your powerful Word of truth. I choose to renew my mind, to replace my thoughts with Yours, so I can honor You with my life.

THE BATTLE IS THE LORD'S

"All those gathered here will know that it is not by sword or spear that the LORD saves; for the battle is the LORD's, and he will give all of you into our hands."

1 SAMUEL 17:47

As a young man, David stepped out in faith, and the Lord used his victory of killing the giant Goliath to propel him toward his future. His act of bravery is inspiration for us to battle our own giants, to step out in faith in God's power. And like David, whatever the outcome, our single step of faith may open or close doors in God's plan to move us forward toward our destiny.

For David, killing Goliath gave him favor with King Saul, who made David a leader of the nation's army. David's military successes, in turn, earned him respect and even the adoration of the people. In God's perfect timing David became Israel's greatest king.

So where could your path lead if you faced your Goliath? God wants you to defeat the giants in your life. It's time to fulfill all that He created you to be and destined for you to do. He's filled you with purpose, and He wants you to live it out.

God, I choose to face my giants. Help me defeat them and move forward fulfilling all You've called me to do.

LIFE ASSURANCE

"I will put enmity between you and the woman . . . he
will crush your head, and you will strike his heel."

GENESIS 3:15

In the garden of Eden, God foretold that a woman's offspring (Jesus) would crush the Enemy's head. Much later, when Jesus died and was raised again, His victory did that—and bought us freedom. Freedom from sin, freedom from death, and freedom to live unhindered by the Enemy. Yes, he still tries to harass us, but we have authority over him. We have power to defeat him because of Jesus living on the inside of us. *"Greater is He who is in you, than he who is in the world"* (1 John 4:4 NASB).

I like to think of it this way: Jesus died to give you not only *life insurance* for when you die, but also *life assurance* here on earth *today.* You are free to walk through life here confident of His presence with you and His love for you. Free to be who He made you to be. Free to do all He created you to do. Even the freedom to unashamedly approach God and enjoy daily fellowship with Him.

Today, remember your freedom! And walk in it. It is yours, won by Jesus and given to you.

Praise to You, Lord Jesus, who defeated death
on the cross! All praise to You, my Lord and
Savior, for doing that because You love me.

RECOVERING A MASTERPIECE

Cleanse me with hyssop, and I will be clean;
wash me, and I will be whiter than snow.

PSALM 51:7

In the early 1990s, the international art community witnessed a dramatic shake-up. A famous early-seventeenth-century Caravaggio painting, lost for two hundred years, was rediscovered. Titled *The Taking of Christ*, this painting had disappeared in the late eighteenth century. Through a series of exciting events—triggered by a random discovery by two graduate students in Rome and ending with an art scholar's visit to a Jesuit priest's residence in Dublin, Ireland—the painting was recovered.

For many years, *The Taking of Christ* had been wrongly identified as a replica painted by another artist. So it had been devalued and casually passed through several owners. When it was found, the question of its authenticity remained, but as experts painstakingly removed layers of dirt and discolored varnish, the high technical quality of the painting was revealed. *The Taking of Christ* truly is a priceless treasure.

Similarly, *you* are God's masterpiece. *You* are extremely precious to Him. Even though you might feel like used goods, damaged by sin, abuse, or your own poor choices, and discarded by someone who did not recognize your true value. No matter how many layers of the world's dirt, grime, and pain cover you, God will restore you to your original and priceless value. He will make you a masterpiece, whiter than snow.

Lord God, may I yield to Your restorative touch. I long to walk
in confidence that You consider me a priceless masterpiece.

REFRAME YOUR PERSPECTIVE

Give thanks in all circumstances.

1 THESSALONIANS 5:18

Most of us spend a fair amount of time regretting what we don't like, what we don't have, and who we are not. On some level, thinking constructively about these things can spur us to action. But mostly, they just bring us down. So instead, try this today: when you find yourself thinking this way, give thanks for what God provides.

Consider this a kind of reframing of your perspective: "God, this is not the job I wanted, but I thank You that I have a job. This is not the house I wanted, but I thank You that I have a roof over my head. This is not the marriage I expected, but I thank You that we are working on it. These are not the ministry results I was praying for, but I thank You for this opportunity to serve. Lord, I want You to hear my heartfelt thanks for what I have, for what You have given me."

You can do this reframing—and you can start now. Whatever your circumstances, thank God for what you do have. At the same time believe that He—whose plans for you are good—is able and faithful to take you where He wants you to go and to give you what He wants you to have.

Lord, I do have much to be thankful for. Help
me choose to see the many ways You are a
good, gracious, and generous God.

SCATTER AND SHARE

"As you sent me into the world, I have sent them into the world.
For them I sanctify myself, that they too may be truly sanctified."

JOHN 17:18–19

You have so much to offer to people who don't know Jesus: your salvation story, your friendship, your service. Yet for those of us who have been involved in church for a long time, it's easy to get so involved with Christian friends and activities that we let go of relationships with unsaved people.

God wants us to consciously choose to stay connected to people who don't go to church. He wants us to influence people with whom we have no present relationship. He wants us to share the gospel with the lost in our sphere of influence.

Yes, He will always want us to be fully engaged in Christian community, but remember that church is the place where you go to be trained and strengthened to do what God has called His people to do: scatter the seed of His gospel.

Where do you spend time with people who do not know the Lord and need to hear about Him? Wherever it is that you can scatter! At your kids' school events, the gym, your workplace, your community. Wherever you go—go scattering seed!

Thank You for the mission fields You have given me, Lord.
Help me build relationships, listen carefully in conversations,
and love with Your love so I can share Your gospel.

COUNTING THE COST

Then the men were exceedingly afraid, and
said to him, "Why have you done this?"

JONAH 1:10

Our fight-or-flight instinct can save us from all manner of dangers. But when it comes to God's difficult calling, how do we check that voice that says, *"Run away!"*?

God sent Jonah to Nineveh to "preach against it, because its wickedness has come up before me" (v. 2). A tough and unpleasant calling. But Jonah so disliked the people there that he "ran away from the LORD" (v. 3). Jonah went to Joppa and bought a ticket for a voyage in the completely opposite direction!

It's easy to judge Jonah for such blatant rebellion, but the truth is we often do the same thing. If you want to flee from God's purposes, you will always find help. The Devil will always—metaphorically speaking—make sure that a ship is in port to take you as far outside the will of God as possible. But the price of the fare for that getaway is always far heavier than the price of obedience. Comparatively, Jesus' yoke is always easier and His burden is always lighter (Matthew 11:30). Make the hard choice—the right choice—and choose what's better in the long run.

God, I wholeheartedly embrace what You've called me to do. I run hard after You and all that You have for my life.

NOTHING WASTED

And now, do not be distressed and do not be angry
with yourselves for selling me here, because it was
to save lives that God sent me ahead of you.

GENESIS 45:5

Okay, so he might have acted like a brat. And his father kept it no secret that Joseph was his favorite son. And Joseph wasn't wise when he shared the dream of his older brothers bowing before him. I can just imagine how obnoxious they thought that was. But did Joseph deserve to be thrown into a pit to die (plan A) or be sold into slavery (plan B)?

Of course not. But they both happened. As a slave in Egypt, Joseph dealt with false accusations and unfair imprisonment. But after he interpreted Pharaoh's dreams, Joseph was assigned to the highest position in the land under Pharaoh. As Joseph's story unfolds, even his own dreams were fulfilled: his brothers did bow before him years later when they traveled to Egypt in a time of famine and asked for food. By then, Joseph had matured. His response to them was wise and gracious: "You intended to harm me, but God intended it for good to accomplish what is now being done, the saving of many lives."

You can read all of Joseph's story in Genesis, but the point is this: just as God didn't waste Joseph's hard times, God doesn't waste your hurts. Not. A. Single. One.

Lord, thank You for working out Your plans for good in
my life, and giving me hope for a redeemed past.

"HAVE YOU SEEN MY DAUGHTER?"

"If a man owns a hundred sheep, and one of them wanders away, will he not leave the ninety-nine on the hills and go to look for the one that wandered off?"

MATTHEW 18:12

I was in a London bookstore on Oxford Street, one of the busiest streets in the world, when I lost my three-year-old. I'd looked away from Catherine for just a moment, and when I turned back around, she was gone. Vanished! I looked out at the teeming sidewalk of people, first confused, then frantic. I ran outside in search of her. I climbed on top of a mailbox, screaming, "Catherine! Catherine!" I stopped strangers: "Have you seen my daughter?"

Then I saw her. She had just walked around the corner to the children's book section and was sitting behind a bookshelf, mostly hidden. While I had been frantic, she had been reading.

I will never forget that feeling of panic. Maybe you've experienced that horrifying feeling. You feel physically ill. Your heart beats violently. You feel hopeless and helpless and crazy to find your child.

Likewise, every single second of every single day God's heart beats passionately for every lost person. So many need rescuers; so many need others to help; so many are simply sitting still. Yet each of them is God's precious lamb, missing treasure, beloved child. He seeks them—as He seeks you—as a loving parent would.

Thank You, God, that You always come
for us when we wander.

"AND IT WILL"

"Ask and it will be given to you; seek and you will find;
knock and the door will be opened to you."

MATTHEW 7:7

No one has to teach children to ask for what they want. They are naturals: "Mommy, can I have that? Daddy, I want this. Can I have it?"

Our heavenly Father invites and expects us to do the same. "Ask," He says, "and you will receive."

Of course we sometimes wish that we could pray and—*zap!*—God would answer our prayers. But three little words separate the asking and the receiving: "*and it will.*" Jesus said, "Ask *and it will* be given." In my Bible those three words take up about half a centimeter, but I know from experience that the "and it wills" of life can sometimes take years. Asking is easy and receiving is fun, but in between the asking and the receiving there is always an "and it will" of unspecified length.

I think the Lord gives us these "and it will" times so we don't get so caught up with the receiving that we ignore the One who is giving. Waiting is an opportunity to become more dependent upon and intimate with the loving God who is responding to our request. So embrace your "and it will," and never forget the love of the Giver.

*Gracious, generous God, show me how to be more focused
on You, the Giver, than on the good gifts You give.*

THE ROLE OF A LIFETIME

Put on the new self, created to be like God
in true righteousness and holiness.

EPHESIANS 4:24

I have an actress friend who amazes me. She plays so many different roles, yet she can keep them all straight! How does she keep from running out onstage and delivering the wrong lines in the wrong costume? Despite whatever role she's currently playing, she never loses sight of who she really is—her true identity.

Just like this actress, every single one of us has many different roles to fulfill every day—and they can change at any moment! We are pulled in so many different directions by people around us and their expectations or needs.

The only way we're able to "morph" from role to role and not end up mixing them all up is by doing what my actress friend does: remembering who we are at our core. In other words, who you *are* is not determined by what you *do*. Your *do* is not your *who*! You are more than just a function. Who you really are can be found only in Christ. Not in gender, ethnicity, socioeconomic background, education level, or career status. It lies in who you are in Christ—beloved, saved, and wonderfully made.

Jesus, thank You for establishing my identity in You, beyond any role I play. I am glad to be known and loved by You.

BEHIND THE SCENES

Answer me when I call to you, my righteous God. Give me relief
from my distress; have mercy on me and hear my prayer.

PSALM 4:1

Have you ever felt like your prayers were just bouncing off the ceiling? Did you wonder if God was even listening? Let me reassure you: God is *not* ignoring you! He *is* hearing you. And He's answering you—but it's a process where you have no idea what He is doing in the heavenlies and behind the scenes.

Perhaps, for your best interest and someone else's, God rearranges ten thousand other things in order to answer your request. (That takes time!) Or, more specifically, maybe you have prayed for years for a certain friend to be saved, and—nothing. But unbeknownst to you, God is at work, moving a Christian into your friend's town for a job at the company where she works—all so they will have a spiritually significant conversation over coffee. Elsewhere, God is arranging for a Christian band to come and play in that person's town—and for someone else to give your friend a free ticket to the concert. The workings of God are infinitely complicated, but He weaves them all together for His glory, and for the love of His children.

Trust that He always hears you and is at work behind the scenes to answer your prayer!

Lord, You are a master choreographer. Keep me mindful
of this when I'm waiting to see an answer to my prayer.

THE SECRET OF CONTENTMENT

The LORD turn his face toward you and give you peace.

NUMBERS 6:26

You've undoubtedly seen those infomercials featuring the most amazing products that you never knew you needed! One day I found myself wanting to order an EZ Egg Cracker. Having discovered that this device existed, how could I possibly continue to crack open eggs with my own hands? *But*, I realized, *I was content cracking eggs by hand until I saw that infomercial . . .*

Life is a little like that, isn't it? We are relatively content until we hear about the next gadget, update, house, car—and need to have it! In fact, every marketing campaign out there is designed to make me discontent, until I have *that thing.*

The apostle Paul, however, found contentment not in any infomercial product, but in the toughest of situations—while he was in prison. That's because real contentment never can be found *out there*; you only can find contentment *in Christ.*

The grass is not greener somewhere else; it's greenest wherever you water it. If you nurture and water your relationship with Jesus Christ on a daily basis, you will be content regardless of your circumstances. You already have complete, full access to the secret of contentment: His name is Jesus.

Jesus, Your peace and contentment is such a countercultural trait! But how freeing. Please help me to be content, consistently nurturing and watering my relationship with You.

THE POWER OF THE CROSS

The message of the cross is foolishness to those who are
perishing, but to us who are being saved it is the power of God.

1 CORINTHIANS 1:18

We hear so many voices telling us to be strong, to assert ourselves, to give it all we've got. What we don't hear so often is where that strength is supposed to come from. We can scrape the bottom of our barrels to muster enough power to change things, to control things, to protect ourselves, but there's no reason to rely on our own limited power, when we could relax and rely on Christ's unlimited power—which is freely available to us.

To live a life transformed by your gracious God, let go of your perceived power. When you find yourself struggling, remember the power of the cross— the resurrection power that brought Jesus back to life.

Focusing on the power of the cross is an essential and hope-giving practice. After all, you can't heal yourself from your past hurts, but the cross reminds you of the resurrection power shown in Jesus' victory over sin and death. God uses that same power today to bless His people—to bless you and me—with the ability to forgive, with healing, and with transformation.

Lord, thank You for the power of the cross and
Your victory over sin and death. And thank You
for using that power for my good, to bring healing
and freedom, to make me more like Jesus.

GIVING THANKS

Give thanks to the LORD, for he is good; his love endures forever.

PSALM 107:1

I want to point out something today that may be a relief to you. You know we are to be thankful in all circumstances, right? But when life is difficult and your heart is breaking, you aren't expected to run around wildly thanking God for the painful circumstances. God doesn't call you to be some kind of spiritual masochist. Nor does He call you to deny what you're feeling. What God does call you to do is to thank Him *in everything*—not *for everything*—in the midst of whatever is going on in your life.

In other words, we're to remain thankful to God for all He has done in the past and is doing for us now. "Give thanks *in* all circumstances; for this is God's will for you in Christ Jesus" (1 Thessalonians 5:18). God wants us to give thanks because He is good, even when our situation isn't.

When times are difficult, you can be thankful that God has an overarching plan for your life that will not be diverted. He is a sovereign and gracious God. Remembering His faithfulness to you in the past helps you not be so thrown off course by life's mishaps. Thankfulness is a gift He gives you that changes your heart, gives you strength, and keeps you moving forward.

Lord, giving thanks reminds me of Your great love. I give thanks to You, for You are good.

CONNECT THROUGH THANKS

Let us come before him with thanksgiving and
extol him with music and song. For the LORD is the
great God, the great King above all gods.

PSALM 95:2-3

When I miscarried between my two girls, I was so disappointed—but praise and thanksgiving started me moving forward. In our darkest hour, Nick and I went to church. Surrounded by our friends, we worshiped—even through our tears. As we thanked God for what we did have, and praised His holy name, our hearts changed. They lightened. And the atmosphere around us changed.

When you face something difficult, start by thanking Him. He loves you so much. He has given you eyes to see the colors of this world and ears to enjoy the sounds of birds singing, babies laughing, and music that stirs your soul. Respond by delighting Him with words of praise and gratitude. Of course, music is a natural vehicle for your thanks too. I believe it is an untapped treasure chest of praise that can shift the atmosphere of a room and help change our perspectives, uplifting us toward the heart of God.

Today, strengthen your connection to your Father with thanks and praise. I cannot tell you how this simple act has helped me to keep going in the toughest times.

*Lord, I have so much to thank You for—that I'm
alive today, that in You I'm strong, that You love
me unconditionally. I praise Your holy name.*

NEW ROOTS

As for me and my household, we will serve the LORD.

JOSHUA 24:15

Once, when I was in England for a women's conference, I stumbled across a small shop with a sign that read, "Discover your roots—family history available inside." Since I was adopted, I decided to try the name "Caine," as my husband, Nick, is from good English stock. *Who knows?* I thought. *Maybe I married into royalty!* I was startled from my daydreams when the woman behind the counter handed me the results.

Turns out, Nick's ancestors were far from royal. The list was dotted with criminals, convicts, paupers, and pirates! Although Nick's family tree was gnarly, looking at the past gave me a new perspective on the future. The lives of our future descendants would be so different. I laughed, knowing that because we had chosen to follow Jesus, our lives *and* future generations would be changed. A family history that had once been defined by immorality, poverty, alcoholism, and criminality would now be characterized by faith, love, peace, and joy.

We all have the power to leave a legacy. Whatever our past, it never has to limit our future. Because of God, we always have the power to chart a new course. We can fulfill our destiny and realize our dreams. We can impact and influence future generations.

God, thank You for including me in Your family
tree. I pray that I will leave a legacy of faith,
love, peace, and joy for future generations.

CHURCH FAMILY

The righteous will flourish like a palm tree, they will
grow like a cedar of Lebanon; planted in the house of
the Lord, they will flourish in the courts of our God.

PSALM 92:12-13

This is the season when most of us connect with family—holiday meals, outings, parties, and fall festivities light everything up. But regardless of how much you enjoy your natural family, know that you have another, larger family who wants to support and celebrate with you as well—your church family.

God designed our church families to birth us, nourish us, and launch us—just like a mother does with her children. For nine months with each of my girls, my body was their entire world. In there they had all the nutrients they needed to grow and develop. In the same way, the church is to our potential what the womb is to a growing baby. Just as an embryo must implant itself in the wall of the uterus so it can grow, we too must implant ourselves in our local church in order to see our dreams become a reality.

The local church feeds and nourishes our potential and dreams through a steady diet of praise and worship, Bible-based teaching, and relationships with people who help us. This Thanksgiving season, connect yourself with all your family—both natural and spiritual. Plant yourself in God's house, and flourish in His peace and provision.

*Lord, thank You for Your church—my spiritual
family here on earth. Help us flourish together.*

MEMORIZE, REMEMBER, AND TREASURE

He predestined us for adoption to sonship through Jesus
Christ, in accordance with his pleasure and will.

EPHESIANS 1:5

The Bible is full of strong defensive weapons that you can carry with you and use any time, any day—especially when the Enemy or the culture around you tries to tell you what you are or what you are not. That's the perfect time to remind yourself of these absolute truths:

- I am adopted (Ephesians 1:5).
- I am accepted (Ephesians 1:6).
- I am forgiven (Ephesians 4:32).
- I am predestined (Ephesians 1:11).
- I am raised and seated in heavenly realms (Ephesians 2:6).
- I am created for good works (Ephesians 2:10).
- I am called to eternal glory (1 Peter 5:10).
- I am more than a conqueror (Romans 8:37).
- I am an overcomer (John 16:33).
- I am never forsaken (Hebrews 13:5).

I can't emphasize it enough: memorize, remember, and treasure these promises. Then when you need to remember who you are, you'll have the solid rock of God's Word to stand on.

*God, You make so many victories possible for
me. Thank You for making me who I am!*

CO-LABORERS

[Jesus] told them, "The harvest is plentiful, but the
workers are few. Ask the Lord of the harvest, therefore,
to send out workers into his harvest field."

LUKE 10:2

There comes a point when our devotion turns to action—and that action doesn't have to be glamorous, because Jesus is looking for *co-laborers*, not *co-stars*.

Jesus told the disciples that the workers were few in the harvest of souls. And they still are today. Let's determine to be a generation of co-laborers who are not afraid to get dirty, to work hard in unrecognized positions, to touch the untouchables, to work for the freedom of the oppressed, and to get involved in the lives of those who are lost and hurting. We all like to *tell* a good story—but *living* one requires hard, fearless work and a slog through the mud of this hurting world, with the power of Christ behind us. So let's put in our sweat equity for Jesus.

God hasn't called any of us to be heroes. The only Hero the world needs came thousands of years ago, and His name is Jesus Christ. Instead, God has called us to be workers. He's created us to do good works—not to live a life of comfort and ease (Ephesians 2:10). So let's ask Him where our field is, and let's get to work.

Lord Jesus, show me where You want me to
co-labor with You. I commit to do the "dirty
work," in your power and strength.

MOTIVATING MENTORS

Remember your leaders . . . and . . . imitate their faith.

HEBREWS 13:7

As you travel your Christian journey, it can take a lot of strength at times to keep going—to keep believing. One thing I learned that has helped me tremendously to stay strong, faithful, and forward-looking is a lesson I learned long ago: make the faith of others a motivator.

In other words, look to your mentors—the ones who inspire you. When I look to my pastors and other leaders in the faith, I get so inspired by their tenacity, courage, and dependability. I think that if they can do it, then I can do it too. Although I can't imagine what it would be like to spend a lifetime cleaning the wounds of lepers and helping the lame in India (my challenge would be with the fact there is no running water in many places), Mother Teresa's story helps me believe that maybe, just maybe, I can do half as much for humanity in my lifetime as she did in hers.

Read the stories of people who have achieved great things. Surround yourself with people who love Jesus and are living for Him. As you do, you will see God moving through them to make His kingdom come to earth—and you'll be inspired and empowered to fulfill your destiny!

Lord, thank You for working through the lives of
others. Help me draw strength and motivation
from them to keep moving forward.

MAKE FRIENDS WITH YOUR FUTURE

Commit your work to the LORD,
and your plans will be established.

PROVERBS 16:3 ESV

Perhaps you're looking forward to your future with excitement! Perhaps you're nervous, scared, or avoidant. Either way, I want to encourage you to make a conscious choice that will help you on your faith walk: make *friends* with your future.

How do you begin making friends with your future? By making sure your relationship with the past is healthy first. It wasn't until I was willing to sever myself from wrong thinking, wrong beliefs, and past hurts that I could truly believe that God had great things waiting for me in my future—"an inheritance that can never perish, spoil or fade" (1 Peter 1:4). Nothing, and I mean nothing, has to keep us out of God's great future that He has planned for us.

So if there are lingering effects of your past holding you back from your future, go to God. Let Him walk you through that healing process. Let Him help you forgive, let go, and move forward. Then make friends with your future. I believe the best is headed your way!

Lord, I'm grateful You have Your eye on my
future. I look forward to fulfilling my purpose
and all the good plans You have for me!

FAITHFUL IN THE LITTLE THINGS

---

*He has brought down rulers from their thrones
but has lifted up the humble.*

LUKE 1:52

Sometimes our Christian walk is not very glamorous—especially if we're in that season of being faithful with the little that's in our hands while we're waiting for the next season in life to come (Luke 16:10). During that time, it's easy to wonder, *Where's the victory? Where are all the wins?*

But never despise small beginnings (Zechariah 4:10). The way toward my dreams of speaking for God began with a lot of work at a youth center in Australia that wasn't very glamorous. I remember painting walls at 2 a.m., cleaning toilets, handling administrative tasks, and even writing funding proposals so we could keep the doors open. But during my six years there I developed the skills and character necessary to do what I'm doing today—and dream even bigger dreams.

I genuinely believe I would not have been blessed to step into what God had for me if I had despised my time serving at the center. If we're not willing to be faithful in the little things, we won't get to reach our dreams fully formed.

Wherever you are today, be faithful. Right. Where. You. Are. Start serving and doing whatever needs to be done—even if that's changing the toilet paper rolls between church services. If you will, then He will move you forward at just the right time.

Lord, I will be faithful in little, believing You to give me much.

A NEW COURSE OF HEALING

If any of you lacks wisdom, you should ask God, who gives
generously to all without finding fault, and it will be given to you.

JAMES 1:5

A button is pushed. A trigger is activated. And suddenly, you find yourself
in emotional upheaval. But don't worry: these moments of turmoil can be a
signal that more healing is on its way.

Once, when I was hurt by a valued friend, my old shame came out of
nowhere. It blindsided me and exposed some old wounds I'd thought were
long healed and some shame-based toxic waste I thought I'd shipped off to
Jesus. As the hurtful situation unfolded, I was tempted to conclude that I was
being judged—and falling short. Still very sensitive to criticism and fearful of
rejection, I wanted to withdraw.

I also began to feel I was the problem, a feeling that triggered my black-
and-white thinking: I am either loved or unloved, accepted or rejected, wanted
or unwanted. Nothing is ever in-between. I was tempted to make adjustments
so others would feel more comfortable. My people-pleaser tendencies definitely kicked in!

It was powerful to know I could turn to God and ask Him for help—and
He healed me even more as He helped me process what had happened and
walked me through healthy responses.

*Lord, thank You for being with me as I travel my
healing journey. I look to You as it continues.*

THINKING BIGGER

The Lord has made the heavens his throne;
from there he rules over everything.

PSALM 103:19 NLT

In all my plans, in all my dreams, whatever step-by-step goals I set, I am always thankful that God's thinking is definitely bigger than mine. "'My thoughts are not your thoughts, neither are your ways my ways,' declares the Lord. 'As the heavens are higher than the earth, so are my ways higher than your ways and my thoughts than your thoughts'" (Isaiah 55:8–9).

The picture we see for our future is often based on our limited experiences, resources, expectations, socioeconomic backgrounds, traditions, education, and culture. But God is not contained by any of these.

- Where we see lack, God sees opportunity.
- Where we see failure, God sees potential.
- Where we see containment, God sees refinement.
- Where we see weakness, God sees strength.
- Where we see death, God sees life.
- Where we see what is or has been, God sees what can and will be.

As our perspective comes in line with God's, we begin to see our dreams fulfilled. So act on your plans and your vision, but remain open to God's course-altering perspective—and let it guide your way.

Loving God, thank You for Your crystal-clear
vision of my life. Thank You for helping me see
every circumstance through Your eyes.

WILDERNESS BLESSINGS

He brought his people out like a flock; he led
them like sheep through the wilderness.

PSALM 78:52

When the children of Israel left Egypt, miracle after miracle happened in the desert. God parted the Red Sea—and they crossed on dry ground. Then God defeated the Egyptians as they drowned in the sea. Then God gave the Israelites food from the sky and water from a rock. Over and over again, God miraculously delivered them.

But could they see it? Not exactly. They'd been delivered from physical slavery in Egypt, but when they looked toward the promised land, nothing but desolate wilderness stretched as far as they could see (Exodus 16).

The wilderness was a vast place of unknowns, yet it was also a land of great purpose. In the wilderness God gave His people opportunities to trust Him, to walk in faith, to remember His goodness, to develop thankful hearts, and to become people of worship. But they constantly stumbled and complained. They weren't quick studies.

Let's try to do better. If you are in a wilderness right now, look around you. Look for the ways He is providing for you in the desert. As you keep moving forward, trust God, walk in faith, remember His goodness, become more thankful, and develop a heart for worship. Trust Him that He is leading you *through.*

Lord, I choose to be thankful in this wilderness season.
Thank You for all the ways You are providing for me.

YOUR VALUABLE CONTRIBUTION

They devoted themselves to the apostles' teaching and
to fellowship, to the breaking of bread and to prayer.

ACTS 2:42

When you think, *No one is going to miss me; it doesn't really matter if I show up to church or tithe; no one is going to notice*, remember that God has placed you where you are for a reason, and your fellowship with other believers is important.

You definitely notice when one tiny member of your physical body is out of place, don't you? When I displaced my ACL during a skiing accident, I didn't even know I *had* an ACL. But when that tiny ligament behind my knee slipped out of place, it crippled my whole body with pain and put me in a brace for weeks. The small, seemingly insignificant parts of the body can have an astounding effect when they're out of fellowship with others. The apostles understood this. That's why they were devoted to one another.

Whether you're that ligament, elbow, knee, foot, or one of the more "celebrated" and "glamorous" parts like the mouth or eye, know that God has set you in your place. When you devalue your contribution, you cripple the body and tire out other parts who have to compensate for your absence. You are valuable—and everyone really does need you!

Lord, I devote myself to You and to the place You've called
me to serve. Thank You for using me to help others flourish.

DOING IT ALL

"Seek first the kingdom of God and his righteousness,
and all these things will be added to you."

MATTHEW 6:33 ESV

For years, we have been told we can have it all, be it all, and do it all. But, the fact is that the pursuit of having and doing it all has left many women disappointed, exhausted, and stressed.

In our disillusionment, we can even begin to think there is no possible way we can manage a strong Christian walk with everything else we have to do. The truth is, you can have it all, and you can do it all—but we need to discover what God's definition of the "all" is first.

It doesn't mean we can have anything we want, or that we can have everything simultaneously. What it does mean is that what we have should be the result of seeking first the kingdom of God—and then Him adding to us.

When it's God who adds the "all" rather than us trying to strive for it on our own, we don't have to be stressed, overworked, or anxious about trying to keep something we cannot obtain on our own anyway. If we simply continue to put God first, He adds it to our life according to His perfect will and His perfect timing.

*Lord, I'm thankful that Your "all" is what I really want—
and that You make it possible for me to receive it.*

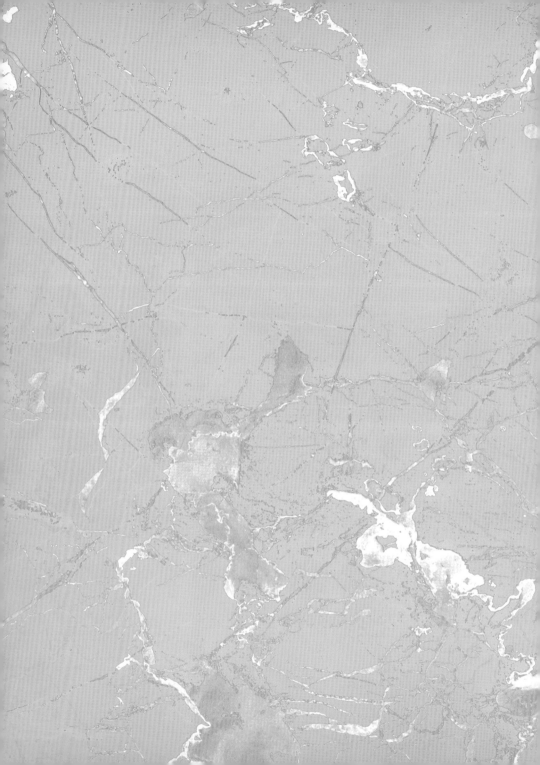

DECEMBER

Look to the Lord and his strength;
seek his face always.

CHRONICLES 16:11

CHOOSING THE MESSINESS

Elisha sent a messenger to say to [Naaman], "Go,
wash yourself seven times in the Jordan, and your
flesh will be restored and you will be cleansed."

2 KINGS 5:10

As you know by now, healing is a step-by-step, day-by-day process. It may not happen overnight, but it can come in unexpected ways.

The Bible tells of Naaman, a valiant army captain who was stricken with leprosy and wanted to be healed (2 Kings 5:1–19). When he learned about Israel's prophet Elisha and his connection to God, Naaman—with his chariots and his horses—stopped at Elisha's house. Instead of seeing him personally, Elisha sent a messenger to Naaman with instructions: "Wash yourself seven times in the Jordan."

Naaman became angry. He had expected the prophet to wave his hand, invoke the name of the Lord—anything that brought instant healing. Not to be told to go into the muddy Jordan River seven times!

Naaman's healing was a messy, muddy process—just like it is for us. And like Naaman, we have to choose to heal and choose to trust that if we do what God, the Great Physician, asks, we will be made whole. We have to accept that healing is almost always messy—mentally, emotionally, and spiritually. But even in our mess, He is always gentle with us as we experience healing, growth, strength, and wholeness.

Lord, no matter how messy the journey is, I move forward to receive healing. I want to be whole—spirit, soul, and body.

TRUST IN WHO?

Trust in the LORD with all your heart and do not lean on
your own understanding. In all your ways acknowledge
Him, and He will make your paths straight.

PROVERBS 3:5–6 NASB

God wants us to trust Him instead of ourselves—and yet it is a reflexive action to trust only ourselves, and no one else, including God.

We can know in our heads that we need to trust God, but it is certainly not our default mode. Our natural instinct is to hunker down and protect ourselves—rather than open up our hearts to God. But God created our spirit to want to engage with Him and trust Him.

When you find yourself resisting trust and embracing control, when you find yourself leaning into self-sufficiency or self-protecting, step back and pause. Recognize that you're pulling back into trusting only yourself instead of trusting God fully.

When you find yourself veering onto the path of your own understanding, stop and "acknowledge Him." Open your heart up to His love and His leading. Let Him guide you and make your paths straight.

Lord, I trust You with all my heart. I choose not to
lean on my own understanding. I acknowledge You
and invite You into my heart and the details of my
life, trusting You to make my paths straight.

YOU ARE WELL ABLE

---

*See what the land is like and whether the people who
live there are strong or weak, few or many.*

NUMBERS 13:18

There's new land in front of you, and it's time to move into it. But maybe you've felt overwhelmed about how to move into it—into the ministry, the career, the relationship—whatever it is that God has called you to. Perhaps what you need is a team of leaders like Joshua and Caleb encouraging you.

When the Israelites were ready to step into the promised land, a nation occupied the land. So God had Moses send twelve leaders to scout it out and report back (Numbers 13). Ten of them came back saying that the land was big, the cities were fortified, and the people were larger and stronger than the Israelites. Those ten could see only the obstacles, and they incited fear in the people. Joshua and Caleb, however, saw the same exact obstacles, but came to a very different conclusion. They saw only the possibilities and the favorable outcome. They said they were well able to overcome.

Whatever land is in front of you, find leaders to speak truth into your life like I am speaking right now: *You are well able to take the land. You are well able to overcome and conquer. You are well able to move forward, receive that promotion, walk through that door.*

Lord, thank You for sending me leaders to
encourage my faith. I believe I am well able.

GOD WANTS TO DO SOMETHING *THROUGH* YOU

"Even though [the friend] will not get up and give you the bread
because of friendship, yet because of your shameless audacity
he will surely get up and give you as much as you need."

LUKE 11:8

What is the longest you have prayed for something? Six months? Five years? Ten? When you have prayed long and hard about something, the question you probably most want answered was, "God, why is it taking so long? I have been praying and praying and praying."

God's answer is nearly always, "I need to do something *in* you so that when I answer your prayer, I can do something *through* you."

As you wait for God to answer, know that God is also teaching you to be persistent and faithful. He's teaching you to be faithful with the small things He has given you—to be faithful when you haven't yet received the answer to your prayers, so you will be a good steward when you do receive your answer.

So, keep praying faithfully and audaciously. And when you receive God's answer to your prayers, remember that this is just the beginning of what God has for you, because as Luke wrote, He wants to give you as much as you need. He wants to do a brand-new thing *in* you, so He can do more *through* you!

*Lord, I am audaciously persistent in my prayers. I trust
You and thank You for what You want to do through me!*

PREPARE THE WAY

"I will send my messenger ahead of you, who will prepare
your way"—"a voice of one calling in the wilderness,
'Prepare the way for the Lord, make straight paths
for him.' " And so John the Baptist appeared.

MARK 1:2-4

One December morning, my daughter Catherine jumped into our bed at 5:30 to declare, "Mommy, it is only twenty days to Christmas. I am so *excited*!" Needless to say, I did not share her excitement at that hour. But I realized how much I do love the Advent season—the season of preparing for the coming of Jesus. Each year, we remind our children that Christmas is about Jesus entering into the world, and Santa is not the reason for the season—although he does bring presents to our place.

In the Bible, John the Baptist prepared the way for Jesus. But how can we prepare people today? I believe God wants to use us in our normal, seemingly monotonous, everyday lives to introduce people to Jesus. Imagine how we would live each day if we believed that every encounter we had and choice we made about how we spend our time, talent, and treasure were part of that preparation process.

In this holiday season, let's prepare people for the One who can bring true meaning, peace, love, joy, purpose, and forgiveness. Let's prepare them to meet Jesus.

*Lord, show me how to prepare the way for You in
the hearts and minds of everyone I encounter.*

GOD GIVES HIMSELF

But he stands alone, and who can oppose him? He does whatever he pleases. He carries out his decree against me, and many such plans he still has in store.

JOB 23:13–14 ESV

What could possibly be good about disappointment? Only this: the possibility of God's presence.

I find it interesting that the word *appointment* is right there in the word *disappointment*. That wordplay reflects what I have seen in my life again and again. Disappointment *takes* something from us: a dream, a piece of our hearts, maybe a whole chunk. But disappointment *leaves* something too: a lesson learned, an opportunity, the possibility of choosing change.

The Enemy, however, would like us to feel such deep disappointment that we never find our way back to God or His plan for us. He wants to convince us to stay stuck in our disappointment in hopes that we'll miss future God appointments. But we don't have to let that happen.

When Job faced massive disappointment, and he asked God a lot of anguished questions, God never did provide answers as to why Job's life had unfolded as it did. What God did give Job was Himself, and as it turned out, that was more than enough to propel him onward toward a brighter future— one where God restored to him far more than he ever had before.

Lord, thank You for redeeming all of my disappointments.
I believe for a better future than I ever imagined.

DRAW CLOSE

---

*Immediately her bleeding stopped and she felt in her
body that she was freed from her suffering.*

MARK 5:29

Healing is possible for you today—mentally, physically, or emotionally—whatever you need. And the journey to receiving your healing begins with drawing close to Jesus. That's what the woman who bled for twelve years did.

Her persistent bleeding forced her to stay hidden and out of the public eye. *Unclean* is what her religion called her—a cultural label that caused her deep shame. Desperate for a cure, she spent all her money on doctors who couldn't help.

She lived chronically weak, I imagine, from the continual loss of blood. She dealt continually with hygiene issues. Her condition literally dictated how she spent every second of every day of her life.

But one day this desperate woman caught a glimmer of hope: she learned that Jesus was in her town. This miracle-working Jesus was doing what doctors could not. The blind were seeing; the lame were walking. *If only I could touch Him . . . Or maybe if I could just touch His clothes . . . He has healed others. Surely He could heal me as well,* she thought. Hope. For the first time. She drew close and touched Him, and Jesus healed her. So draw close to Him—and take your first step toward wholeness.

*Jesus, I draw near to You and receive Your
healing power in every area of my life.*

GOODBYE, INDECISION

Who, then, are those who fear the LORD? He will
instruct them in the ways they should choose.

PSALM 25:12

We make thousands of decisions each day—what to get at the grocery store, which outfit to wear, how to spend our day. And each choice takes energy from us. Sometimes there's so much small stuff to decide about that it's easy to see why we avoid making decisions about the big stuff.

Indecision has gotten the best of me on a few occasions. I've learned the hard way, and perhaps you have too, that *indecision can cause us to miss our dreams.* Sometimes we choose to sit on the fence and procrastinate for so long that the opportunity sails right by us. We may even try to spiritualize our indecision by convincing ourselves we haven't heard from God. Yes, we need to ask for the Holy Spirit's leading, but I believe there are some decisions God is waiting for us to make before He opens or closes a door.

So be brave—don't avoid decisions. You can even start small as a way of working this habit into your life. I dare you: the next time you're in a restaurant, pick something from the menu before asking everyone else what they're having, and stick with your choice. Seize the day! Make a decision and surprise yourself!

God, I want all my decisions to glorify You. Thank You for
the courage to choose, and the wisdom to choose rightly.

LIMITLESS

God said, "Let there be light," and there was light.

GENESIS 1:3

Imagine a straight, uninterrupted path between you and what God has called you to do. The way is completely open, all obstacles removed. Inspiring, right?

Now think of how things *really* are. Did you immediately think of everything in your way? Did your mind go straight to all the reasons why you couldn't even begin to accomplish what God's called you to do?

That very human response doesn't consider what God brings to the assignment He's given us—which is all His power backing us. No, God won't normally remove all the difficulties from our path, because difficulty is part of this fallen world. But God does give us His power to help us overcome—and His power made the universe out of nothing!

So what are you facing? There's no prayer too big for Him to answer. No problem is too complicated for Him to resolve. There is no disease He cannot heal. No heart He cannot mend. There is no bondage God cannot break. No need He cannot meet. No enemy He cannot defeat, and no mountain He cannot move.

There is nothing God cannot do. He created the heavens and earth, and He lovingly created you for your purpose. He will get you to your destiny!

God, I make You bigger on the inside of me than the obstacles I face. Great are You, Lord! And great is Your power!

THE REASON FOR OUR HOPE

Always be prepared to give an answer to everyone
who asks you to give the reason for the hope that you
have. But do this with gentleness and respect.

1 PETER 3:15

As I've traveled the world, I have noted above all else an absence of hope. People are despondent, lacking any sense of purpose or anticipation about the future. I see this hopelessness influence the media, politics, the arts, people's personal finances, and society at large. But as followers of Christ, it doesn't have to influence us.

Christians live according to a different set of principles from those who don't know Christ: we have hope. No matter how bleak international affairs, national headlines, local news, or our family lives may be, we can hold on to Jesus and the hope of healing and heaven that He made possible. He is a secure and eternal anchor for our souls. If our ultimate hope were in people or anything this world offers, we would be drifting and lost. But our hope is in Jesus Christ, who triumphed over sin and death.

Jesus came to change the hopeless state of the world! That's why Peter tells us to be prepared to share Him with the parched souls who cross our path. As we lead them closer to our Lord, hopelessness falls away.

Lord, thank You for the eternal hope You bring. Please
help me always be ready with Your name—Jesus!—
when people ask me about the hope I have.

WHY DIDN'T ANYONE TELL ME?

We proclaim to you what we have seen and heard, so that
you also may have fellowship with us. And our fellowship
is with the Father and with his Son, Jesus Christ.

1 JOHN 1:3

Don't you hate it when you look in the mirror and you notice a huge piece of spinach between your teeth from lunch *five hours ago*? You mentally retrace your steps and think of all the people who must have seen it but didn't say a word! *Why didn't anyone tell me?!* you wonder.

Or what if you were walking and talking with a friend, not paying attention, and—*BAM!*—you walked straight into a pole! Your friend had failed to point it out to you. As soon as you pick yourself up, you would ask, "Why didn't you warn me?!"

If someone nearing the end of life asked, "Why didn't you tell me about Jesus?" imagine how that person would feel. And what would you say? We live in a lost, broken, and hurting world, and we know that people can find purpose, wholeness, and healing in Jesus. If we don't speak up, who will? You can make a difference in someone's eternal future. Because you know what's at stake, you can push past hesitancy, fear, or anything else that might keep you from sharing the life-changing news of your Savior.

Help me, Lord, to be winsome, wise, and
genuine when I tell people about Jesus, my
Savior, my Lord, my Redeemer, my King.

PREPARE FOR TAKEOFF

"I bore you on eagles' wings and brought you to myself."

EXODUS 19:4 NKJV

The flight attendant was standing in front of me, wearing a yellow safety vest and an oxygen mask. Although I had heard the safety message a trillion times, her proximity to my seat compelled me to feign attention! And it's a good thing I tuned in. Most flights I have been on are uneventful, but on that flight, turbulence hit. And during those scary in-flight moments, I desperately recollected the safety message:

Life vest under the seat [check]

Put on oxygen mask first before assisting others [check]

Know where the exits are [check]

Place yourself in the brace position [check]

Why do I share this? Because the Christian life is like taking off on an unpredictable adventure! And though many days will be great, there will be days when turbulence hits. On those days, I want you to know instinctively how to brace yourself and get into position to weather whatever comes your way. I want your first response to be to trust in God—knowing that He is the skilled pilot who has everything under control.

So stay in your own seat, strapped in, holding steady and on course. Remain calm and full of confidence that the One who brought you this far will surely get you to your destiny.

God, I'm so excited to move forward on my journey.
Thank You for Your instructions in Your Word. Please
keep me mindful of them when turbulence hits.

THE BEST OPTION

I say to myself, "The LORD is my portion;
therefore I will wait for him."

LAMENTATIONS 3:24

You've got options. It's as true today as it has ever been. And we like to keep our options open. We often don't want to commit to anything too soon because something better might come along—don't want to accept that invitation because we might get a better one, commit to that job, school, or relationship, because we don't know what's ahead. Our options are limitless. We can even order our coffee thousands of different ways!

But, that kind of "options open" lifestyle can't coexist with our choice to follow Jesus.

At some point, we have to make a dramatic decision—take a defining action—to follow Jesus' way and no other way. By saying "I will" to Jesus, we say "I won't" to other "options" in this life—just the way saying "I will" to my husband, Nick, when I married him meant an "I won't" to all other men. So when we are lured toward the many things that claim to give us hope in this world, when we face other gods, other priorities, other "options," let's say "No." Let's reject the idea of any plan Bs.

Today, let's stop weighing our options. Let's choose Jesus once and for all!

Lord, please help me simplify my life, letting go of all the options. I choose You and Your ways today.

FROM FEAR TO FREEDOM

Set me free from my prison, that I may praise your name.

PSALM 142:7

It was easier to help my daughter Catherine face her fear of rainstorms than for me to face my fear of flying, but I learned a lot by helping Catherine. Namely, you can't run from fear, because fear is inside you. The only way to deal with fear is to face it head-on before it takes over your life.

Catherine's fear started when we were once caught outside in a violent storm. It wasn't long before I saw that she feared storms so much she was willing to forsake opportunities for fun and friends to avoid storms. I knew that if she didn't conquer her fear, it would become more entrenched.

So on the next rainy day, I scooped up Catherine, and we headed outside. At first she cried, but then I began to jump and stomp in the puddles. I laughed at the sky and rejoiced in the rain. Surprised by my complete absence of fear, Catherine stopped crying and began to laugh. Soon she was stomping in the puddles with me.

Now I can't keep Catherine inside when it rains. She grabs her sister, and they put on their rubber boots to run into the puddles.

And me? I faced my fear, too, and today I fly almost every week—fearlessly.

Lord, please give me wisdom to know how
best to face my fears so I can experience the
grace of Your deliverance and freedom.

CAUSE AND EFFECT

"In everything, do to others what you would have them do to you."

MATTHEW 7:12

The law of cause and effect is very real in our Christian walk. When we live in such a way as to reveal Christ to the world, it makes an eternal difference in people's lives. They notice and become curious, hungry for the truth. For example:

- When we live a morally pure life, we show a dark but watching world that God has determined the best way to live.
- When we live a God-first life in a world of competing options, we demonstrate the value of making God our top priority.
- When we live "green," people see that we love God's creation.
- When we forgive instead of harboring offense, we illustrate grace.
- When we serve "the least of these," we reflect God's compassion and true leadership.
- When we fight for justice, we show our awareness of the incalculable value of every person.

Your actions and choices matter—even when you aren't aware that they do. People watch you, listen to you, and learn from you—much like your children do when you don't realize they are observing and absorbing. So, consciously use your influence wisely and show the people in your realm of influence who Jesus really is—the true Savior, who gives them hope. The only One who can give their lives meaning and purpose.

Lord, help me use my influence wisely, to make a difference, to lead others to become Christ-followers.

BEAT THE FAITH-SHAKERS

I trust in your unfailing love; my heart rejoices in your salvation.

PSALM 13:5

Your faith will grow through the uncertain and the unknown. As tempting as it might be to stay where you are, living with the certain and the familiar, your faith won't grow if you never move forward. Our Enemy has quite the set of tactics to keep you in that place of stagnation. I call those tactics faith-shakers.

My list is by no means exhaustive. But I've found that believers who conquer these tactics with *unshakeable* faith are well equipped to handle just about anything that comes their way. Faith can defeat everything on this list:

- Negative circumstances
- Fear
- Failure
- Unmet expectations
- Relational strife
- Weariness
- Opposition
- Hopelessness

When you find yourself dealing with one of these faith-shakers, fight back! Choose to accept the situation or emotional state as an opportunity for you to see God work. Yes, the Enemy wants to keep you from looking to God and trusting Him. But God wants to use those situations and emotions to grow your faith, and He is far more powerful than the Enemy. Know that God is at work at these times and strong to help you, as He always is.

Thank You, God, for helping me recognize enemy
tactics so that, in Your power, I can both stand strong
when I encounter them and expect to see You work.

HOPE WHEN YOU'RE HOPELESS

Then Peter got down out of the boat, walked on the water and came toward Jesus. But when he saw the wind, he was afraid and, beginning to sink, cried out, "Lord, save me!" Immediately Jesus reached out his hand and caught him.

MATTHEW 14:29-31

The storm raged and waves crashed around Peter as he stepped out on the water. Beginning to sink, he cried out to his Savior. And "immediately," Jesus caught him. So when the storms of life rage and waves of hopelessness crash around you, may you—like Peter—cry out to Jesus and stretch out your hand. Jesus will extend His, and you will find yourself back in the boat, Jesus by your side, the winds gone, the waters calmed, and yourself back on course.

Storms will arise, and you'll feel as if you're sinking. When you do, look to the only Life Preserver who can both save you *and* calm the storm. Choose to believe in God's presence, power, and promises despite your circumstances. Then you'll find yourself marveling, like the disciples did: "those who were in the boat worshiped him, saying, 'Truly you are the Son of God'" (Matthew 14:33).

Trust Him to bring healing, transformation, freedom, and hope, even if your problem seems as big as a raging sea. Trust Him knowing He always will catch you.

Trustworthy Lord, even though I cannot see You, I choose to place my hope and faith in You. I know You have a way beyond what I can see.

DO SOMETHING YOU'VE NEVER DONE BEFORE

Sing to the LORD a new song, his praise from the ends of the earth.

ISAIAH 42:10

I read an article many years ago about an order of French nuns whose average age was ninety. The journalist asked the secret to their longevity and their response was twofold: they committed to keep their minds active by continually reading and learning, and every month they did something they had never done before. If it works for ninety-year-old nuns, it will work for you and me!

Why not try the following:

- Research the Web or read a book about a subject you know absolutely nothing about.
- Learn a new language.
- Enroll in a college or night class in something you've always been interested in but never thought was very practical.
- Develop a new skill.

Personally, at this stage of my life, I'm working on my master's degree so I can grow in my calling as an evangelist. I'm learning so many new things as I'm reading books I never knew existed. So try something new that will enlarge you—spiritually, mentally, and emotionally. If you will, you'll take on the capacity to carry more, and you'll find new things to praise our loving God for.

Lord, thank You for helping me enlarge my capacity for life—and ultimately for You!

CHOSEN INCLUSIVELY

---

*You are a chosen people, a royal priesthood, a holy nation,
God's special possession, that you may declare the praises of
him who called you out of darkness into his wonderful light.*

1 PETER 2:9

Most of the time, when you make a choice—of what to have for dinner, what college to attend, what person to marry—you choose *exclusively*. What I mean is that you select something and exclude everything else. You make your pick, and essentially leave the other choices behind. God, on the other hand, has a way of choosing *inclusively*—and that's how He chose you.

God chooses everyone, all the time. He never chooses one person at the exclusion of another. He loves each one of us—all of us—so much that He paid with His Son's life the price for our forgiveness and reconciliation to Him.

When you comprehend the magnitude of what it means to be chosen by God, it makes you feel qualified, confident, and eager to share the truth about forgiveness and reconciliation with others. You want to say to everyone you meet, "God chose you too!" What a privilege to help others discover that they, too, have been chosen *by* God and *for* God. What a privilege to share the gospel and disciple others in a growing relationship with God.

*Thank You, God, for choosing me, adopting me, loving
me, and using me to share Your good news.*

ASK GOD THE BIG QUESTIONS

Now I know in part; then I shall know fully, even as I am fully known.

1 CORINTHIANS 13:12

How do you (or did you) get ready for a night out with someone new? I bet you put a considerable amount of time into hiding all your imperfections and looking your very best. Yet as you got to know that person, and as you built trust, I bet you relaxed and let your image go a bit. You grew to feel you could be yourselves together in sweatpants in front of the TV. You became comfortable showing the real you. That's because with increased intimacy comes increased honesty—which is exactly what God wants in His relationship with you.

As your relationship with God moves from casual dating to a daily commitment, it's essential you quit trying to perform for His acceptance and just be real. It's essential you invite God to stir up all that's in your heart. And you can start with asking Him:

- to ignite your passion.
- to reveal areas in your life that might need some work.
- to give you a clearer picture of His plans for the future.

Honesty with God can only bring you closer to Him, so don't be afraid to be honest—and ask Him for His honesty in return.

God, please show me how to drop my defenses and be open with You, so I can hear what You have to say to me.

HE'S GOT YOUR BACK

Because of the LORD's great love we are not
consumed, for his compassions never fail. They are
new every morning; great is your faithfulness.

LAMENTATIONS 3:22–23

It wasn't an especially long flight, but it was a memorable one.

"We are having trouble getting the landing gear up," the pilot said, "so rather than continue on to Raleigh, we'll have to turn around and try to land in Chicago."

Try? That's a word you never want to hear in midair.

I gulped as I sensed fear spread up and down the aisle. Some passengers began to bow their heads and pray aloud. Others started to cry.

True to form, my husband, Nick, began quietly praying for us—not at all in fear, but calmly and thankfully. Nick committed the pilot, all the passengers, and a safe landing to the Lord. Then he leaned into me and whispered, "We'll be fine, Chris. He is with us, and He has our backs. You don't need to be afraid of anything." With that, Nick squeezed my hand, put his seat back, and closed his eyes. Then, believe it or not, he drifted off to sleep.

That's the kind of faith I want! Today, if life feels out of control and you're not sure how things are going to turn out, remind yourself of God's faithfulness. Even as you adjust to emergencies or "try" to land your plane, trust that He's got you.

Great is Your faithfulness, God! Thank You for
peace as I deal with the unexpected.

SHOULDER TO THE PLOW

One day while Moses was taking care of the sheep and goats of his father-in-law Jethro . . . the angel of the Lord appeared to him as a flame...God said..."It's time for you to go back: I'm sending you to Pharaoh to bring my people, the People of Israel, out of Egypt."

EXODUS 3:1–10

When the world tells you, "Market yourself; sell yourself; build your portfolio," remember that God is the one who promotes you.

In the Bible, when great heroes of the faith were called, they were always *working*, not promoting themselves. David was shepherding, Elisha was driving oxen, Moses was taking care of his father-in-law's animals. Diligently, dirtily, and thanklessly, they worked through danger, stench, and discomfort. And because God saw them working hard, He spoke to others on their behalf and anointed them. Do you think their "gifting," "calling," or "sweet spot" was laboring in the fields? No! They were created to be a king, a prophet, and a father of faith. But they each worked hard where they were *before* God promoted them.

If God has assigned you, He will find you! And He tends to work with those who are already working! When you align yourself with God in faithfulness and diligence, He will work on your behalf and get you to your destiny.

Lord, I choose to work diligently and faithfully
right where I am, knowing that You will speak to
others on my behalf. You will promote me.

A CHANGE IN THE ATMOSPHERE

Seek peace and pursue it.

1 PETER 3:11

When you think of a holiday atmosphere, what comes to mind? Perhaps it's baked goods, family laughter, warm fires crackling. Or, maybe what comes to mind is not the perfect snow-globe Christmas, but an atmosphere of tension that comes from past hurts, strained family relationships, loneliness, or loss. I want you to know today that whatever atmosphere you're walking into this holiday, you can change it. You can carry in a new atmosphere—one of joy and peace.

No matter what is going on around you, remember that the joy of the Lord is your strength (Nehemiah 8:10). By making Jesus the center of this season, you can experience the peace that passes understanding (Philippians 4:7). You can be the peacemaker, the joy bringer, the carrier of a different atmosphere—because you carry the light of the world (Matthew 5:14). You can point others toward the Light that dawned at Christmas so long ago: Jesus Christ.

Fill your heart and home with His love, joy, peace, kindness, generosity, laughter, warmth, and celebration. Think of family or friends who need to be forgiven, embraced, included, and loved. Why not determine to make this the year *you* cross that threshold and make a move toward forgiveness, restoration, and reconciliation? In His strength, you can bring the good news to the world around you.

Jesus, I am so grateful You came. Please help me bring Your peace into every situation I enter.

GOOD NEWS, GREAT JOY

The angel said to them, "Do not be afraid. I bring you
good news that will cause great joy for all the people."

LUKE 2:10

I love the Christmas season! Don't you?

I love the anticipation on my girls' faces and in their hearts . . .

I love the smell of our Christmas tree . . .

I love the mess (did I say that?) . . .

I love the extended family time . . .

I love planning gift giving (my primary love language) . . .

I love the food (of course) . . .

I love looking at all the lights and displays with our girls . . .

And I love that for a period of time, in the midst of hyper-consumerism, secularism, a man in a red suit being transported by reindeer, and a world full of pain, heartache, challenge, and adversity, we get to exalt the name of Jesus. We get to declare to the world good news for all people.

So in the rush of the season, remember the heart of today's verse: Our message is *good news*! Our message brings *great joy*! Our message is for *all people*. Let's determine that to keep a joyful spirit at Christmas, we won't get cynical or judgmental, but we will actually live and look like people with good news to tell! We'll invite everyone—and never exclude anyone—to our table.

God, thank You for the gift of Your Son and the
good news. Thank You for filling my heart with Your
Spirit's joy, so I can share it with all people.

THE CHILD IS BORN

For to us a child is born, to us a son is given, and . . .
he will be called Wonderful Counselor, Mighty
God, Everlasting Father, Prince of Peace.

ISAIAH 9:6

Today, as we rest in thankfulness, peace, and joy for Jesus' birth, let's also remember how He came: as a baby, in a barn, to a teenager and her husband. God always has used the odd and unusual to work His will—and Jesus was His masterpiece.

Remember how God chose the foolish things of the world to shame the wise, and the weak things to shame the strong (1 Corinthians 1:27)? How foolish must Mary have looked when she came to Joseph and said, "It was an angel"? And how foolish Joseph must have looked to accept her! Imagine how weak must that tiny baby have looked, lying in the feeding trough, relegated to the barn because there was no room in the inn. And yet . . .

Mary gave birth to the Messiah, and Joseph helped raise Him. That holy baby defeated hell and death. And the same Spirit that brought Him to life lives inside of you. So today, as we praise God for His mysterious ways, let's joyfully agree to be a fool for Him, and to be part of His miraculous workings here on earth!

Lord God, I am amazed by the beauty of Jesus'
coming, of the foolish things You use to work Your
glory on the earth. Hallelujah, Christ has come!

TREASURE UP THESE THINGS

Mary treasured up all these things and pondered them in her heart.

LUKE 2:19

The gifts have been opened, the parties are over, and the leftovers are in the fridge. Aside from all the treasures under your tree this season, God invites you to treasure in your heart the wonderful things He's done, just as Mary did.

The baby Jesus had come, and Mary and Joseph were no doubt full of joy and relief. But a little ways away, in a field nearby, God was reaching out to those you'd least expect. A jaw-dropping display of angelic glory was appearing to a group of ragtag shepherds, telling them a Savior had been born in Bethlehem.

They hustled to Bethlehem to meet this baby, worship Him, and "spread the word concerning what had been told them about this child" (Luke 2:17). In the meantime, Jesus' mother "treasured up all these things and pondered them in her heart."

May this time of celebration also lead you to treasure up what God has done for you through His Son. Treasure up the blessings He's given you, the way He loves you, and the ways He's spoken to and acted for you. Like Mary, ponder them deep within. Let the celebration of Jesus' coming continue in the quiet thankfulness of your heart.

Lord God, the things You do and have done for me are spectacular. I treasure, savor, and remember them, and thank You with my life.

SPREAD HIS LIGHT

In [Jesus Christ] was life, and that life was the light
of all mankind. The light shines in the darkness,
and the darkness has not overcome it.

JOHN 1:4–5

Look outside at night, and you might still see the twinkling of Christmas lights. Let them remind you today that on your street, in your circles, in your life, your opportunities to shine God's light into the darkness are countless, and the needs are desperate. Yet no darkness is so dark that it can't be broken by Christ.

This became so real to me when I visited the prison camp in Auschwitz. I realized that crimes against God's children are no less evil today than they were during World War II, and perpetrators are no less cruel. Evil exists throughout the world *now*—not just in history.

I also know that same darkness will be with us until Jesus returns with new heavens and a new earth (Revelation 21:1). But He isn't here yet, so you and I have the joy of shining His light to dispel all the darkness around us. Together, with God's help, let's shine brightly into one life after another spreading God's great joy. Let's share His grace, His love, and His hope. Until every person we meet is living the light with us.

*Thank You, Lord, that Your light in me always
overcomes the darkness and brings light to others.*

THE GOODBYE BARBECUE

[Elisha] took his yoke of oxen and slaughtered them.
He burned the plowing equipment to cook the
meat and gave it to the people, and they ate.

1 KINGS 19:21

To get to your purpose, you'll need to leave some things behind. Once you feel the pull of the possibility of where you're destined, you'll never be satisfied with where you've been!

When the great prophet Elijah called young Elisha to his destiny, Elisha first kissed his family goodbye (v. 20). Then he said goodbye to his livelihood: he broke up his plows, butchered and barbecued his oxen, and fed the people with the meat. Then, he "set out to follow Elijah and became his servant" (v. 21). There was no plan B for Elisha! And there's no plan B for us when we set out to follow Jesus.

Are there some things or people you need to fondly kiss goodbye today in order to follow Christ? Do you need to bust up some plows and barbecue some cows? Whether it's a relationship, a habit, a sin, or even a redistribution of your time and resources, you will undoubtedly need to set some fires and give some goodbye kisses in order to set out after Jesus and become His servant. Ask God today what you need to let go of, and for strength to light that match.

Lord God, I want to follow You without a contingency plan. Show me what I need to say goodbye to today.

MAKING PLANS

Direct my footsteps according to your word; let no sin rule over me.

PSALM 119:133

The end of the year always brings with it a time of reflecting, setting goals, and "new year, new you" resolutions. As you think about your resolutions, let me challenge you to keep them flexible. Because flexibility will enable you to keep stretching and reaching out, always being open to those who need a helping hand—to those we didn't expect to run into.

In other words, try loosening up your life enough to be ready for divine interruptions. Don't structure your days and goals so rigidly that you lock out God from working in the middle of them. It's too easy to book our calendar so full that we run from one activity to another, leaving only Sunday morning church as a time for meeting God. That's not what He wants—and it's really not what you want either. You want Him by your side throughout the day.

So build margin into your life for God to bring divine interruptions. He longs to walk with you into each moment of every day, loving you, leading you, guiding you. Build margin so you can hear Him talking to you—and margin for you to talk back. Just be flexible because, as I always say, "Blessed are the flexible, for they will not snap!"

Lord, I put You at the center of my plans this coming year. Help me hold lightly to them and firmly to You.

LACKING NOTHING

"I will heal my people and will let them enjoy
abundant peace and security."

JEREMIAH 33:6

For all the tests, trials, and struggles you've been through this year, recount them and filter them through the revelation of this scripture: "I'm convinced that the testing of my faith produces perseverance and that I must let perseverance finish its work so that I may be mature and complete, not lacking anything" (James 1:2–4, paraphrased).

That means you are closer than ever to not lacking anything! What good news. You are well on your way to a lackless life. You are growing mature and strong. And in the coming year, the new tests, trials, and struggles will make you even stronger. God is perfecting you, and He reveals not yet fully healed areas so you can be healed and whole for the next level of your calling, relationships, and purpose. As you keep pursuing Him, I believe you will be mature and complete, not lacking anything. God said so, and He is at work completing you.

So be open in the coming year for Him to reveal even more areas where you can grow. As you do, you'll find that He is giving you everything you need to live this life in abundant peace and security.

*Lord, I look forward to the day when I lack nothing in
You! Continue to reveal new places for me to grow,
new tasks to do, and new ways to be complete.*

OFF WITH THE OLD

Speaking the truth in love, we will grow to become in every
respect the mature body of him who is the head, that is, Christ.

EPHESIANS 4:15

As you celebrate New Year's Eve and reflect on what God has done in your life
this past year, remember His life-giving truths for every day of the coming year:

1. Fear is banished (1 John 4:18).
2. Love is stronger than death (Romans 6:9).
3. Good triumphs over evil (2 Corinthians 2:14).
4. Our needs can be met in Christ (Philippians 4:19).
5. Captives can be set free (Luke 4:18).
6. Hope can be restored (Romans 5:5).
7. Diseases can be healed (Matthew 8:17).
8. Peace can prevail (John 14:27).
9. Joy can reign (John 16:24).
10. Failures can be redeemed (Romans 8:28).

Our hurting world also needs to know the truths above, truths that flesh
out what it means to have Jesus as our Savior and Lord.

So I encourage you to continue in the journey toward putting off the
old—whether it's shame, fear, hopelessness, or something else—and putting
on Christ. Speak up so that no one misses out on hearing about all that our
almighty and all-loving God longs to do for them.

Lord, I continue to mature in Your love,
sharing the truth as I go. Thank You for Your
presence with me every step of the way.

NOTES

MARCH 15

1. Brené Brown, "Shame v. Guilt," January 14, 2013, http://brenebrown.com/2013/01/14/2013114shame-v-guilt-html/.
2. Judith Stadtman Tucker, "Motherhood, Shame and Society," interview with Brené Brown, Mothers Movement Online, http://www.mothersmovement.org/features/bbrown_int/bbrown_int_2.htm.

ABOUT THE AUTHOR

Christine Caine is an Australian-born, Greek-blooded lover of Jesus, activist, author, and international speaker. Together with her husband, Nick, she founded the anti–human trafficking organization, the A21 Campaign. They also founded Propel Women, an organization designed to celebrate every woman's passion, purpose, and potential. Christine and Nick make their home in Southern California with their daughters, Catie and Sophia.

ChristineCaine.com
A21.org
PropelWomen.org

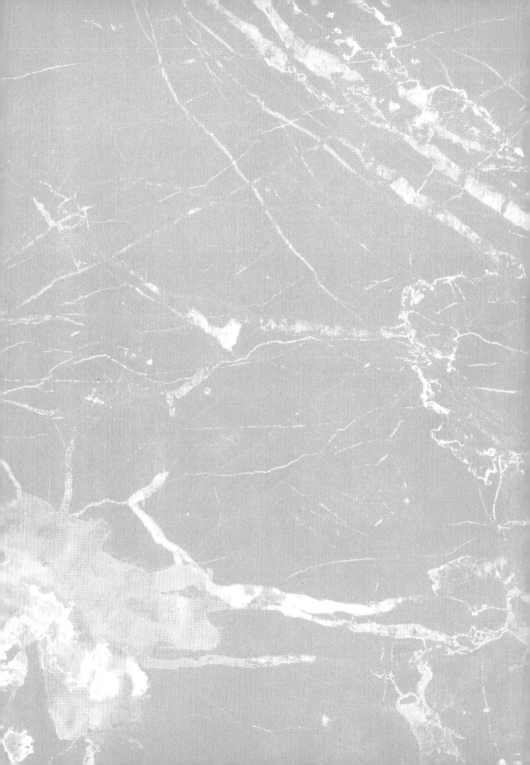

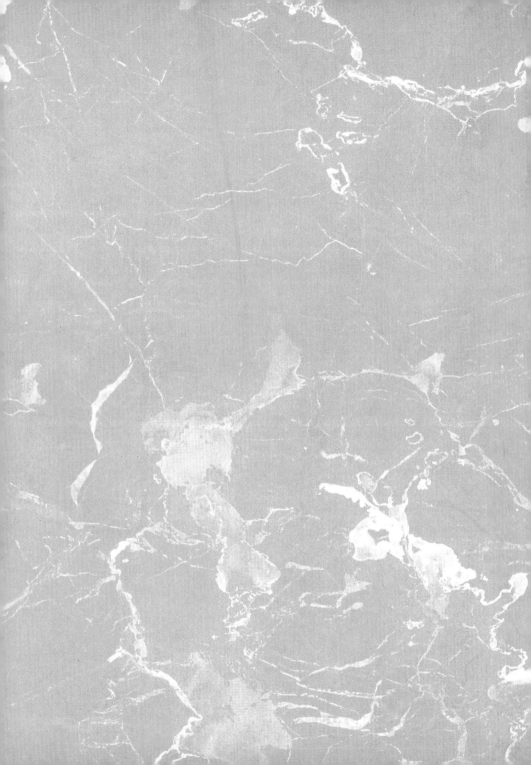